The Sculptor

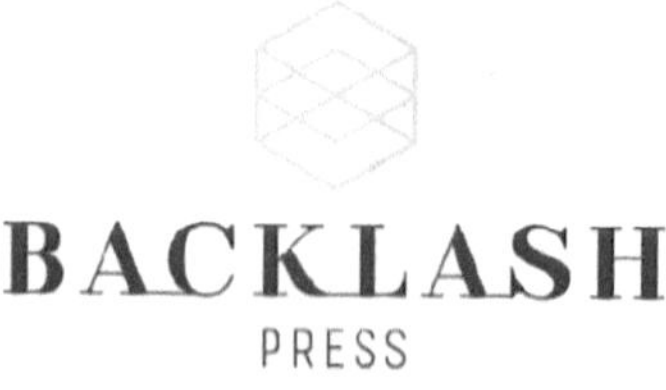

A pioneering publishing house dedicated to creating intelligent, vivid books. Established to inform, educate, entertain and provoke.

A Backlash Press Book

Published 2015, 2024

backlashpress.com

Illustrations by Robert Littleford

Printed and bound by Ingram

ISBN: 978-1-9162666-2-9

The Sculptor

Gret Heffernan

Backlash Poetry

American Dangerous: Renée Olander

Bombing the Thinker: Darren C. Demaree

Burial Machine: Jacob Griffin Hall

Clay Unbreakables: Natalia I Andrievskikh

Into The The: Robin Reagler

Phantom Laundry: Michael Tyrell

Tattered Scrolls and Postulates: Joseph V Milford

The Arsonist's Letters: Michael Tyrell

The Life in the Sky Comes Down: Bruce Bromley

Unfinished Murder Ballads: Darren C. Demaree

Backlash Journals

#1

#2

#3: Provoke

#4

Isolation

#5

The Ballad of Elora Winter

Evergreen, her throat unseen,
Landscape dark increscent
Wisp and by, the clouds and I
Gone but reminiscent.

Winter morn and shadow scorn,
Breastbone cups a locket
Photo bare, her lost black hair
Empty blinded socket.

Ride the Down and into town
Twilight amniotic
Bruised sea quay, a boat they see
Concealed in waves a trick.

Blood channel fare to take you there
At the helm the deceased.
Split Irish Sea and soon you'll be
In morning light, Passage East.

Heart that's flayed, open ribcage
The coast she cries her loss

Close your eyes should she surprise
Her form an albatross.

Shriek of luck, your sight she'll pluck
Collect with which to find
The soul she lost, the fury it cost
The world she longs to blind.

Cut Backstrand, green kelp and sand
Dune wind and sorrow fed
Swim the bay without dismay
Just sing to the undead.

'Tis song you need, go, God speed
I pray you dream no beast
When tide is high, scarify sky
Steer clear of Passage East.

Lorelie, sweet Lorelie,
Daughter, dearest ghost.
Lorelie, please Lorelie,
Rise, restore your host.

Contents

I believe that nothing is more abstract, more unreal
than what we actually see.

Giorgio Morandi

Elora Winter

Dear Lorelie,

All stories are love stories and this one, despite its unearthly nature, is no different. I thought I'd tell it when I wanted to feel absolved but the pure intentions of my crimes are forgiveness enough. In the end, you only have yourself to pardon or condemn. And I choose to live, if that's what you can call it, and so, I'm writing you now because I'm leaving this house.

I've stayed here in the hope that you had survived and would want to find us. This letter will be waiting for you, and should you be alive and curious, know that I plan to head west. I'm hoping it will burn some things out of me. I think of you every day, every day, but I've come to realize just how long the life is ahead of me. And how much time it takes to reconcile time. So.

Come for me if you like, I'll leave a trail of work and show you how best to live, for there is an art to being reborn, to knowing what we know. You are not as alone as it seems. There are others like us.

I suppose it might have been different. By different I do not mean better, but it strikes me sometimes how simple it all might've been had I just yielded to my marriage to Arlo. How Birdie, Jacques, and I might've been saved from the heartache we've learned to carry and how good people might still be alive. Jacques is gone. Is he dead? It's hard to say. To move forward, I have to believe he is, but that means acknowledging that there are cells and pits in me that will never repair, that have ended with him. Though, I've learned that life is about tending more than anything else – tending wounds, tending loved ones, tending dreams – and had I not crawled out of myself, had I chosen to yield, I wouldn't have met Jacques, or you. I wouldn't have known spectacular love, I wouldn't have become the woman I am, cuts and all, and so, despite the anguish we've caused, I know that I would change nothing. Nothing. Not even my death.

I love you. I've loved you from the moment of your conception. Love is the beginning and the end of all life. Surely, that must spare us.

What else is there to say?

Apart from everything.

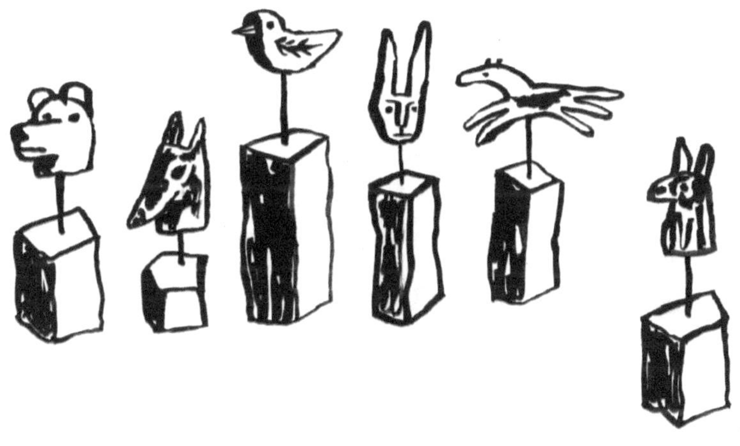

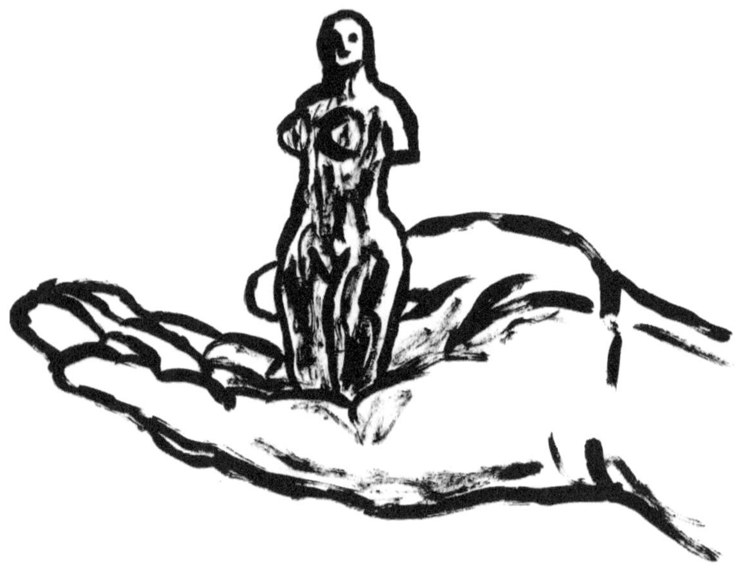

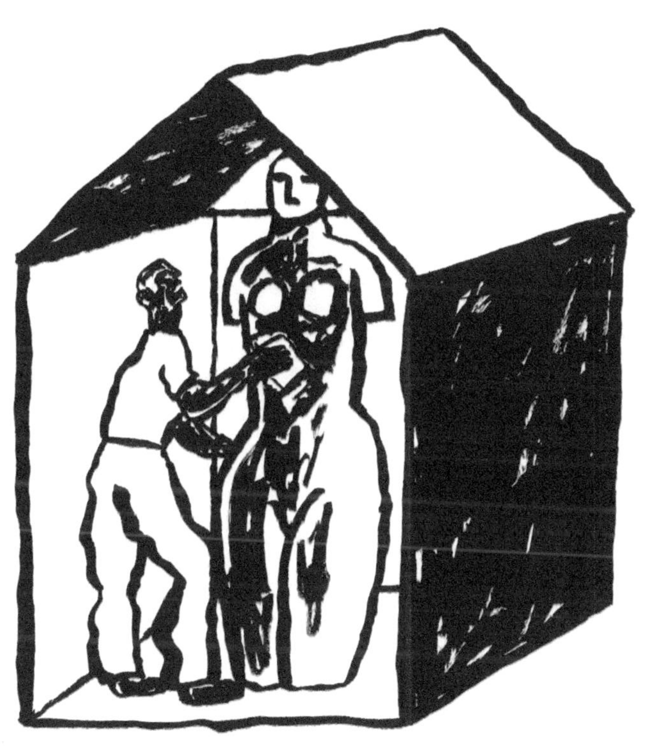

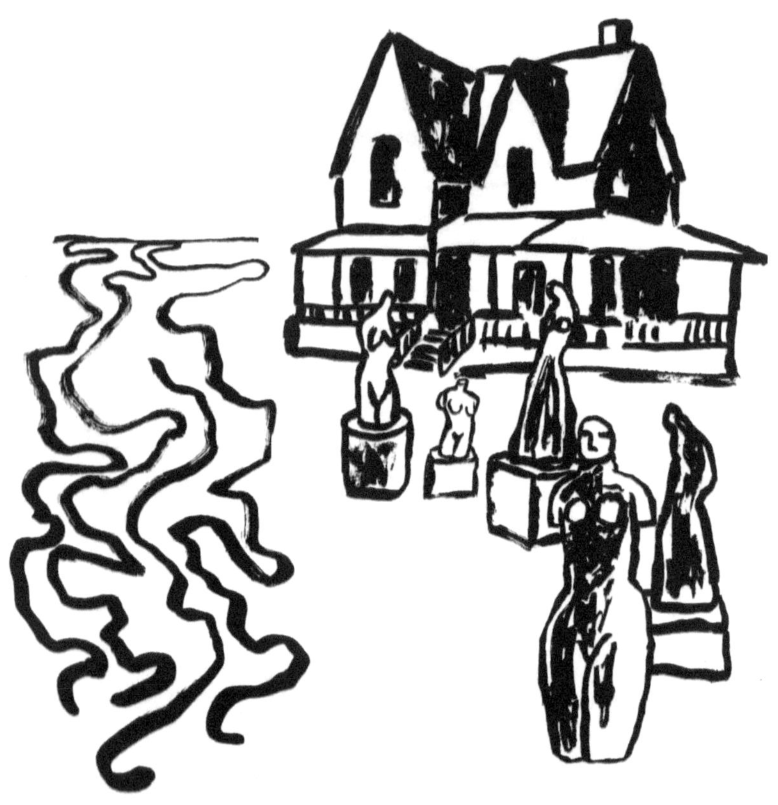

Birdie Dubois

When I first met Stan, there were sparks of a silly and flirtatious variety. We just knew how to talk to one other. It was too easy, which, on reflection, was one of the problems. We were both living in Chicago at a moment of personal reckoning. I was creating what would become known as my photo boxes, though I've never been entirely happy with that name, but who am I to criticize art critics? Plus, it keeps the stories inside my boxes underestimated and ordinary, so hidden in plain view, therefore, safe.

I guess that description summarizes my life now.

However, back then, I was anything but concealed and wanted nothing more than myself and my artwork, my photography, to be eternally on exhibit. I had just graduated from art college and finance was a factor, so I had to spend three days a week working as a tea caddy and paper pusher at a solicitors' firm. The other days were spent building a meagre livelihood in photojournalism, which I hoped would eventually support my art career. It was all rather tiring and uninspiring. So, when I heard that a diner was paying, actually paying, artists to hang their work on the walls, I filled a suitcase full of photo boxes and skipped lunch.

Stan had just finished his degree in English literature. He was trying to write a novel about a Polish family who immigrated to Chicago and opened a restaurant. Obviously, it was modelled after his parents, whom he adored, and who had recently left him in charge of Stan's Diner, suitably named, on Walnut and 43rd, while they snow birded in Florida. Stan's Diner was one of those places with original mint and black Formica tables. It had deep-red leather booths, brass fixtures, and neon. It was pristine and I loved it straight away.

When I walked in, Stan was behind the counter, writing. I quietly sat in a booth, opened my suitcase, and took out my photo boxes. He slipped his notebook in his apron and came over to take my order. We ended up sitting and talking for three hours. I got fired from the solicitors' firm, but I didn't care, because I had my first exhibition, plus, I'd met a man who was so charming that I lied about liking sauerkraut.

Over the next few weeks, Stan let me work at the diner until I found another secretarial job. Our relationship was tender and fun, too enjoyable, in fact, for me to take it seriously. It was a time when I thought love needed to be difficult, intense, and earned though challenge, if it was to be eternal. I let him go too easily. I see that now. But I also see why it was a mistake I was destined to make. Plus, he could have made other choices as well.

His parents decided to take early retirement and permanently move to Florida, so overnight, Stan inherited Plan B. He's called the diner Plan B for as long as I've known him, long after it was obviously Plan A or even, the Only Plan. And, the "great Polish American novel" evaporated, as did our romantic relationship because Melissa rang.

Stan had briefly dated Melissa, an actress on and off stage, prior to meeting me. He ended the relationship because, to use his Narnia-esque description, he was Edward and she was Jadis, beautiful, cold, cunning. And, as it turned out, three months pregnant with his child. Stan did the right thing, because Stan always does the right thing, which is why he remains to this day, both miserable and my greatest friend. So, he moved in with Melissa and began expanding the diner's menu beyond boiled meat and pickled delicacies.

My pride was shattered and, parenthetically, my leg. I had been photographing a steel workers' protest and had my leg crushed. I was photographing demonstrations a lot at the time and garnering quite a reputation for magazine work. A police officer grabbed my camera, punched me to the ground, and purposely trampled, with, ironically, steel caped boots, my camera into my femur. He was easily a hundred pounds heavier than I was and it was a vicious attack. The paramedics had to pluck glass and plastic from my thigh. My scars looked like buckshot. The whole event was sickening. Incidentally, nothing happened to the police officer and my complaint was never taken seriously. It was as if the constabulary were happy to see me fall, as though I deserved the punishment. I had a reputation for taking opportune photographs capturing officers who were in the pockets of landlords, factory owners, politicians or other white-collar criminals. I was pretty shaken up and my nerves were a wreck.

Stan came to visit me in hospital.

"Do you want the good news or the bad news?" he asked.

"There's good news?" I answered and he sat down on the bed beside me.

"I served the curator/owner of Vertical Gallery a zapiekanka and he wants to speak to you about an exhibition."

Vertical Gallery was known for launching artists careers and was considered one of the best galleries in Chicago.

"The owner of Vertical is Polish?" Zapiekanka is a Polish open-face sandwich.

"Shocking, right? But, aren't you happy?"

"No, that would be awful for business. What's the bad news?"

"Melissa doesn't want you working at the diner anymore."

"What? Fuck Melissa."

"That's how we got here in the first place. Look, I know you've been through hell recently, but this gallery thing is a real opportunity for you Keet." Keet is his pet name for me, short for Parakeet, you know, the Birdie connection, cheesy, but it worked for us. "An exhibition there could change everything, plus, it's decent money."

"For an artist."

"For an artist, yes, but I'm thinking that you won't need much at Idlewild."

I looked at him, "What are you talking about?"

"I've been thinking," he said.

"Well, stop."

"Why don't you go to Callisto for a while? You could rest, create, take photographs, think. I can help move your things. Marge can look after you until your leg is better. After the opening, the show will look after itself. Wouldn't it be nice to have some time away?"

I guess I agreed because I needed to recoup my power somewhere quiet and Callisto was certainly that, but quiet places tend to boil underneath, as I soon found out. The gallery put on a sole exhibition of my photo boxes, leaked information about my attack, which did wonders for my PR, especially since I attended the private viewing in my wheelchair, and most of my photo boxes sold within a weekend. Alone and deflated on the inside, triumphant and heroic on the outside, the reviews were as much about my bravery towards adversary as they were about my work. It was said that I was heading to Idlewild to create my next show, but I knew I was going to hide my repair and broken heart.

My parents were originally from Chicago, and I was born there, but when I was five and about to start school, they bought Idlewild in Callisto, Illinois, with the idea of living off the land and starting a smallholding. Idlewild was an old farmhouse near the Mississippi river and named after the famous steamboat. People always assume my parents were hippies and I must correct them by explaining that they were naturalists. Hippy is a word that's lost its original meaning and it undermines my parent's bravery. They opted out of commercialism, which was about making a quiet stand, not the 'peace sign' propaganda that generally enters a pedestrian mind when alternative lifestyles are mentioned. Don't get me wrong, I care little for how people choose to live, provided it's kind, after all, who am I to judge? But I make this distinction because I need you to get a sense of Idlewild's atmosphere. It was gentle and remote. Unobtrusive and unadorned. Forgotten, though not forsaken, all in all, a place of inhuman enchantment where time was something you could slip in and out of with ease.

Little did I know, Jacques was living in a similar space, in Canada, and learning to create what would become his finest sculpture. I think about this often. How artists live in a slipstream of places. Some ideas we are born into and others, are born from us, but it is the ability to enter the wash and warp time and memory that makes us creators. Idlewild was a place of creation.

That's what my parents did. They grew food, herbs, and created things, which is a virtuous way to live. My mother created paintings and my father created songs and they both created me. I had the notion that I could reinstate a sense of peace within myself upon my return, but it was difficult, because I hadn't been there since the death of my father, ten years prior, and I was filled with anxiety from the steel incident. Anxiety from Stan. Anxiety from creative recognition. I boarded the train chock-full of tension.

My mother and I had moved back to Chicago after my father's death. She was from Midtown before it was trendy and still had friends, family, and her small apartment. We kept the house because it was what my father would have wanted, plus, we could walk to Idlewild from the Amtrak station. We always thought we'd return for the summers or weekends out of the city, though we never did. My mother never had the heart to be there without my father and I wasn't keen to go alone, then after my mother died, I tried to forget about it all together. But it wasn't abandoned, as we'd left it under the care of Marjorie Johnston, a herbalist and Callisto resident, who sent us occasional updates and jars of homemade chutney.

The Sculptor - Gret Heffernan

Marjorie, or Marge, rang the night before I left with news concerning stay. Her sister from Minneapolis had suffered a stroke and was moving in with Marge until she'd fully recovered, so Marge could no longer be at my "beck and call." However, because Marge seldom presented a problem without offering a solution, she said, "I've just received a letter from that Canadian cousin of yours, Jacques Beaumont."

I groaned in annoyance, but it is an extraordinary story really. You see, my father and Jacques's father, Mathis Beaumont, were both the bastard children of some la-di-da general in France. Of course, my father didn't know this, he only knew that he'd been in foster care in Montreal and then adopted by a family in Chicago. Actually, he never knew he had a half-brother in Canada. Mathis got in touch with us after he found out about my father when he had to apply for his passport to come to America, he was a nature photographer, and realized that his stepmother, an affluent Parisian, apparently, had listed my father as Mathis's next of kin. She wanted nothing to do with her husband's illegitimate children. Can't blame her really, it was an out-of-sight, out-of-mind scenario. Anyway, Mathis contacted us a year after my father had died. Now Jacques sends Christmas cards and the occasional letter to Marge, because she is the only one that replies.

"And you opened it?"

"Well, it was addressed to me. I am the one who keeps in touch with him, you know, if you wanted a letter addressed to you, you should have made an effort. Not everybody knows a sculptor in Canada, it's interesting," she said.

"Fair enough. What did he say?'

"It said he's looking for a place to work in America. He wants a change of scene, just for the summer, and I thought your mother's studio would be perfect. He could live there and fix the roof, tend the garden, in return for his room and board. I'll come every day to help, but you'd also have the security of having another person around, and that person would be your cousin, so nobody would talk."

"I don't care about gossip."

"Well, you might not care about gossip but, I, on the other hand, have to live here."

The barn had been renovated for my mother to use as a painting studio. It had a modest bedroom, bathroom, and kitchenette. I had Marge move the canvases out the year my mother died but understood the roof needed fixing. I had a broken leg, a broken heart, and an idea for a series of photo boxes that would require peace and quiet, so my first response was no, no, another person in my space would be too intrusive. However, the steel incident had weakened my confidence and I was nervous of being entirely on my own, in the countryside, which had begun to seem unbearably rural. The idea of a fellow artist seemed like destiny, all the same, I was sceptical.

"What's he like?"

"He's a proper gentleman. Obviously, I've never met him in person, but we've been communicating for years. Manners like the queen. It seems like a pretty ideal situation to me, don't you think? Fated even, I mean, how the devil will you manage the stairs?"

That settled it. How would I manage the stairs? I looked outside the window at the U-Haul that Stan had packed with all my earthly belongings. I was preparing to leave first thing in the morning. My apartment was empty but for a single suitcase in the corner. I had a ticket for the afternoon train to Callisto. "Okay," I said, sealing my fate, "tell him he can stay for the summer. But just the summer."

Elora Winter

Time and the creative process have taught me that when we speak, we speak to multiples. Most of whom are unknown. So, as I'm writing this letter to you, I know Jacques is here with me, I can feel him listening, just like I can feel my future self, once all of this is over, waiting for me. I do not know if you are in this world or another, the same is true for Jacques, but, nevertheless, you are with me, Lorelie, every time I dive into the place where ideas are born, it is your hand that rises up and grabs mine, the life I have yet to live, is for you. You need to understand who I was if you are to know who I've become.

To begin with, the woman I was when I married Arlo embarrasses me. Shame is too strong a word. I've dealt with the shame and minimized it to mere embarrassment. I don't know how to explain this part of myself in a way that you'll appreciate, except to say that, I was at a stage when I needed help and he was the only one that offered. Our paths are generally determined by the help we receive or don't receive and that's not just true for the young. Things were harder for me because I had no form of guidance, financial or otherwise, and Arlo supported me throughout my father's funeral. It was as simple as that. I know it seems irrational, but I mistook relief for love, and he was kind in the beginning. Don't get me wrong, he deserved to die in the end, but I'll never forget how he valued my singing. He took it seriously. No one that I was close to had done that before. Singing was my passion. My voice is the only thing I miss about my old self, so it is no coincidence that when I first met Jacques I was singing.

Arlo had gone to collect Birdie from the station. I had wanted to come with him, but he insisted on going alone. I think he wanted to judge Birdie for himself before I rekindled any kind of friendship with her. He claimed that there wouldn't be enough room in the car, that she was citified now and was bound to have loads of luggage, plus the wheelchair, etc., etc., so I waited for him to leave and walked to my spot on the river. It was a small outcrop of sandstone that barely jutted over the water. The wind had cracked and hollowed what was once a large boulder so that it resembled a beetle's open wings or a split and upturned bowl that faced the water. It was my own personal amphitheatre for between each wing was a flat rock just big enough for me to stand upon. It was where I composed my songs, you see, I loved folk music, folklore, long before I became its subject. Ironic, isn't it? I remember the song I was working on, it was about a ghost that haunted the coastline of Passage East, Ireland, where my grandmother was from. It was the last song I ever wrote as I can no longer write music. I am not able to hear it in the same way, to feel it, but I remember I had these lyrics in my head:

Evergreen, her throat unseen,
landscape dark increscent
wisp and by, the clouds and I
gone but reminiscent.

I sang them over and over again trying to pry open the next verse when, suddenly, I felt him there, standing behind me and listening. I turned around and he just nodded, "Sorry to disturb you," he said, and began to walk away, intent to leave me in peace.

"Wait," I called out after him, "aren't you Birdie's cousin?"

"Yes," he walked back and stuck out his hand, "Jacques, and you are?"

"Elora."

"Elora," he said, and again, "Elora, nice to meet you, you have a beautiful voice."

Then, as soon as he was gone, the next verse arrived, complete and whole:

> Winter morn and shadow scorn,
> Breastbone cups a locket
> Photo bare, her lost black hair
> Empty blinded socket.

And I knew I should stay away from him. And I knew that I wouldn't.

Birdie Dubois

I appreciate how it's human nature to try to treat facts like stories, to mould them into our own sense of understanding, even, a fact like death. You may think, well, either a person is dead, or they aren't, but then, there are different interpretations of death, of life after death, and that's what makes it all so difficult to unpick. A story is the agency of the heart, and we all know the heart has its own rules of explanation. But, sometimes, something happens that knocks every sense of interpretative balance completely off kilter. And, afterwards, it becomes impossible to speak about the facts until they offer you a truth you're willing to accept. You just must wait until your need to tell the story is bigger than your need to understand its surrounds. Until there is an assemblage that needs to take place despite what resulting construction may come of it.

On the writing desk beside the window, where I sit now, there is a photograph of my great aunt Mary. I look like her. I've carried this photograph with me all my life. I don't know who took it. I used to pretend that she was speaking to me through the photo, that, somehow, I was the photographer, and I could talk to her, that my stories, my artwork, were all a part of our conversations. Elora has been a part of that conversation. So has Jacques.

I see this photo every day. It's a black-and-white snapshot of Mary sitting cross-legged on the grass beside a bicycle leaning against a tree. She's wearing 1930s wide-leg trousers, a white button-down shirt, and a short scarf, which I imagine being red, tied around her neck. Her feet are bare, and I can see that they are wide like my own sturdy yoga soles. I know that her eyes are hazel because I've been told that mine are identical to hers. We are people that look better in person or in a photograph than on paper, because our humour is our most attractive asset. Her mouth is smiling and open, as though she were speaking to someone she loved, leaning forward with her index finger pointing up into the air, mid-sentence, And then ..., she says, in my mind, wide-eyed, we have the same bushy eyebrows and thick brown hair. She wears hers cut in a short bob and curled around her ears. Amelia Earhart style.

When I was a teenager, I had this repeated mini daydream, a flash really, where Amelia, Mary, and I kept leaning over a table covered in maps and pointing, then we'd laugh and take a drink of coffee. That was it. Repeatedly. I wrote a story about it titled, "Conspirators," which was terrible and, hopefully, buried deep in an irretrievable hard drive somewhere. I can't find it anyway.

But then, years later, I wrote the short story, "Instruction in Cartography," where I fly over my own body like a map. I wrote it in calligraphy on a map of the state of Illinois. It was my first real installation piece, before the photo boxes, and I fell in love with containing landscapes inside of landscapes inside of landscapes. I loved restricted tiers. It makes one tunnel inward. The piece won a prize but, it's funny, I didn't make the link between that daydream and those two stories, in fact I'd all but forgotten the daydream, until I was in a street market in New York and saw a pair of aviators wings laid out among the bric-a-brac and, just like that, I remembered. I made the connection, in short, because I was ready for it. I pinned those wings, alongside a duplicate of Mary's photo, to burnt hide that I placed inside a cigar box. It was the first piece to sell at Vertical. What I'm saying is that connections hit us when we are ready to apply them.

I try to be the type of woman that I imagine Mary and Amelia Earhart befriending, and that idea has literally been a measure of my character, crazy, right? Maybe. But the other thing that's struck me recently is how we all perform for an imaginary person who we identify as being what we'd like to become, or, at least, impress. That we seldom, maybe never, measure ourselves against who we presently are but, instead, who we hope to be or have already been. I just knew my imaginary characters' names.

I'm explaining this because meeting Jacques and reconnecting with Elora felt like a thing I'd been chosen to do. Some introductions are chosen. Not to suggest that Jacques is someone that I'd like to become, on the contrary, but I'm aware now that through knowing him and trying to comprehend what happened to him, I'll become more fully who I was intended to be. I don't know exactly what this means, which is why I'm speaking about it, why I feel I need to strive for some sort of productive witnessing, because we are not merely the singular versions of ourselves, but rather a combination of narrative and cellular histories. So, perhaps, if Jacques's life shows me how to die with dignity, then maybe Elora's is there to show me how to be reborn?

I arrived at the station in Callisto on a June afternoon. The air was full of heat and river mud. A wheelchair was waiting for me, as was Arlo Donnelly, Callisto's only police officer and, from what I remembered, a total dickhead. "Thanks a lot Marge," I thought sarcastically, still, she didn't know a police officer had broken my leg, so I couldn't completely blame her. I let him help me from the platform, which makes me cringe when I think about it now. I hadn't realized Arlo still lived in town. I thought that he married Elora and they moved to Minnesota or something like that. The last I knew of him was in high school. His father had bone cancer and it was brutal. I remember my mother used to make him tonics for the pain. His own mother, Dorothy I think her name was, had run off with the volleyball coach when Arlo was young. I didn't know him well in high school. He was a bully, and I was always behind a camera. Also, I was a few years younger and, well you know what high school's like, those kinds of age gaps mattered, but when he picked me up from the station, we were in our twenties and a year or two here or there was nothing. He spoke like we'd been great friends.

"Hey now, a little birdie told me you was coming back to Callisto," he laughed at his own bad joke. "Ha, ha," I said.

"Welcome home. So, what happened to your leg? Here, lemme get that," he took my suitcase.

"Let's just say I got on the wrong side of the law," I said.

"You were always a little rebel rouser," he said. "Somebody was bound to slow you down sooner or later."

"I could take offense to that," I said, joking, but also serious.

"Well don't, cuz I didn't mean offence, only that time's a leveler. See? It's that temper I'm talking 'bout. Lord knows we could do with a bit a spirit 'round here," he helped me into the car, folded the wheelchair and stuck it in the trunk.

"I hear you have visitor staying," he said, as he wedged himself behind the wheel.

"A cousin, yes."

"You know him well then?"

"No, not really."

"That don't make you nervous at all?"

"Should it?"

"Well, a woman on her own ..." His voice trailed off.

"I can look after myself, thank you, Arlo," I said, and he laughed.

"How about I check in on you from time to time?"

"Thanks, but that really won't be necessary. Marge is coming around every day and I'm able to walk a little way with crutches," I said. "Plus, Jacques is my cousin."

"Jack?"

"No, Jacques, it's French," I said, and he huffed.

"Marge won't be able to haul things around," he said.

"Stan is there. I'm sure things are already where they need to be," I said.

"Stan?"

"A friend from Chicago."

"Aaaah," he said, insinuating something sexual.

"He's moving my boxes down with his pregnant wife Melissa," I said, resenting how I felt the need to redeem my reputation. Why had I lied about them being married? It just seemed easier but, still, it made me angry at myself.

"Ah," he said, reaffirming my character once more.

I sighed. I'd forgotten the subtle meanings behind the variations of "Ah" and all the other intricate mannerisms of my previous life. It was not a complex system and Arlo was not a complex person, but still, it was draining.

"So, I heard you married Elora Winter?" I said, trying to change the subject.

"Yep, it's Elora Donnelly, 'bout, oh, four years ago now," he said.

"Any kids?" I asked and he stiffened.

"Not yet."

We drove up the driveway. It was long and gravel and sparsely fringed with willow trees. They were larger than I remembered, of course they would be. We had planted them as a windbreak because a strong wind from the prairie had a habit of shaking our car. The house was a typical clapboard early 1900s farmhouse. Behind it, the river cascaded like a memory pulled from my mind and sprinkled with sun. I was back home. Hollyhocks bobbed against the machine shed. Forsythia and the red barn. An old plough in the field with white hydrangeas growing around it. It was all a bit William Carlos Williams.

"I wonder if there will be plumbs in the freezer," I said, and Arlo gave me a sideways glance as if I'd gone crazy.

Stan and Marge were talking on the porch. They both waved and Stan walked towards the car. Arlo steadied the wheelchair and Stan opened the door.

"I can do it myself," I said, as Arlo leaned forward to lift me.

I balanced on my good leg and flopped in the seat. Melissa was in the van. When she saw Stan and I talking she rolled down the window. I waved. She didn't.

"Arlo, can you give us a minute?"

"Sure," he said, and joined Marge on the porch.

"How are you?" Stan asked.

"I've been better."

"Yeah, sorry we weren't there to pick you up. It's getting complicated, you know, pregnancy hormones and all," Stan looked over at Melissa. "I've unpacked everything. Marge has arranged the house and it looks amazing. I had no idea your mom was such a talented painter. I think you are going to be really happy here, Keet. Anyway, I got you this," he pulled a moleskin notebook out of his pocket.

"What's it for?" I asked.

"It's to write about your experience, your trauma," he said.

"Soulful journaling Stan, really?" I teased and he relaxed.

"I know you hate that kind of crap. I just don't want you to get an emotional blockage or anything." He is sentimental despite his tattoos, ice-coloured eyes, and bald head.

"Blockage? You make me sound like a drainpipe. However, I would have totally gotten behind a Tantric for Trauma course."

"Stop it, otherwise I'll be forced to sign you up to the Painting the Body Whole Again watercolour class offered at the Methodist Church," he winked, then cleared his throat. "Are you sure you're going to be okay here?"

"I'm sure. I'll be fine. I'll return to Chicago as free flowing as a Mr. Muscle sink," I tapped the journal.

"No, really, Keet, I'm a little worried. It's, well, rural."

"Don't be."

"I don't know how not to be. You're the best. You do know that don't you?"

"I know."

"I have to go," he said, and glanced towards the van. "Sorry."

"I know that too," I said.

He wheeled me to the porch, kissed me on the forehead and drove away. What I didn't know was that, tragically, a month later, Melissa would lose the baby and Stan would stay to help her emotionally and, after that, I guess he'd stay out of habit. But I was enthralled by Jacques and Elora by then and everything was different. Thinking about that day now, it seems like a final brush of innocence for both of us.

I couldn't watch him drive away. It was too painful. I heard the wheels on the gravel and forced myself to look forward. This was my life now and Stan was right, there were things I needed to figure out. I tucked the notebook into my satchel.

Unkempt evergreen hedges were positioned along the front steps leading up to the porch, where Marge stood waiting for me with a cup of tea in her hand. Arlo walked down the steps holding my crutches. I slowly climbed the stairs and kissed Marge on both cheeks.

"How European," she exclaimed and gave me a big hug. "It's so good to have you back," she said, "wait until you see what I've done with the place. Arlo, don't you have somebody to arrest or a donut to eat or somethin'? I'm sure Birdie here is tired and doesn't want you hangin' around like a song on repeat."

"It's nice to know some things never change," I said to Arlo, feeling a bit embarrassed for him.

"Ain't that the truth," he said, and tipped his hat towards me, "I'll let you rest up. Lemme know if you need anything," and he got in his car.

"Thank God for that," said Marge, "the man makes my psyche hurt."

"Well, he is pretty painful to endure," I said.

"More'en that. I've never liked him. There's just something, you know, something about him I've always thought was mean."

She hit the nail on the head. Took a sip of her tea and squinted in the distance. "Christ on a biscuit, who's that?"

I looked. A tall, thin figure walked slowly along the river towards us.

"My darling cousin, I presume," I said with a smirk.

Jacques Beaumont

The first thing Jacques brought back to life was a field mouse. He was just a boy and had found the mouse dead near the woodshed. It was in perfect condition, as though it had simply keeled over and stopped breathing. There was no blood or entrails pushing past its tiny, splintered teeth, yellowed brown near the gums. The creature seemed unconscious and when he picked it up, he half expected it to wake and bite him, but it just lay in his palm like a bit of stiff pelt. He couldn't believe his luck. It was perfect for carving. He had a block of pine in his bedroom, already smooth and soft as toffee, just waiting for this mouse and his chisel, as if the two were fated, which, he'd eventually come to understand, they were.

He ran up the stairs to his bedroom. The room was hot and breezeless, even with the window open, and he began to sweat as he laid the mouse carefully inside a towel-lined shoebox. Every corner was cluttered with animal bones, rocks, snakeskins, beetle casings, feathers, eye knots of wood, and sketchbooks like a dragon's hoard of found things he loved to carve.

He studied the mouse's body before he placed the box on his desk and took up his chisel. The mouse was the first dead creature he had ever carved, and he wanted it to be faultless. It took him hours to replicate the mouse's delicate features accurately, and he lost all sense of time in process, yet when he'd finished, the mouse and the figurine were virtually identical. He looked at his work in admiration, for focus had seemed to melt into his hands, as though his hands were acting extraneously from his body, from somewhere close, yet distant, like the future. He held the figurine lovingly to his chest and as he gripped the carving in his hand, he found that he knew, instinctually, how to will the mouse alive. He squeezed and prayed and slowly, as though blowing up a tiny balloon, the mouse's body began to take form. He heard the mouse's legs as they began to scratch against the cardboard. He peered into the box and watched with disbelief as the rest of its body softened and twitched to life.

He tipped the shoebox on its side and the mouse hurried out. He remembered looking, awestruck, at the carving in his hand and wondering if it had had something to do with the mouse's revival? His mind said no, of course not, but something deeper, something historic, said yes, yes. Resurrection was not a term he understood then, and everything he felt was based on a bewildered sort of reflex. A roar flooded his ears, his mind, and vision with the snowsquall of confusion. Before he could think another thought, the mouse ran across his desk and quickly leapt out of the window, plummeting to the ground. Jacques could see the dark splat of its small body like a squashed grape, then it stood, dazed and bloodied, but very much alive, and ran away.

And now, as a man, he remembers that was the precise moment that time revealed its fluctuating existence to him. How the power of the mind, when released from the body, can overlap time and that no thing, no shape, or idea is ever truly static or linear. It was inside such a space that he met Elora. Inside the fervent overlap. There are people in the world that direct this alteration and there are people in the world that simply adjust. Jacques was one of the directors, as was Elora, and when he resurrects her into her full reawakening, she will realize how much he loved her then, loves her still, and will love her always.

Jacques picks up a wooden medallion from the kitchen table, places it inside his palm and opens and closes his hand like a blinking eye. He used to dream that he had eyes in his hands. What would she say? What would she want said? Some nights the frost behind his eyes suffocates him. It weaves one pattern furiously over the other, until it grows into a single block of ice that he has to crack himself out of. He walks through his mind then, breaking open his sculptures with a hammer and chisel. His past bursts from their wooden skulls like trapped black flies. He remembers now. That summer there had been a plague of bluebottles. He remembers everything. He sits down at the table and begins sketching a fly, a bear, an onion, a pint of jam, mountains. A young woman who loved to sing. Elora. A river. A bird. A murder.

Pine Creek, Ontario

Mathis Beaumont was a photographer because he needed a layer between himself and his obsession with grizzly bears. It worked like glue inside a crack. It united and divided the fact that he was both man and bear. The lens allowed him to filter. It wasn't until after Mathis had disappeared that Jacques began to fully understand the use of his father's filter and how you can grow one, like an invisible fingernail, in order to tolerate yourself.

Their house had stood in a valley of mountains like a block of soap inside a green dish. It was a two-story rectangle of worn clapboard. The lake beside it was completely still and reflected another house, watery and surreal, like another world he could jump into. This was the view, the dimension, his mother preferred, and in the spring, when it was clear that she was ill and wasn't recovering, she moved her chair to the window and watched the mountains tremor in the water, as though working up the courage to stare at the real thing. Hibernating season was over and his father was away.

"You've got to chew the fruit to see the pit," she told Jacques, speaking of his father's absence. "His expeditions are the closest he gets to chewing himself. Passion is like that. Like chewing yourself. That's the way it is with people. I didn't choose him. You think I'd choose a lunatic? Lord, no, he just happened upon me. And he didn't choose that blasted bear. She was just always his. And it's true your father's half mad, but let me tell you something, he feels fear and he loves anyway, and that's a darn sight better then fearing nothing and loving nothing and living half dead. You got that? Half mad is better living than half dead."

She looked out the window towards the row of pines that wrapped around the base of the mountain and protected their valley from the cold rock. She picked a piece of loose thread from her cardigan and rolled it between her thumb and forefinger. It was one of her lucid moments and he sat beside her on the sofa. She reached over and put her hand on his knee.

"But not you, no. You've got the look of the hell bent."

She looked out the window again. The pines were dark frayed knees against a denim horizon. The sun was low and golden in the sky.

"It'll snow," she said. "It'll snow before the week's out. It may be April, but I know the goddam weather."

She took his hand and stroked it as though he were a small child.

"Someday," she said, "Someday you'll have a bear and it will eat you," she sighed. "Or you'll chase it," she sighed, "but probably both."

And so.

The thought that he might be full of real and imaginary bears was an idea that Jacques carefully folded up and placed inside his heart like a note inside an envelope.

Mathis Beaumont's unusual affection for bears could be traced back to his devotion to a particular ushanka, also known as a Russian trapper's hat. It was a wild and magnificent possession for a child living in the south of France. One could argue that the hat saved the emotional life of young Mathis Beaumont, for even as a grown man, he could close his eyes and glaze the boy he once was until that child shined bright enough for Mathis to feel a soft fur against his eyelids. Indeed, it was the fur that made the hat truly wonderful. It was stitched from the hide of a Russian Urrissi bear, a distant relative of the North American grizzly, and gave Mathis the warmth he would eventually use to draw the line his life would follow.

But before that, others drew it for him.

Mathis was the illegitimate child of General Jean Philippe Beaumont, a French nobleman with a preference for Haitian women. The year was 1905 and two things happened that irrevocably transformed Mathis's future: his mama, a beautiful Creole housekeeper, died and Jean Philippe Beaumont was diagnosed with syphilis. In a desperate act to save his soul, as well as rejuvenate his marred member, Jean Phillippe moved his illegitimate son to his least favourite countryside residence, Château de la Colline Pourpre, an hour east of Aix-en-Provence and a million miles away from the streets of Paris. Mathis was given a hot bath, a hot meal, and a cold English governess. Despite his one act of kindness, Jean Philippe perished and Mathis, in accordance with French law, inherited his financial birth right. His stepmother was furious and immediately shipped him to a boarding school in Montreal, Canada, as far away from Parisian society as his passport allowed. It was a dream come true for Mathis. He placed the ushanka on his head, boarded the ship, stood at the prow, and watched the Atlantic shove them to Canada. Land of the Grizzlies. Two years later the world went to war, and Mathis, for the second time in his life, had been saved by another's vanity.

A peculiar fascination seldom exists without a sensible origin. General Jean Philippe had always refused Mathis cuddly toys because he claimed they were emasculating. His playthings were restricted to weapons, and while the governess wouldn't be so bold as to give Mathis a secret teddy, she did offer him the ushanka his father was given during a Russian post. After dinner his governess would read from one of Jean Philippe's prescribed war novels and Mathis would snuggle up to his hat. They sat by the fire in the winter and on the terrace during the summer. Mathis listened and rubbed the hat across his cheeks. The fur dampened with his breath and soon grew matted inside his small, tight grip, and it was through this affection that his uncanny interest in grizzly bears grew. This was an interest his father was happy to endorse, so that by the time Mathis left for Montreal, he was practically an expert on the subject. He saw his life as running parallel to the solitary and nomadic existence of the grizzly bear. After boarding school, he packed his camera equipment and made the long journey towards Ontario, where he bought a modest house in the middle of nowhere and began to pursue his passions in peace.

His love of photography did not have such obvious origins. It couldn't be pinpointed, but almost certainly dovetailed with his relationship to light. Light and its ability to replace words. Unspeakable, unfathomable words that stitched his memory with radiance. Indeed, his memory was held together with light. Candles in a room and his mother singing, dancing, praying. Men with lanterns in dark streets. A fire in a barrel. The cold moon through a crack in his bedroom ceiling and the glare of wet rocks against a cloudless sky. His mama lighting the desk lamp and the mountains moving from pink to purple like heavenly ships. He was a prism of his memory and in every direction he turned, light catalogued and defined him, so when his father gave him a Brownie camera for his birthday, it felt like the final benediction of an internal instrument that had long since been playing.

During his first few years in Pine Creek, he watched the light religiously and hardly spoke a word. He planted a garden. He read, and reread, the books he'd brought with him. He spent months away tracking, mapping, and photographing the grizzlies in his area. He had pictures of them fishing, mating, clawing the earth, and sleeping in large, soft piles. He grew accustomed to the smell of his body and the voice of his mind. It was like meeting an entirely new person. He knew hunger, danger, and thirst. He watched the bear and learned the mimicry of survival. He tended his garden and thought of himself as supremely happy.

But restlessness is the thorn of happiness, and one evening he found himself standing on the Nose, a boulder that jutted out from the rock face, and staring at the lit windows of a distant town. The next morning, he came down from the mountain and enquired about a room for the night. It was 1930 and the wheat prices had fallen so drastically that tens of thousands of farmers had been forced to leave their land. The country had gone into economic ruin and the innkeeper turned him away as though he were another vagrant until he produced cash from his wallet. The money was too much for the innkeeper to resist and he gave Mathis a room. From the window Mathis watched horses pull cars their owners could no longer afford to fuel. Entire families were shoeless and begging. The sound of his voice shocked him, but not so much as the desperation of humanity.

An hour and a clean face later, he trudged camera and tripod through the town, offering bread to those that would pose for him. He was told that the horse-drawn cars were called Bennett Buggy's. Many of them had been turned into homes with blankets and the few household items the travellers could carry stashed away under ripped seats and inside glove boxes. He took a photo of a soiled child nursing from a breast like a small pillow of air pushing from a ribcage. No one had the energy to complain. Their eyes reminded him of animals in the dead of winter. Many traded halves of bread for drink, which was another form of hibernation and he learned to feed the children first.

When he could no longer endure what he was seeing, he walked to the edge of town and into the woods. He set up his tripod and camera forty feet away from an old Ponderosa with the intent of capturing something more alive than the life he'd just witnessed. Which is exactly what happened, because when he looked through the lens, he saw Nora, sitting at the base of the tree and staring straight at him. The lens had turned her upside down. He could see that she was brown and beautiful even on her head.

"I've seen those. They say one can steal your soul," she said.

"Why don't you try it and decide for yourself," he said.

She moved in front of the lens, looked through it and immediately lurched back. He caught her; it was like holding a deer in his arms. She pushed away from him and brushed herself off.

"Sorry," he laughed, but she was not amused. "I should have told you the lens turns everything upside down," he said. "Try it again."

He felt her go quiet, so quiet that the silence between them became an understanding. She was chewing her tongue. He watched her and although she didn't move, she reflected a feeling of intrinsic life, like a tree trunk. She was small and steady. Industrious, he thought, a wren. Her whole body jolted, and he heard the shutter snap. He looked in the direction of the photograph and saw nothing. She emerged from the focusing cloth with a smile.

"Perfect," she said and walked off into the trees. She didn't bother lifting her muddy skirt and petticoat. He stared after her until she disappeared and then wondered if she'd been real. Strange things can happen to a lonely man, he thought, and then: Wait. Am I lonely?

Back in his dark room, weeks later, he watched the image of a small cardinal emerge from a dish of chemicals. It was sitting on a branch. Its chest was all puffed out as though it were just about to sing. So, he thought, not a wren after all. A cardinal. He spent the rest of the afternoon colouring its feathers red. The next day he framed and hung the photograph on the wall. It reminded him of snow before it's been stepped in. Pristine and perfect.

Day after day the cardinal sang to him. He couldn't stop hearing it, so busied himself and made a stew. Venison, juniper berry, tarragon. He stirred the pot and noticed the hand that held the spoon did not resemble his own. It was as hard as dark grit stone. He stopped and took inventory of himself. His body was calloused and scarred, ugly even, but his mind, his inside felt remarkably supple, as though he'd become the perfect design of a clam.

Perhaps, he thought.

Perhaps that's the way it is with work that you love?

Perhaps a strong body, makes a strong mind that unfastens inside?

It begins with something small. An idea. A hat. Two cells. A cardinal in a tree. Yes, he thought, yes. He wanted to share this revelation with someone; he looked at the photograph hanging on the wall, and then at the mountain beyond. He tasted the stew, it wasn't ready yet, and there was time to weed and water his garden before dinner. He'd need a hot meal inside him for the twoday hike it'd take him to reach his bride. He never gave it a second thought.

He arrived in town on a Sunday. There was a market, and the street was bustling with beggars, whores, greengrocers, businessmen, and ladies. He found her right away. She was wearing a hat that shadowed half her face. Her clothes were not new, but they were clean. She stood next to a stall knocking on a watermelon to test its ripeness. When he asked her to live with him, she imagined his eyes and his mouth visible in the night. The fever had taken her entire family. She had just enough money to survive the year, and all thoughts beyond that accompanied a panic so great that she often wished for death. She said yes.

Their life was peaceful. He spent all autumn and winter improving the house to her liking. He whittled her two cats for the mantelpiece and made a wardrobe for her dresses. He carved swirls of wind on the banister and leaves on the woodwork. He hung up his photos of birds, at her eye level, not his, because he knew she liked them, yet all the same, when spring arrived, the walls seemed to tighten.

"There is no other way to keep me," he told her, and left.

She learned that marriage to an artist is seasonal, but a quickening inside her told her that soon she'd have another to keep her company.

In the mountains and at home in his darkroom, Mathis hunted. He was a hunter of light. A hunter of illumination, where nothing remained untouched.

When Nora told him that she was pregnant, he thought of her womb as a camera, the captured seed was a slide and cells multiplied an image into view. When the baby was born they named him Jacques, and were you to hold his skin up to the sun you would see a series of slides:

An infant nursing on a rocking chair.

A barefoot child catching frogs.

A boy floating on his back in a pond and clouds racing their reflections over him.

A teenager standing in the silence of a snowy wood.

And so on and on. Each image, each slide, a single molecule building the picture of Jacques and Mathis was there and he wasn't there, like light through the trees, the presence of Mathis was dappled.

The year that Nora fell ill was the year Mathis met Callisto and something inside him stepped from one room into another, entirely. He hadn't realized he'd been made of rooms.

He tracked the female bear for days through trees heavy with vine. The ferns were waist high, and the ground was wet and buggy. Her urine smelled like a woman's heat, and he felt her around every corner, so strong was her presence, that birds startled him, so did the rain. How could he have been so careless? His equipment was getting soaked. He walked back to his campsite, crawled inside the tent, and laid his camera out to dry. Rain fell and slid down the tarpaulin, while he sat grumbling and picking at things, a hair from his hat, dirt from his fingernail, fluff, finally, he got up and walked outside.

There she was.

A silver freight train of steam. Callisto reared up and he tasted the hot spray of her breath, saw her yellow teeth, her nostrils spat. What could he do?

He always had a wild heart.

He felt a part of himself incinerate, every bit of him burned with sweat, the rattle of her spit sawed the air, and a crack between them, like wood catching fire, catching instinct, struck. The animal in him rose up to greet her; she lowered, grunted, and walked away. It was terrifyingly simple. He named her Callisto, and when he returned in the autumn, Nora noticed that a part of his soul was, indeed, missing.

It was the part that looked at her, only. He told her he'd been struck by lightning, he told her about Callisto, and she knew photography had stolen him once and for all. Over time Mathis and Callisto came to resemble one another, as though his photographs were captured mirrors, so that by the time Jacques was a young boy, he couldn't think of his father without thinking of Callisto. The two seemed fixed together like a handshake, like an ancient pact.

When his father's sleep had little growls inside it, Jacques knew he'd leave the following day. He always left during his black soil dreams and usually returned with the first snow. Nora would stand back and wait while Jacques ran to him and pounced. He'd laugh and stand there, letting Jacques empty his pockets of presents, glossy feathers, and stones with pictures on them. The snowflakes were penny sized and landed on their sweaters in patterns and melted. They would enter the warm house. Their discarded boots left puddles full of firelight. Mathis would reach inside his pack and give Jacques his whittled animals, then sit in his chair and speak for the first time in weeks.

The carvings were enhanced by his narrative. Jacques and his mother would draw up their knees under blankets, listen, and drink tea. Magnificent, faraway sentences flew from his mouth like feathers dislodged from the hunt. It entranced them and the carvings were dry talismans they spun inside their hot hands. He told his stories beautifully. He did not speak of his solitude, yet it was there, within the shadows that flicked against the wall, like black flags, as they sat inside the half said.

The light in Canada was completely different to the light in Provence. It was not supple and affectionate and wheaten. It was arresting and sharp or nothing, and how an artist used this light deserved, demanded even, a certain level of stateliness that bears naturally cultivated.

The photographer is his light.

The photograph achieves an immortality that is familiar because the picture is both real and unreal. As soon as time is fixed, it's gone, but the photograph remembers and throws out a tentacle of recognition that's entirely personal to the viewer. It's this disconnect of familiarity that haunts us, like a ghost in our clothing, the presence of a secret.

Years passed, and Mathis's photographs improved, because his secrets grew to the point where his obsession was almost revealed. Almost. The almost kept it spiritual, kept it art. If Mathis's pictures were able to whisper, they would undoubtedly speak of transformation.

For what becomes of a human who becomes their own beast?

What becomes of a human that doesn't?

That summer before Nora's death, Mathis came home early, but he was not himself, there were no rocks or feathers in his pockets, and he spent most of his time in his darkroom.

It was the summer of bluebottles.

Jacques remembers walking down the stairs in his pyjamas. The room smelt of vinegar, lemon, and unwashed hair. His mother was scrubbing tiny black spots from the woodwork with a wire brush and had already taken large circles of paint off the walls. Her actions were becoming increasingly manic, though this word did not factor into his vocabulary, and he saw her as possessed. Her peach housecoat was hanging half open and covered in white paint flecks. Her feet and knees were filthy and stray strands of hair kinked like black spider legs from her messy braid. Her arms stopped moving when she heard him, and water dripped from her elbows into a puddle on the floor.

"It's as if we've been cursed," she said.

He let the comment hang in the room like an unheeded warning. What was there to say? He blinked at her. She was right. He went and made a cup of tea.

The summer heat had produced a plague of black flies. Bluebottles created a hive of iridescence between the storm windows and the house felt as though it was floating inside a crawling sea.

When the flies first arrived, Jacques helped his father remove the outer windows. The morning was yellow, hot, and still. Their valley was scorched bland, and the mountains rose like stone omens. The flies burst forward and landed a shiny glove on Jacques's face. He gagged and swallowed one by accident. His father pointed up to the black ribbon twisting out of view, and his mother, on the porch, began a round of applause. Mathis and Jacques joined her, and a row of pines that pitch-forked the sky caught the sound of their clapping as it skipped across the field. The sun had made them dizzy. Inside the house, Jacques drank a glass of water to dislodge the wing he had caught in his throat.

Of course, it had been useless, as the flies returned in droves, and like an organized army, they left black spots, smears, and swirls on the woodwork and in corners. They bit and drew blood, and when they died, they left their flaky carcasses across the floor. Their tiny black bodies crumbled under Jacques's bare feet. All summer long he picked wings and antennae out from between his toes.

Jacques pulled a chair up to the window and drank his tea. A fly squeezed through a small hole of broken sealant at the bottom of the window frame and whined with freedom. He put his tea down and waited. It landed and protracted its arms like windshield blades. He placed his thumb on top of it until he felt a pop, then walked to the back door and flicked its body towards the dry ground. It scattered with the others like blue-black scabs on a head of sedge grass.

Beyond the field, his father's boat rolled to shore. He had been fishing, and Jacques had heard him leaving at dawn, heard his zipper, his heels in boots, the turning doorknob, and then the peaceful nothingness of a person who has left. The window was a patch of early morning lavender and chilly shadow, and he fell back to sleep curled under his quilt.

Jacques walked down to the pier. The fish hung from a tree like a line of silver darts. His father reached up, cut the line, and threw them on the ground where they flapped droplets of musky water against Jacques's legs. His mother, dressed and composed once more, stomped down the hill drying a knife on her apron. Her hair was secured with clips. She did not look at Jacques. Instead, she looked at the fish and whistled her approval. Mathis smiled.

Jacques squatted next to his mother and helped her unhook the fish mouths. She chopped the heads off the smaller fish and gutted the rest. She gave him a newspaper full of entrails and fish heads.

"Bury it," she said, and grabbed his arm.

His father was walking back to his boat.

She squeezed his arm and didn't blink.

He knew she wasn't talking about fish guts. He thought of her in her peach housecoat. He pushed her hand off his arm and she softened, recoiled.

"I'm so sorry. I'm so sorry, squirrel. I'm just tired, that's all," she said, as she lifted her face towards the sun. "I'll get better."

"I know," said Jacques.

She looked at him. Her eyes glistened like two bluebottles and infected everything.

A flock of geese flew overhead, noisy as a crowd of bicycle horns, and he watched them land on the lake. It was incredibly still, and the geese smeared across its reflected mountains like raindrops across a canvas. There was disruption all around him. He buried the fish guts in the garden and walked back to the house.

His mother was in the kitchen chopping onions. There were tears streaming down her face, so she hadn't noticed the onions turning pink.

"You're bleeding!" Jacques said.

She stopped, dried her eyes on her sleeve and looked down with amazement at the cut between her thumb and forefinger. It was long and deep. She dipped her finger in the pool of blood, licked it, and grabbed a tea towel. The blood mushroomed through the cloth like a red cloud.

"It's nothing. Here," she gave him the knife and swatted flies as she ran down the hallway. He finished chopping the onions.

He knew she hadn't felt a thing.

There were other clues. Once she dropped a spoonful of chilli on the floor and when she couldn't pick it up, began banging her hand against the wall. His father had been away on expedition and by the time he returned, the bruise was a pale yellow as if someone had rubbed a dandelion across her knuckles.

After his eyes adjusted to it, he saw it everywhere.

To him the word illness meant stomach bug or cough. It meant hot soup, not sudden outbursts of vowels like loud, frustrated claps. It meant blankets, not dead hands. Her hands were the first to lose their feeling. They were battered, bruised, and cut. He knew when she could feel because she'd ask him to sit next to her, then she'd run her hands up and down his arms, his chest, stopping to feel his heartbeat, through his hair, and then softly, softly across his face and cheeks.

By the end of the summer her arms were as thin as a child's. They were ropes she wrapped around herself as if trying to hold together the pieces of a shipwreck. In her eyes she carried the same mysteriousness of the sea and could not be helped or predicted or guided. Her illness was like a superstition his father refused to talk about. The problem was that his father was not a seafaring man. He was a woodsman. He knew wood and very little of water. He was not prepared to learn something new. Sometimes it is simply the refusal of change that initiates change so suddenly.

It was the risk that made Mathis feel alive, the risk of losing, not his life, but the intensity of the moment by coming one step too close. He began to crave the adrenaline that stretched like a trip wire between himself and Callisto. The camera was a way to trap that vertigo through explosion, flash, in a box that he could take apart with his hands. If he could, he would have taken himself apart. He would have reassembled himself. It was violent like that. It was violent in the way that making love is violent, for what is essential for our survival, can also drive us beyond our own control. He could not control himself or his desires any more than he could control

Callisto. But. He could house the two of them inside a slide, so that he owned his weakness, and like a magician, he could revive them from darkness and into the focus of light.

Jacques and his father were collecting firewood.

"I notice you haven't been carving," his father said.

It was true. Resurrecting the mouse had scared Jacques and he'd been afraid to carve since. What if it happened again, or worse yet, what if it didn't? It had felt so natural that Jacques now wondered if it had actually happened at all. His father took a small shell from his pocket.

"Look here," he said.

It was a small thing. A seashell deep inside the capacious lungs of the forest like a perfect pink cyst. His father held it up.

"I found this in the forest. It happens sometimes that an echo of the past can make its way to the surface. The seabed that produced the shell a million years before the forest grew proves the soil's legacy, but the forest cannot remember anything beyond its own existence and has no recollection of the watery beginnings it feeds from. We live inside our enclosures," he said, "and occasionally, we wake up inside the wrong one. Your mama, my mother, was Creole and would be upset with me for saying that. There are no wrong enclosures, she'd say, the soul learns what it needs to know for its entire journey. She was a guide. A translator of enclosures. Some people thought she was crazy. Others thought she was wise. Crazy or wise, my photographs guide me, soothe me, and she taught me that there is no other way to live. I want to tell you this." Mathis placed the shell inside of Jacques's hand. "When you find your essence, be true to it. If you are a shell that wakes inside a forest, do not deny the ocean, guide it. Guiding is a part of your legacy. There are fossils of your mama inside of you."

The shell in the forest, thought Jacques, as he looked at his father, the bear in the skin. The creator within.

The Sculptor - Gret Heffernan

The starling arrived the next day. It has been killed for sport by one of the cats and left beside the front door as a present. Jacques picked it up and inspected the two clean little holes inside its chest. What if it had fledglings? A power is not corrupting if it's used for good, he thought, and carried the bird upstairs.

Wood is perfect for re-embodiment and invites touch because it, too, is cellular and composed of tissues, so cell attracts cell and regrows cell. It burns, its wounds leak, and it has a memory and turns to stone, like our bones, when they're petrified, yet retains a warmth that is unduplicated. This warmth, like the warmth of a human, comes from the sharpening or growing of a core, and must first endure tools, both brutal and smoothing. Age quickly possesses cellular entities, and the perfect sculpture begins to erode as soon as it's created. Like humans, the earth lays claim to the reusing of molecules from the beginning. Our molecules are intelligent, yet fluctuating, and therein lies their precious ability to mutate.

Jacques's mama, his father and now Jacques himself were all born with the ability to harness life's forces. We are taught the laws of physics, and, without question, these influence our universe, but the forces that dominate our species are the laws of emotional acumen. Jacques's lineage understood that physics and intelligence could be interchangeably influenced through ritualistic prayer. Sculpture is his form of prayer; his father's was photography; his mamas was voodoo. It is an old wisdom and Jacques was born into it.

As his ability to resurrect small animals matured, it was as though the forest knew, so brought to him it's recently perished. He built a long shelf above his bed and placed all his resurrections on top of it. There were lots of mice and birds, a few rabbits, and a single glorious vixen. He had found her by a stream. Her coat was wet and solid with frost. He didn't have a piece of wood with him that was fox sized, so decided to try with the small bit of maple he had in his satchel. He sat down beside her and began to carve and pray. The water gently rocked her beautiful, russet form, from her white throat hung miniature icicles. He thought of how he would use a hot poker from the fire and gently singe her forelegs and the tips of her ears black. When she was awakened, he'd locate the black flecks in her eyes.

She did not run away from him like the others had but stretched her limbs and took a drink of water, before looking directly at him and walking into the wood. For a moment, Jacques wondered if she might speak to him, so abundant was her spirit, and he felt their organisms align. The vixen reminded him of how his mama would have been, a majestic survivalist, a mystery outside of the mind's field.

When you understand this, when you begin to live outside of your enclosure, it is not inconceivable that the essence of one thing might fall into another. That a vixen might resemble his mama, that lives should link, though this was never the physical case with Jacques. His arms were arms, not wings, his hands were hands, not claws, but through them he could raise the shells from the soil. In resurrecting you never produced the entire personality, rather the substance that was the strongest, so when his mother began to lose her mind, he carved and carved her hands, for they had always been the strongest.

A pair of loons called out inside the crickets' hum. Jacques put down his book and went to the open window. His mother was sleeping. The sun was sinking, and Jacques could see Mathis rolling a large log from the woodland. A trail of bulldozed grass stretched all the way to his darkroom. When Mathis reached the door, he turned it upright and wrapped his arms around it with his face against the bark. It looked as though he were wrestling someone. Jacques heard the log thunk in the corner.

Jacques left the house and followed the trail of bent grass to the edge of the woods. The forest floor was springy, covered with pine needles and mossy stumps like half-hidden trolls.

Mosquitos shrilled through the ferns and spiny thicket, a few owls piccoloed off the dense alders, where small funnels of evening lit up the occasional tree, but otherwise the canopy was evergreen thick. One of these funnels spotlighted a split tree trunk that sat in the ground like a shard of glass.

It reminded him of his mother's hands.

It was an old wound and leg-thick branches lay on the ground. It was beautiful wood, soft and easy to manipulate. Jacques picked up as much as he could carry and walked back to the house. It was almost dark and orange holes were glowing from his father's darkroom. Jacques piled the wood on the porch and squat down to choose a piece to carve. It was smooth, unknotted, and the size of a forearm.

He let his knife decide the shape the wood would take. The forms he was carving at that time transcended classification, like a sigh or laughter transcends language. He drilled small holes in the bottom of each sculpture and stuck them on a stick fixed inside a block of wood.

He thought of them as sensations. His mother called them shrunken heads. He placed them in his bedroom window, where their shadows cast strange boulder shapes across the floor. He liked the view between them. Sometimes he carved a certain shape purely to break the view, to crack the space around it, and rift the surge of atoms like a bubble in a life that's sedimenting.

He was learning to carve himself, to thumbprint and convert the wood into his own creation. He looked down at his carving and saw that it was becoming another small, cupped hand. He imagined removing his mother's hands at the wrist and replacing them with ones of his own making. They would be beautifully carved with stars for knuckles and diamonds for fingernails.

Mathis's darkroom was a shed without windows that sat twenty paces from the house. Each wall had three fist-sized holes for ventilation and when Mathis was developing his photographs, he nailed a flat board over the holes. It had been days since Mathis had left his darkroom, yet the holes remained uncovered. Through them,

Jacques could see small movements of light, shadow, and once, even an arch of piss. Mathis ate carrots, string beans, rolled-up bread, anything that would fit through the holes. He refused to open the door.

Nobody was allowed to look inside. If Mathis needed something he pushed his lips through the wall like a slug and shouted. Jacques passed him screwdrivers, long sticks, tacks, and wildflowers. Jacques saw photographs glossing the walls and a thick silhouette in the corner. He wondered if it was the log he'd seen his father rolling and squinted towards the figure.

"Take your eyes off her. You have no business looking at her," his father said.

His eye floated like a knot in the wood.

"Father," said Jacques, "tell me what you are trying to do."

"I'm saving her," said Mathis.

And Jacques knew that he was talking about his mother, that he was trying to save Nora, that Callisto and Nora were not separate in his father's mind, but joined, somehow, in essence. That he was trying to summon Callisto in the hope of giving Nora strength.

"Let me," said Jacques.

"No," said Mathis as he closed the small window.

Mathis had been inside his darkroom for five days when Nora started throwing things at the wall. The objects she threw grew twice their size in the long autumn light and hit the wall like monsters.

Jacques took the knives and scissors from the kitchen drawer, threw them in a bag and left. She didn't notice. She was caught in a rhythm. He walked past his father's darkroom, three holes flickered with gaslight, and all the way to the lake.

He sat cross-legged on the dock. The reflection of a few stars lay trapped in the lake like fireflies in a black jar. Nude fish mouths wrinkled the water's skin. He took his knife and a small, unfinished carving from his pocket. It was a pawn. The last piece to his set. He and his father played chess during the winter when the bears were hibernating. The sky was as dark as it would get on a full moon and behind him the house anchored like a bright ship.

The lake held even the Milky Way.

At its bottom the fish slept with stars on their backs.

He thought about this. He thought about the burn of possibility.

He walked back to the house. His father was still in his darkroom, softly singing. Cold air rushed him through the door. She wasn't asleep, instead, sat in a pile of torn clothes and didn't look up.

"You're too hard on things," she said, mending one of his shirts.

The needle stabbed her thumb. The stitching was large and irregular. On the table he could see little pinprick indentions scattered across the surface like beads. Mathis opened the door and Jacques hardly recognized him. His face was smeared and hairy. There were many things different about him, but the most noticeable was the smell.

"Look at how useful I am," Nora said, holding up a crudely darned shirt. "Aren't I useful?"

The first snow came and lasted for days. It drifted ground level with the windows ledge and cast a strange bleaching light into the house. Mathis began digging a path to the woodpile. The shovel scraped inside silence. Outside there was a crow. Inside, Nora slept in a puddle of sweat and moved in and out of consciousness. Jacques made a beef pie for dinner and listened to a mouse nesting in the roof.

Mathis turned his face towards the mountain. It was always snowing on the mountaintop, and if Mathis had remained on the mountain for too long, he began to feel as though he were drowning in the white glare. His eyes would start to search for structure and colour, an edge, a deepening in the path, and that's when he would know that it's time to leave. He often drank the sight of the first flower he'd come across, poking like a beautiful hand through the snow, his descend into the green valley could melt him with its suppleness. He knew there was no thirst like the thirst for the green and living world.

He thought about this as he stacked a wall of wood behind the stove. He wanted to say something meaningful to Jacques who was reading at the table. The smell of cooking beef filled the room, and Jacques could feel the cold from his father's body as he stood above him. There seemed to be no way to undo what had been done. He closed his book and looked up at his father in his overcoat and work gloves.

"She's stuck on the mountain," Mathis said, "but you're not."

It explained everything and nothing at the same time.

"I'll only be away for a little while. Remember your uncle in Illinois."

"Don't," Jacques implored.

"I promise I'll come back."

In the morning Mathis was gone. Jacques woke to a cold house, dressed, and went to light the stove. He placed the kettle on top of the hob, put on his boots and damp coat, and went outside to replenish the wood basket. He didn't want to touch the wall of wood his father had built. As soon as he opened the door his moisture instantly froze. His breath hung in front of his face in little exhales of fog. Above him, stars like lighthouses filled the morning sky.

He walked to the logs stacked alongside the house. The black tarp that covered them had frozen to the wood, and when he jerked it free, he ripped off the top layer of bark. The logs were icy and smooth in his bare hands as he threw them into the basket. Birdsong took the sharpness out of the air. He could hear his mother coughing upstairs. The kitchen was warm when he returned, and the kettle was boiling. He put the full basket next to the stove and made two cups of tea. On the table was another letter from his cousin in Callisto. It felt like his father had left it on purpose and Jacques tucked it away in his coat pocket.

Months passed and blizzards came and went. His mother slept through it all in her sweat. Her breath rose and fell with effort. It snagged on every gurgle. Jacques melted snow on the stove and spoon-fed her. Their larder was nearly empty and everything fresh had long been devoured. In the evenings he read or whittled or did anything to avoid confronting the inevitable. The piano beside the sofa beckoned him with its promise of irregular noise. He didn't want to wake her. Sometimes he put the lid down and played intense, inaudible songs.

Time was both fast and slow.

Then, one evening, he found himself standing at the door to his father's darkroom. Hibernation was close to death, he thought, perhaps he could carve Callisto and bring his father to him. A key on a string dangled from his gloved hand. Jacques had nearly stopped believing his father would return. It seemed like their only chance. The sound of his boots crunching in the snow and the owls echoed in his lonely chest. His heart was beating fast. His mother had stopped eating all together. It wouldn't be long. She was mumbling in her sleep when he left the house.

He needed the strength, however forbidden, that his father seemed to find inside this room. He was desperate. He looked up at the moon, white stone cut by black branches. He opened the door and stepped inside.

It was black and smelled feral. He switched on his flashlight. It shone a yellow spot on the floor while his eyes adjusted. He was afraid to look at the walls. He was afraid but did it anyway and what he saw repulsed and fascinated him.

They were covered with pictures of Callisto. The pictures were framed with mud. He smelt it. It was bear faeces. Inside the scat his father had placed little stones and twigs in interwoven patterns. Feathers and bits of flower were delicately pressed into his finger swirls. It was disturbingly beautiful.

He saw her in the corner.

He shined his flashlight on the carved image of Callisto, but she wasn't exactly a bear. Her face was more human than bear. Her paws were human hands. She was serene, almost perfect, and adorned with wreaths of withered wildflowers. Large clumps of fur were glued to her body. Her eyes seemed to plead for release. There was a cough behind him, he turned and found his mother standing just beyond the door, clutching her nightdress to her throat.

"You shouldn't have done that," she said. Her voice was a whisper.

She was barefoot in the snow. Her frail body quivered underneath her nightdress and her eyes were wide and wild. She looked like a ghost.

"You scared me. What are you doing out here, it's freezing, you'll catch cold. Come on. Come back inside," he said, but she just stared at him.

"You shouldn't have done that," she said again.

"Done what?"

"Gone inside," she nodded towards the shed.

"I was just locking it up," he said.

She was beginning to scare him. Her voice was incredibly flat, but her face was hateful.

"Liar! Now he'll smell you and never come back!" she shouted and lunged towards him.

Her teeth were bluish white in the moonlight. Her fingernails dug into his neck. He tried to push her off, he didn't want to fight her, he kept shouting at her to stop, but she was vicious. She clung and bit. Her body, her skin was hot and jagged. He couldn't believe her strength; her bones were sharp and powerful, and her face was a scream. She was tearing out his hair when he seized her hand. Her mouth attacked his glove and she bit and spat until she reached his skin. He smacked her and she fell back into the bloodied snow. She was spitting with exhaustion.

She let him pick her up and carry her back into the house. She was shivering by the time he put her in bed. He pulled the blankets up to her chin; she said nothing and closed her eyes. He fetched another blanket from his bed to wrap around her shaking body. When he returned, he saw that her head had fallen off the pillow. He gently placed his hand behind her neck and lifted. She was unconscious and limp, but alive. He knew she couldn't stay alive for long. He wanted it finished and complete, so leant down to her ear and whispered.

"Don't be afraid. I'll bring you back."

During the night, he put his hand under her head and listened to her breath as it slowed to a stop.

He couldn't stay, there wasn't enough food, yet he couldn't leave her there, nor could he bury her as the ground was frozen solid. So, he collected her body and walked to the door. Outside the world was quiet, but for his footprints and the crystalline clouds of his staggered breathing. Wisps against a starry sky. He knew what he had to do.

He walked slowly towards the ravine.

It was deep and hidden and he threw her down it like a stick. Her nightdress billowed before she began to descend. There had been nothing left of her, he consoled himself. Heavy flakes of snow added another layer of silent insulation. There was no sound. No wind. No mouse, owl, or fox. His animal had left as well. His animal was at the bottom of the ravine.

Now he needed noise. He clapped his hands. He leapt up and ran aimlessly in circles, shouting, screaming, and kicking snow into the air, until he collapsed and rolled himself into a ball. The snow melted around his heat. It cooled his forehead.

He was wet and tired, so tired. Inside the house looked warm and golden. There were parts of himself he could not feel. He rose and walked towards the door. He closed the door behind him and locked it. He lay down by the fire and fell asleep.

Her eyes filled his dreams.

All night, her body slowly disappeared beneath a skin of snow, his dreams.

He slept the following day. The next evening, he entered the woods. The pines were black. The birch trees appeared to be made of silver moon skin. It made him look at his own hands, un-gloved in the freezing air, chapped, stark, and, he now realized, capable of death as well as rebirth, life. She had died in his hands. He had held her head like a large frozen egg. He shook her a little, just to be sure, as though death were something one could crack out of, as though she might rattle a clue.

Weeks passed and snow fell and with each new carving he tried and to crack death, yet failed to bring her back, though he could feel his power growing and he knew he needed to leave.

The morning sky was white and startling, and he stood underneath it alone. It no longer felt so heavy. He couldn't stay in Pine Creek. But what if his father came back? It was possible that he was just stranded at a post in the mountains and would return in the spring. Anything was possible.

Jacques walked into the garage and flicked on the light. The slender trunk of pine was resting like a patient on his workbench. He removed the sheet with the flair of a magician. I'll begin with the head, he thought, its shape and hair, I'll save her face for last. He would have to choose her expression carefully and he hoped that by carving her body first, her form might explain her desired countenance. It's important that she has a choice, he doesn't want her to feel forced or manipulated, so he listens to the wood and the life still inside it, akin to a faint heartbeat.

He began to tear away each piece of her bark as though it were a fresh scab. He used his hands and a small chisel. Anything electric he feared might jolt her, and that is not what the wood wants. She's alive, but he needed to build her emotions, and for creating her persona he relied on listening to the wood. He delicately turned her over and peeled the bark from her other side. She is the length of a head and torso. He ran his hands down the cylinder of her figure. The gesture was intimate and if she were awake, she'd shiver. The wood splinters where it's knotted and he began sanding her back to a smooth, honeyed bone.

Initially there is often a sense of mutilation that remains until the sculpture has come to life, not alive in the way that blood knows it, but life as resurrection through smell, through touch, and that captured narrative we screw into ourselves to hold our memories together. Once they grasp that his purpose is to remake them as solid and strong, his marks move from scars to inscriptions and the relationship begins.

In the beginning, during his activation, the time that he now thinks of as the period when he was learning how to resurrect, his sculpting was frenzied and raw. He'd race through forms that were often muddled with misshapen animals, digging, cutting through layers to get to the bottom of himself. Now, each new sculpture arrives as an instruction of crystalline precision that he can feel expanding beneath his eyelids like frost.

He expected her to return as a bear, but she didn't. Perhaps Callisto was dead, he thought, perhaps his father was trying to resurrect the bear inside his shed?

When he'd finished, he held the sculpture and prayed. There was nothing, he felt nothing, no jolt, no rushing assembly of molecules like the pouring of grains into a jar. It didn't work, he thought, I've failed and a darkness inside him ruptured. And his lonely heart was a thrown brick breaking through ice and sinking in the black water beneath the expanding cracks. He could feel it waiting at the bottom of himself. That evening, he sat down next the fire and wondered where to go. He thought of America. How bizarre it had been that his father had had a brother in Callisto. What were the odds? We are only our chances, our risks, his father had once said, there is no such thing as a coincidence. A destination that seemed both close and far away. He craved an expedition, a place where he could sculpt in peace and learn to develop his gift of resurrection. A place where he could bring his mother back, healthy and sane.

He flipped the pages of the encyclopedia and when he reached the Mississippi, he stopped. She was vein blue and Callisto, Illinois was attached to her like a cyst, like a knot, like a fist.

It is easy to get an American passport when you have money and are the grandson of a French general. Over the following days, he reported his mother missing, shipped his books, his tools, a few sculptures, his father's photography and his French cutlery. He planned to stay in America.

The night before he left, he took his carvings from the shelves and held them one by one. He opened the encyclopedia to Illinois, placed it on the table, and stood his carvings around it in a circle. On the page he wrote, "I am here," just in case his father returned, but also because he wanted to preserve the moment he began living his own life. He imagined dust coating the page and the Mississippi like a fine ice. Soon birds will nest and splat Illinois with their tiny white meteor explosions.

In the morning, he carried a single bag to the train.

It was as loud as a tunnelling dream. It had silver bones, bolted joints, grilled teeth, he stepped inside its snarl and clicked open a glass eye to breathe. Only the icicles near the steam dripped on the platform.

The mountains were ripped charcoal drawings pasted to a blue sheet and as the train left, they began to smudge. He moved his thumb along the dark pines that bearded their bases. Enormous black lakes, like oceans, mirrored beside him. He was the only passenger in the compartment and could let himself think aloud, could let his mouth hang open as he stared at the racing. When night fell, he saw a single light ahead. A station, he thought, or America, whatever it is, I'm heading straight towards it like a ferocious black moth. He opened his arms like wings.

All the way there he imagined he was sitting by the Mississippi riverbank. Skips of gold were on the swells. The sun was hot and the sorrow in him gagged like a sheath he'd swallowed. When I'm ready,

The Sculptor - Gret Heffernan

he thought, I'll begin pulling it from my ears, my eyes, my nose, and it will slip from my fingers and land on the water like a grey scum, it will float downriver, it will break as it slams against the ocean, it will break, and dissolve and I'll never see it again. Then I'll be empty and free for the wind to inhabit, he thought, he dreamed, the wind.

Callisto, Illinois

The walk from the station took him an hour. It was a different country's heat. He followed the map, stayed close to the river, and stuck to the path. There was sun everywhere, warm and penetrating, and the sky was a breaking open kind of blue. It occurred to him that the clearest view of a place was from a distance.

Already, Pine Creek seemed like a life away, another life that belonged to someone that resembled him. He had begun to think of himself as a person he was about to meet when he heard her, Elora, singing between two rocks. Each with their own identity, as though looking down in soundless appreciation.

The house had two identities as well. From its west side stretched a flat green palm of prairie; a runway for the wind that whipped with paint-tearing force and left bits of timber bare and exposed like grey sores on a body. Its east side gently sloped to the river. It reminded Jacques of an old clown who'd applied only half of his white makeup.

Both sides of the house produced waves, the grass and the water flowed together, so that it was immersed in constant movement, like an island one could walk to. A single track arrowed through grasses and into town, Jacques stood on it, and grasshoppers stuck to his legs. Two women sat on the porch. One waved. But his mind was with the singing woman he'd met by the rocks, Elora, who has arrived like his very own bear, his fascination.

Wake up, wake up, said the world, and he did.

Birdie Dubois

Callisto is a town with a population of 527 and if you were to picture it in your mind you would imagine a Main Street draped with red, white, and blue banners, presumably for the 4th of July. You would see a Benjamin Franklin store with a flag in the window, a central limestone courthouse, impeccably cut grass, and hanging planters of begonias on every lamppost.

Inside the living room of my childhood home there is a brown leather chesterfield with a crochet blanket and green wingback chairs beside the fireplace. The curtains are a golden, almost mustard, cotton, chosen to reflect the sun. The walls are white. The floorboards are bare, with scattered, worn rag rugs. There is a black upright piano in the corner that my mother used to play. On the walls hang her paintings interspersed with my own photo boxes, hung by Stan in neat rows.

Her paintings have had a greater influence on me than any other work I've known, though not many people liked them. "Likeability isn't the point," my mother would say. "The point is to discover what's hiding, and we never like that part of ourselves, otherwise we wouldn't keep it hidden." She painted various shapes of light pastel colours emitting a single shadow.

The shadow was a form different to the shape from which it spread and gave the impression that someone or something was

hiding behind, say, a triangle or an oblong. The shadows are vaguely
human, which means you cannot fix them into a known form, so
they alter with each view. The sensation of this flux, of something
you cannot see, cannot identify, gives the feeling of being watched,
though from a great distance, like standing in the middle of an omen.
And you itch to know what is behind the shape, which you've come
to dislike because you get the sense that somehow, preposterously,
you've put it there yourself, that you've deliberately obscured what
should be in plain view. How wise she was, I thought, how accurately
she'd illustrated human nature.

Marge and I watched Jacques walk alongside the river towards
the house. I remember looking down the road for Arlo's car and
feeling relieved that he had driven out of sight. See, the thing was,
nobody knew beforehand that Jacques was black. It was shocking
because it was a situation that hadn't occurred to anybody, in part
because I was pale to the point of bloodless with brownish-blond
hair, so we just didn't expect that my cousin would be black. Haitian,
as it turned out. I waved. He raised his hand and waved in return. His
body was long and angular. He carried a backpack and a satchel only.

"You must be Birdie," he walked up the porch steps and extended
his hand. "And you must be Jacques," I said, and shook it, "nice to
meet you." He had the weathered, yet sanded hands of a sculptor. "I
take it you're Marge?"

He turned to Marge and stuck out his hand, which Marge
bypassed and gave him a hug, "it's so great to finally meet you at long
last," she let him go and patted him on the shoulder, "now, would you
like a drink or some food or something?"

"Just a glass of water would be nice, thank you, but I can get it."

"No, no, you just sit, and I'll be right back," and the screen door
banged behind her.

"What a wonderful place, thank you so much for letting me stay.
Marge wrote me about your leg, I'm so sorry," he sat down on an
Adirondack chair beside me.

"Well, thanks, it's more of a hindrance now than painful. Listen, I'm afraid we weren't really expecting you for at least another week or more, so I don't know if the studio is completely ready or not," I said.

"It's fine, it's fine," Marge interrupted as she opened the door, "it's not as clean as it could be but I turned the sheets and cleaned out the refrigerator. That's all you need to begin with. We can finish the rest tomorrow. Here you go," she gave him the water.

"Thanks," he said, "if I can help with anything just let me know."

"Oh, don't you worry, I left a list of honeydos on the kitchen table," she said.

"Well, I appreciate it and am more than happy to lend a hand. It's beautiful here," he said and finished his water.

"Right then," she took his glass, "there's time enough for chitchat later, let me show you to your accommodation. I need to get home and give Muriel her pills."

"No rest for the wicked," I said, and he smiled. "Stop over later after you're settled."

"Will do, nice to meet you," he said and followed Marge across the lawn.

Until that point, I hadn't really noticed that Callisto was entirely white. I'm ashamed to say that it hadn't particularly occurred to me. Back then, there were many things I wasn't aware of, like how even air has a prejudice, and cooking and clothes, and, most importantly, ideas. Racism when it's obvious is easy to detect, but I've come to understand that it is racism's dormant hidden areas, like the shadows in my mother's paintings, that are the most transformative, the most vicious. Marge sensed it too. After she showed him to the studio, she came back into the house to grab her car keys and said, "Do you think he knows he's landed in the whitest town in America?"

"If he does, he doesn't seem that interested," I said.

"Well, they'll be interested in him, that's for damn sure. Let's be honest, this is small-town middle America and he's the only black person for, what? Fifty miles? I'm gonna worry myself sick. And, you, staying here all by yourself. Good lord, the rumours," she crossed herself, "I'll see what I can do."

"Don't do anything Marge. He's my cousin and he seems nice," I said.

"Nice is beside the point and you know it," she said, and left.

At the time I thought she was exaggerating, but of course the peace wasn't going to last forever. Of course, his arrival wasn't going to become some positive experiment of racial integration. Another thing I hadn't comprehended, because I'd never had a reason to, such is the privilege of white skin, but we were knee deep in clan country. And then, when I began to sense that he was running from something, something bad, well, it was like he'd chosen to hide in an open field surrounded by vipers. Things were bound to go wrong, snakes are bound to strike, and they did, Lord, how they did.

Arlo came over that evening with a punnet of plums. He was newly shaven and smelled of apple shampoo. The light was on in Jacques's studio. Arlo was alone. I felt a flash of fear when I answered the door. Back then, I pushed my instinct away, now, I know better.

"Where's Elora?"

"At home. She's not feeling well. She gets these headaches that come on all of a sudden, and well, hey, has your lodger arrived early?" He nodded towards the studio light and gave me the punnet.

"No. It's just Marge doing some last-minute organizing," I lied. It is hard to convey the reflex I had regarding Arlo. I wouldn't generally lie, but then, I wouldn't generally invite a man who made me feel uneasy inside my house, however, I was afraid Jacques would come outside.

"Thanks," I said, "give Elora my best. It was from a poem, you know, when we arrived, the place reminded me of a poem about plums." He said nothing. Moths pinged against the screen door.

"I wouldn't say no to a beer," he said.

"Okay, um, come in," it was the last thing I wanted and even though it hurt like hell, I made myself put pressure on my broken leg and use the crutches to enter the kitchen. I wanted to dissuade him from visiting me.

"You sure you can manage?"

"I'm fine, honestly, sit down," I called from the open refrigerator, took the bottle out, and hopped back to the living room. "Here you go."

"You aren't joining me?" he asked and I shook my head, no. "Painkillers," I explained.

"What is all this stuff?" he moved the bottle around the room, then took a swig.

"It's my mother's work, mostly, and some of mine."

"Huh," he inspected a painting. "Well, I don't pretend to know anything about it, but it's interesting, I'll give ya'll that. How is your momma anyway?"

"She passed away a few years ago."

"I'm sorry to hear that. I hadn't heard. Cancer, was it?"

"Lung, and that's okay, I didn't expect you to know."

"Ah, well that makes sense, she was a smoker after all."

"No, actually, she wasn't."

"I think you are mistaken."

"I think I would know if my own mother smoked."

"Well, I hate to differ, but I saw her once, behind your garage, smoking a cigarette."

"Just because my mother might have had a secret cigarette once or twice doesn't warrant her deserving to die from lung cancer."

"I didn't say she deserved it."

"You said it makes sense."

"Now, you're just plain overreacting."

"I feel like you've insulted my mother!"

"You are blowing what I said way out of proportion, but I can understand it, with you being on painkillers and all. Plus, you must be tired. I'll leave and let you rest."

"An excellent idea," I said and walked him to the door.

"You get some sleep now, you hear? Rest up and I'll visit you again tomorrow, see if you need anything."

"Arlo, you don't need to visit me tomorrow. I'm fine."

"Uh-huh. Listen, I am truly sorry about your momma, I am. I hope that's the thing you take from this conversation. Now stick those plums in the freezer so they're nice and cold in the morning," he said, and put his Stetson on.

When he left, I stood on the porch and wondered what the hell had just happened. His manipulation wasn't obvious. He had insulted my mother, hadn't he? Or was I just making a mountain out of a molehill? I sat second guessing myself until Jacques opened the door to the studio and lit a cigarette. Figures, I thought and waved him over.

"Evening," he said, and sat on the porch steps.

"Got a spare?" I asked, and he took another cigarette from his shirt pocket.

"Thanks, want a beer? I mean, you'll have to get up and get it yourself and all, but, I wouldn't mind another."

"No problem, sorry, I should have asked if you needed anything," he got up and entered the house, "is the kitchen straight through?"

"Yep, just help yourself," I said, and he returned a minute later with two opened beers.

"It's extraordinary in there. Is that your artwork?"

"Some of it, the boxes are, the paintings are my mothers."

"What do you call them? Joseph Cornell on Steroids?" he asked, and I laughed.

"I've called them lots of things over the years – assemblage poems, box poems, curio poems, pain-in-the-ass poems. I don't really know how they classify exactly, so I let the observer decide that, I just know what I want them to say."

"That makes perfect sense to me. I hadn't realized you were an artist."

"Like you," I said.

"Oh, I wouldn't call myself an artist, I'd say I'm more of a glorified carpenter or something. That's why I'm here, to hone in on my real craft."

"Which is?"

"Transformation."

"Ha! Well, for not being an artist, you certainly speak like one," I said. "But I get it. It's quiet enough to think here, though it must have been quiet in Canada, right?"

"Yes, it was quiet, but there is such a thing as too quiet, too still, which can become the opposite of peaceful," he looked down the empty dirt road and the blackness beyond. "There is nothing unforgiving here, in the landscape, I mean, it's gentle, in Canada, the land, the silence can be fierce," he said.

"Well," I took a drink, "I see your point, but let me tell you something, here, you get that kind of silence, that kind of fierceness from people and don't you forget it."

Our conversations were always meaningful like this, and the pleasantries were few, it was more like – hello, hello, existentialism. I might have fallen in love with him had he not have been my cousin and had I not have been thinking about Stan every minute of the livelong day, which is what happens when you're told you can't have someone, they begin to infect you. So, it was cathartic having Jacques to talk to, and we developed a nice little pattern of solitary, working days and conversational evenings.

His work was interesting to say the least. He carved women. And lots of them. He fashioned together a tripod stand and clamped single poles of fourfoot logs that he'd stripped of bark and planed beforehand. From the spare bedroom window, I could see him working. He worked on three at a time and repositioned them all around the garden. If I had to choose a word to describe how it looked from above, I'd choose rabid. It felt rabid. That's how I knew he was settling something, some recent hurt, or running. In my experience, art, unless it's useful like a bowl, is generally the record of damage or love, which is how truth plays out inside a singular life. In the early days, I thought of asking him, outright, what it was that he was mending, but I knew from my own experience that rarely did the work or any answer represent the whole truth. The point being that he was looking though doing, same as I, and maybe a summarized whole doesn't matter when you're detecting your own story. It's the route that's important, so I let him be.

After about a month, my leg had greatly improved, and I asked Marge if she knew of any cheap cars for sale around town. She arrived with an ancient Toyota pickup – Rusty, I christened her – and I took $200 out of my sock drawer. It felt good to have my independence back and I was tired of relying on Marge to do the shopping, which was her way of keeping Jacques out of town and sight. There are only so many tins of tomato soup a person could eat. Heinz and Betty Crocker were quickly becoming demons that chased me in my dreams. I craved something fresh so drove into town and parked around the back of CC's General Store.

I'd seen Arlo in the window of Rosa's Café no doubt digesting the friedegg sandwich he'd just eaten for breakfast and drinking the rest of his coffee. I imagine at 8:00 a.m. he wiped his mouth on a paper napkin, got up with a groan, put his Sheriff's hat on and walked across the street to CC's Grocery Store. Carrie, CC's daughter and I were in the back to where she'd placed some camera supplies I'd ordered. "I thought I'd save Jimmy the trouble of loading them onto his truck," I told her.

"No problem, just make sure to close the door behind you. Racoons live in that alleyway," she said, "once one got in during a Pepsi delivery and all hell broke loose. Shout if you need anything."

I checked my list. Some film was missing. I was about to walk through the rubber storage flaps and ask Carrie about it when I heard Arlo's voice. He had just walked in, and the following conversation truly exposed the perilous predicament of Jacques.

"Morning," said Calem Carson McKinney III.

"Morning," replied Arlo.

CC's had been in the McKinney family for three generations and, for inheriting purposes, every boy in the McKinney family had to have the CC initials. CC's great-grandfather, Conway Cooper, began the store as an outpost when Callisto was a newly formed river town. Arlo grabbed a basket and stood beside Mrs. Johnson in the bread aisle.

"Lord CC, how many types of bread do you need?"

Through a crack in the flap, I could see how Arlo stood with his hands on his hips, making his belly look even bigger. His skin was the exact colour of his beige uniform. His badge flashed like a silver nipple on his chest.

"Got to cater for all kinds these days," said CC.

"I'll say," said Arlo, "whole wheat? Who eats this crap?"

"You do. That's what Elora buys," said CC.

"No kiddin'? Well I'm getting white. I like white. Whole wheat's for communists," he said, and CC laughed.

"How is Elora anyway?' CC said.

"Good, real good, apart from having the flu again with headaches and all, but, yeah, good," he said, and flung the bread into his shopping cart.

"She must be sick. I never thought I'd see you doing women's business," said CC.

"Yeah, well. When needs must," he said, filling the cart with tins of baked beans. I noticed Arlo's knuckles were swollen.

"Cheer up," CC smacked Arlo on the back. "She'll be jumping outta bed just as soon as she sees you only brought back beer, beans, and white bread."

"She better be. Hey, speaking of Reds, you seen any sign of our new resident? Thought maybe he might've needed some milk by now."

"You mean the lodger out at the ol' Dubois place?"

"That's right," said Arlo, as he began to unload the groceries. "Carrie get over here and help this man. He can barely reach past his breakfast," CC laughed.

"Why? You think he's a communist?" "Hell, I don't know, he's Canadian ain't he? And French. So I'm using my powers of estimation," Arlo said, took a mint from his shirt pocket, and popped it in his mouth.

"Well, what I can't figure out is why on earth anybody would buy a place at the dog end of nowhere?" Mrs. Johnston said, who, until then, had been making a face-straining decision between a blue and a red dish towel. "Lord, the price of livin' these days," she added, looking at the price tags.

"That's a beautiful house," said Carrie. "I guess Birdie's folks just wanted some peace and quiet." She returned to the cash register and began ringing up Arlo's purchases.

"I think it's haunted," said Mrs. Johnston.

You would, you old bag, I thought.

"Yeah, maybe, but in a calm way," said Carrie and her father gave her a look that said, no backtalk young lady.

"Never mind that, it belongs to mad Birdie. That woman wears men's work boots for Christ's sake. I tried to help her out, you know, being nice and all, but the witch put the heebie-jeebies in me. Plus it ain't modern," said Arlo, sucking his mint through his teeth while Carrie bagged his groceries as well.

Tried to be nice my ass, I thought.

"No, but it's close to the river," said Carrie.

"There's hardly a track that runs out there. What'll she do when the rain comes or the snow?" CC said.

"Oh yes, the snow, think of it," said Mrs. Johnston. She stood wringing her hands behind Arlo.

"Was a time when tracks weren't important if you were by the river, but river days are done, long gone since they built the highway, now a person needs a car and a reliable track," said CC.

"Oh yes, the highway. Harold services the car every year, I can't fault him," said Mrs. Johnston.

"Good man," Arlo said, and CC hummed in agreement.

"But do you know what I heard?" Mrs. Johnston's voice was just above a whisper and gossipy, "I heard he was an artist."

"Just like Birdie," said Carrie, "it really is the perfect place for artists."

"An artist! See? What the hell'd I tell you? I'll ask Jimmy about him this afternoon," Arlo picked up his bag of groceries.

"No need to wait," said CC, standing by the window. "Mail van just pulled up outside."

Jimmy walked in. "Morning all," he said, as Arlo approached him.

"Hey Jimmy, you met our new friend yet?"

"Sure have," Jimmy said, smirking so much that Arlo looked as though he wanted to smack that smirk right off his face.

"Well, what's the verdict?" Arlo asked.

"You're not gonna believe this..."

"I already know he's an artist," Arlo interrupted, which annoyed Jimmy, so Jimmy blurted out, "a black artist."

Everyone was silent.

Arlo cleared his throat, "I hope to hell you're talking about intentions."

"No Sir," said Jimmy. "He's colored."

Carrie bristled.

"Colored? What? Nancy told me his grandma was so French she needed a goddamn translator when she called up here, had to search the whole damn county, helped him with his paperwork and all. He's the grandson of a goddamn French general with a bank account to match and you're telling me he's a nigger?"

"You can't say that word!" Carrie said and CC glared at her.

"What're you gonna do?" CC asked Arlo and Arlo looked out the window in thought.

"Nothing but my oath and duty," Arlo said, "and if he orders anything, moves anything, posts anything, shit, if he says anything, I wanna know about it."

"Oh, he's been ordering all kinds of stuff."

"Has he now, such as?"

"Such as home supplies from Sears ... "

"So he thinks he's staying then does he?"

"And, of all things, a shipment of sawed logs."

"What the hell does he need them for?"

"Gladys at the telephone office told me, that he told her, he was a wood carver."

"I told them he was an artist," said Mrs. Johnston, who had been standing there, shocked, holding her groceries for dear life.

"I'll be damned, a creative nigger, whatever next?" CC said and Carrie huffed at her father and stormed out.

"Took the words out my mouth, CC. What. Ever. Next."

I walked to the back of the storage room and started loading my equipment into the car like nothing had happened. CC walked Mrs. Johnston to the car and Carrie came to me.

"You hear all that?" she asked.

"I heard enough," I said.

"You gonna tell him?"

"Do you think I should?"

"Well, somebody from our side should," she said.

"I didn't know there were sides," I said, and she looked at me like I was an idiot. "I think a person deserves to know if they are under surveillance," she said.

"Surveillance? You think he's under surveillance? That seems a bit harsh," I said and, again, she looked at me as though I'd dropped from another planet.

She shook her head, disbelievingly, "Birdie," she said, "I think you both are under surveillance. Be careful and don't be so naive. Things have, well, they've changed since you were last here."

"Have they? Or are we just seeing them in a clear light?"

"Maybe. But it feels different. Arlo's – well, you know Elora Donnelly, don't you? I mean, you were friends with her in High School, right?"

"Kinda, yeah, I guess we were friends, but I haven't spoken to her in years, why?"

"I was just thinking you might want to go and check on her, you know, pop in for a visit and see for yourself what Arlo's become. He'll be at the station by now and she'll be all alone," she said, "might like company."

"She and Arlo are not the kind of people I want to be friendly with to be honest," I said, but I sensed there was something she wasn't telling me, something bigger. She put her hand on my forearm and nodded. It felt like a plea as well as a command. "I'm not asking you to have her over for dinner, just, check in on her," she said, "maybe you can speak to her."

"About what?" I took my arm away and Carrie intensified her gaze, "see for yourself," she said and walked back into the store.

Callisto, Illinois

The Donnelly's lived in a single-story ranch with yellow siding and red shutters. It was down a dead end on an acre plot at the edge of town and where the road ended a tree line began that led to the river.

There was a willow tree that shielded the back of the house from view, beyond which you could see the church steeple and the water tower. An unused swing hung from a low branch. The police station was only a ten-minute walk away, but Arlo always drove.

Birdie made sure his car was gone and parked down the street. She took a deep breath and walked around to the back door. The windows were dark. The legs of a plastic yard duck spun in the wind like a cartoon character going nowhere.

She remembered Elora as she was in high school, back when they had a relationship because Birdie had taught a few of the home-economics photography classes and had taken a shine to the girl. Elora was a few years younger and quite a formidable beauty. She had sewn her own floral and polka dot skirts and designed the layout for the school yearbook, but nothing compared to her singing. Birdie remembered her as having the most beautiful voice she had ever heard.

There was talk of her going to college before her she became involved with Arlo. He was fifteen years her senior and had been married before, to Louise, a good Lutheran until she fell in love with a truck driver. As soon as his divorce was final, Arlo and Elora were married. People shook their heads with pity, but nobody said an actual word. Arlo was known for his temper, which was good for policing, but not for marriage. He came from a family of mean stock. It was said that his daddy thought nothing of cutting the tongue out of a noisy mule.

All the same, Elora made her own wedding dress of ivory lace, long sleeved with a simple V in the front. It showed off her dark hair. She used the same lace to make the curtains in their bedroom window, which goes to show, everyone said, even a damn warthog like Arlo was worthy of somebody's love.

She got pregnant soon after the wedding. They bought a swing and had a barbecue. She sewed blue and yellow and pink bunting to hang in the yard. She filled little jars with homemade lemonade and gave it to the children to drink with red and white straws. There were steaks, cakes, and cigars. Arlo had kept his hands on Elora's stomach the whole time, proving his tender ownership.

Their first miscarriage was public and awful. The church group sent flowers to the hospital, held hands, and prayed. The second was talked about in whispers and the third was hardly mentioned. Elora had become irreversibly tragic. To speak of a dead foetus begets superstition and people avoided it altogether. By then, the curtains were always drawn and Elora would be missing for days, with headaches, the yellow bruising on her skin fading like a forgotten dream. She never mentioned it. She still held his hand. She said things like, "There's time for us yet," and so people decided to leave well enough alone.

Birdie knocked on the screen door. It was open and she peeked in. "Hello?"

The kitchen was dark, but for the dim lines of light that laddered the closed shutters. She saw Arlo's groceries unpacked on the kitchen table. There was a movement at the table as Elora scurried to cover herself, and in doing so, dropped a towel of ice she'd been holding against her cheek, on the floor. "Shit." She reached forward to grab them, grunted in pain, and shook her hair in front of her face, but it didn't cover her eye. It was as round as a black and violet baseball.

"Oh my God, Elora," Birdie knelt beside her, picked up the ice cubes and gave them to her. "I'm so sorry. Do you remember me? Birdie?"

Elora placed the ice inside the towel and back over her eye. Her lip was split under her nostril and her dressing gown was stained with blood. She stank of heat and sweat. She turned away.

"Just go away." She sounded a bit like a ventriloquist when she spoke because her lip was so swollen.

"Elora, I can't leave you like this. I can't. Did Arlo do this?"

"You shouldn't be here." She completely turned around in her chair.

"Nor should you," Birdie said. "Elora, this is insane! I'm not leaving until you tell me how to help you."

Elora turned to face Birdie and removed the towel from her eye. She looked as though she belonged in a morgue, as though she were a creature, not a woman, and Birdie had to force herself not to look away.

"Why are you even here? You're not my friend, we're not friends, I haven't seen you in years and now you just waltz into my kitchen and tell me what to do? Just leave!" Elora readjusted the eye patch and winced.

Birdie lifted her trouser leg and showed Elora her scar.

"See this? A police officer did this, smashed my camera into my leg, so I understand more than you think I do. At least let me get you something for the pain."

She shook her head, "I have what I need," but Birdie could feel her soften.

"I have a place in Chicago, you could stay there, I'd could take you, help you file for a divorce, whatever you need, you know, you could be safe."

"I'm not ready for that yet," she said.

Yet, she said yet, so she's thinking along those lines, thought Birdie. It gave her hope.

"Then a least come and visit me. I'll show you my photo boxes, make you dinner, drink some wine, yeah? We don't have to talk about this, okay? We can talk about anything, anything you like," she put her hand on Elora's shoulder. "I remember you before all of this, please, say you'll visit."

Elora nodded. "But you need to leave now."

"What will you do in the meantime?"

"What I always do." Her eye looked jellied, fake, as though she could pop it out and bounce it around the room as a Halloween trick. "Now go. Quickly, before he comes back."

Spittle had gathered in the sides of her mouth. It was hard for her to swallow. Her breath made the whole room smell of hot copper.

Birdie hated to admit it, but she was happy to leave. She had become aware of the shadowed hallway, the shadowed living room, and the inability to see beyond a window. She wanted light and normalcy. She got up, gave Elora a hug, "I am available anytime day or night," she said, opened the screen door, and walked outside, resisting the urge to run.

Elora Winter

I remember when Birdie came and saw me in my indignity. I kept thinking, after this, I'll go to the river. The water will look spectacular on a day like today. The waves shining like scattered coins. It gave me courage. Small things, small actions, can reap huge courage. A "hello nice to see you" or the sun.

I stared at the place where Birdie had been squatting for a long time, outside I could hear the stupid plastic duck's feet spinning and the irregular squeak of the swing, then I got up and made myself some coffee.

Slowly I climbed the stairs to the attic. The roof was pitched and the boxes of Arlo's parents' house were tucked inside the places too small to stand inside. I pulled back the curtains of the single window. The swell of my face and its ugliness did not surprise me. It was a face I rarely owned. It changed like a barometer around Arlo.

Actually, it erased. So looking at my reflection was like looking at someone else, it was like feeling from someone else; looking through glass is a way to view things safely. I'd spent years looking at myself through a closed window. Disturbed dust settled in a film across my coffee. I wiped my finger across a box, all of this I thought, the erosion of me, collecting. I balanced my mug on the windowsill, opened a case in the corner and took out a small vial. Against the window it streaked the sunlight blue.

Arlo had used the sleeping powders before, years ago, to ease his father's pain. We had our fathers' suffering in common.

"Stuff's like rat poison," I remembered Arlo saying as he mixed it, "it never loses its potency, so keep it safe."

It was not that I wanted Arlo dead, although I'd thought about it often enough, it was simply that I wanted peace in the evening, especially if he was drinking, which was constant. I'd pour him a scotch, slip in the powder, and wait for him to start snoring. Was it so much to ask to walk by the river, to sing, unafraid?

When I was young, I had wanted to be a part of something unreservedly magical. Not beautiful, not lavish, nor even perfect, but miraculous the way cave drawings are miraculous, because they prove our capacity to evolve, and lure us into believing our own possibilities. I was tempted by the primal imagination that inspires skill, the ability to dream the initial dream, and then create what has been dreamt. Then, and perhaps even now, I am mostly my dreams.

I dropped the vial into my dressing-gown pocket and carefully closed the curtains. He would notice something like that; he noticed everything when he didn't want to look directly at me. I needed to put the groceries away. It was important to keep things normal.

Birdie Dubois

As soon as I got home, I started working on Elora's photo box. Creating from a secret, just like sharing a secret, saves it from haunting you. It struck me that although no one investigated their suspicion, the town knew that Arlo beat Elora, and because he was an upholder of the law, the fact that their suspicions went unchallenged, changed the very nature of what the law meant. Across a photo I'd taken of the Mississippi I wrote:

Words,
or their absence,
precede worlds.

But where I'd take it from there it was difficult to say. She was a complicated woman inside of a complicated situation. To reach the core of ideas, it's helpful for me to use figurative allegory alongside words. It's no magic really; people have made the word "magic" silly. It's just an old knowledge that many have forgotten. The mind simply works well with symbols and images. Think of Christ on the cross, wedding rings, the lotus flower, the Star of David, and so on. I use them to move my audience, as well as myself, out of the persona we've created for ourselves. Symbols and ceremony, the two oldest tricks in the book. Like I said. It's no miracle really, just the repositioning of power, just plugging the intellect into an emotion as a way to illuminate understanding.

I found an old beaker in the kitchen. My mother was always keeping random things like this and holding it in my hand made me miss her very much. She would have known what to say to Elora. She would have known what to do. I, on the other hand, hid behind my artwork. I could not place Elora in wood. Wood felt, for the first time, too much like a coffin. In the shed there was an old mirror. After a glass of wine and ceremony to somewhat ease my superstition, I carried it out into the yard and threw a rock at its centre. I collected the pieces and dipped them in a murky wash that I created with phthalo, cobalt, and river mud. I took the photograph I'd taken of the river, carefully cut the sentence out, and randomly cut up the rest.

After the shards of glass had dried, I superglued the pieces and the photos into a shallow ceramic dish. I placed the beaker in the center, took a black Sharpie and wrote "shhhhhhhhh" all around it like a swirl.

Marge knocked on the door.

"You're looking better," she said, and walked in, "I brought you this in case you decide to have a shower." It was a beige nonslip bathmat. I groaned.

"Is this a hint?"

"No, in fact, I'd advise against showering, but I know I can't tell you a darn thing. Keep having baths until you get stronger," she said, "but if you don't, please use this. All this worry keeps me up at night, plus my indigestion."

"Baths bore me," I interrupted.

"See? What I'd say? Not a darn thing. What's this?" She was looking at my broken mirror beaker assembly.

"A broken mirror I glued back together," I said.

"That's bad luck," she took her hand away.

"Obviously," I said, "that's the point."

"Have you been drinking?" She picked up my wine glass and inspected it.

"No," I said, but I could tell she didn't believe me.

"Is it him?" She nodded towards my mother's studio.

"Is what him? You mean Jacques? No. No, he's great to have around. Why would you automatically think he had anything to do with my mood or once-in-a-blue-moon afternoon drinking?" I felt an anger I couldn't explain. I wanted to justify him, to crucify this stupid town.

"It's Elora if you must know."

"Elora Donnelly?"

"Yes, Elora Donnelly, the woman whose husband keeps beating the shit out of her while all you good citizens of Callisto sit tight and do nothing."

Marge straightened her back and placed the wine glass down. "You don't see what we do."

"I see she has an eye the size of a fucking baseball and no intervention," I said, "that's enough to make a pretty accurate judgement, I'd say, wouldn't you?"

"You went to their house? Why?"

"Yes, I went to their house! Why? *Why?* The question is why the hell isn't everyone going to the house and demanding that he be locked up or something!"

"Don't you think we've tried? She's been, well, resistant," Marge said. "It won't work if she's not on board."

"Of course, she's resistant! She's scared shitless!"

"Everyone is! He has connections everywhere – with the law, with the court, and beyond – you don't fully understand the magnitude of what is going on here," she said.

"Beyond what? Why does everybody speak in code? What does that even mean? What's beyond the court? Do you mean God? Or the church!"

She huffed, "practically," she said, and we both turned towards a creak on the porch steps. It was Jacques. He was standing behind the screen door holding carrots.

"Um, hi, this is this a bad time, I'll go," he said. "No," said Marge, "Wait. I was just going," she turned to me, "stay out of this, trust me," she said and I threw the wine glass against the wall. "Okay," said Jacques, "I'm just going to leave these here," he put the carrots on the doormat.

"Your melodrama is going to get us all in trouble!" Marge got in her car and slammed the door and Jacques looked at me in bewilderment.

"Don't leave, come in, the coast is clear, well, nearly," I said and unhooked a dustpan and broom from the kitchen wall.

"Let me do it," he said, "you look like a domestic flamingo balancing on one leg like that," and took the broom from me. "So, dare I ask what that was about?"

"Town politics," I said in a way that shut the conversation down.

He put the glass shards in the garbage bin, "be careful when you empty this," he said, "and don't forget your carrots," he walked down the porch steps.

"Jacques!" I shouted after him and he turned. How could I warn him without being insulting or implicated? I didn't want him to feel wary and yet that is exactly what I wanted him to feel. I just had to be honest.

"I just want you to know that, well, a lot of people in this town are racist. I'm so sorry, I don't know how else to tell you this but, well, just, be aware." He took in the information and slowly nodded.

"Thank you for letting me know," he said, walked away and kept to himself for a few days.

During that time, the idea for Jacques's photo box came to me. I wanted to show that oblivion to colour is a white person's true advantage and racism's silent bullet. I could have spent years walking around Chicago, living my liberal, multifaith, mixed-race existence, without ever coming face to face with the challenges of racism, because I didn't need to. Because I was born the colour of modern society's expectation of success and had chosen to live around people that, mostly, reflected my views, as well as my educational advantages. Here, I was a fish out of water, and so was Jacques, but he retained his usual grace and worked. He constantly worked, though, in my experience, sometimes, most times really, the work understands things before you do. And that was certainly the case.

Elora Winter

I walked beside the stream, baked to a leather map with knife engravings across its bed, until I reached the river and sat down beside the bank. The late afternoon air sat in my mouth like a hot penny. The insects ruled. Their murmur was tidal and scavenging. I breathed deeply, I knew about thirst, about droughts of the internal, humankind. Ideas grew in me like seeds under concrete. I relished the dehydrated world around me, for it meant that I was not alone, that the earth seemed merely my body turned inside out, and a kinship was formed. The sound of the cicadas felt like a heat in my throat. The trees were still and posed in purgatorial moments. The town too, in my mind like a dot on the map edge, and I thought about how places can live like hives and are alive through the functioning of its peoples. What was my function? Of course, I knew, but to know your purpose and to arrive at it, to live it, are different things.

The dirt road that ran parallel to the stream unrolled a parched tongue and soon Arlo would drive down it, but now I had the river. The current was too strong and low to produce a clear reflection, but it was comforting to see the shadows of my face change. The wind lifted off of the water and felt cool against my swollen eye, like a balm of soothing current.

Behind me the windows to the house looked luminous and I imagined that the house was on fire. In my mind, I burned it to the ground, then stood, listening. I am not stuck, I thought, I refuse to be stuck. I thought about the conversation, the safety, Birdie could give me. I could do that. I thought of speaking to someone again, singing again, I could use her voice as a symbol and begin to break the glass. I stopped and listened. The song in me, playing. The dusk that was amniotic. Amniotic –

Ride the Down and into town
Twilight amniotic

I could hear the reeds slop alongside the mud bank, the locusts and the grasses brushing in the wind. I lowered into these sounds and hummed myself back to nothing. Let the song come.

My shadow disappeared into the field behind me as though I'd spilled, I soaked and the days heat fell from me in layers, until I was soft. Imagine moss on bone. The last of the sun descended into the water like a retreating red ship.

The night dropped its lump in my throat, it grew and filled me. I could feel my voice, tunnelling from far away, yet moving closer, I imagined it shaking the water in glasses as it crunched through rock and soil, it began to burn, to push until it burst and shot up through my legs, my pelvis, stomach, diaphragm, and when I opened my mouth again it slid out, like a burning snake through a snowdrift, it cut and sizzled and entered the prairie in one direction, the river in the other –

Ride the Down and into town
Twilight amniotic
(And the verses came –)

Bruised water quay, a boat they say
Concealed in waves a trick.

The Sculptor - Gret Heffernan

> Blood channel
> fare will take you there
> At the helm, the deceased.
> Split Irish Sea and soon you'll be
> in morning light, Passage East.

I sang and it hit Jacques in the stomach with the strength of a bullet through a melon.

He watched me singing. He didn't know the song, but it didn't matter. I sang like releasing birds, like mining, like breaking the clutch of sea. He knew that kind of surrender. He was that kind of surrender.

The music was my representation. The knife that could cut me away from my other self. This was the voice I had known all my life. It moved around me like salty waves, licked the inside of my shell, glossed my cupped belly to smooth. I reached low and collected its cool shape. I held it close to my ear and heard the world, the other world. This was my seashell voice.

That kind of submission makes you do things just to blur the edges of reason.

Jacques dipped below the grass, got down on all fours and started slowly crawling towards me. I heard him, or rather; I heard everything hesitate around him and it stopped me, caught me on its hook. I turned and saw a nothing, so big, so loud, I felt it might swallow me. It made me run.

Birdie Dubois

I found Jacques in the backyard. Night had just begun to set. His lady sculptures were everywhere. He had accomplished so much since his arrival a few months earlier. He had painted the studio white, the roof was nearly refurbished, planted a garden, and the door had new hinges.

"I don't know where you find the time," I said.

"Hey, look at you, a one-crutch wonder," he smiled from over from his vegetable patch. The maple tree in his backyard was full of late summer cicadas. His garden looked fantastic, and he stood in the middle of the rows, harvesting runner beans. I could see small bits of woodchip stuck on his scalp like curly bugs. He stepped out of the rows and smeared soil across his jeans.

"Best time to harvest is in the night. Do you have time for a mint tea?" he said and plucked a slug off of one of his plants. "It's also the best time for pest control." I followed him up the steps to the kitchen.

"So, how are you Miss Dubois?"

"Never better Mr. Beaumont," looking around at his sculptures, "you have a regular harem here Jacques. They're amazing."

"Thanks. Only a few are finished, but yes, I've been busy," he said, "although I haven't neglected my tenancy duties," he pointed to the roof, but I couldn't have cared less. I was fascinated by his sculptures.

"I'll say," I said, "thank you so much."

"Well, thanks for having me," he said and stood under the doorframe and stomped the mud from his boots.

"Your ladies, I notice that they all have similar features," I stopped to look at one of the carvings.

"That's because most are of my mother," Jacques said, "she died. Recently."

I didn't know how to respond, so chose not to, grief was individual, and he was an artist, after all. Crickets in the grass and the river's murmur filled the silence. He put the kettle on. I noticed his knees were sodden, though the soil was bone dry.

"Have you been near the river?"

"Tea inside or out?" Jacques took mugs from the drying rack. Ignoring or avoiding my question.

"Outside but honestly, only if you have the time," I stepped inside.

"I have plenty of time," he said and removed the singing percolator from the stovetop, took mint leaves from his shirt pocket, rinsed them under the tap, and dropped them into two mugs. "Honey?"

"No thanks," I said as I took the mug and blew into it. "That's nice. Thank you. So. You must be finding Callisto inspirational," I said, and nodded towards his sculptures on the lawn.

"Yes," he said. "I'm glad you came over. I wanted to apologize for the other day. I felt like I barged in on something I shouldn't have."

"Please don't apologize, honestly, I feel like we should be apologizing to you. I mean, Callisto hasn't been exactly welcoming," I said, and he laughed.

"I'm not here to be liked," he said, "despite my utter charm."

"How do you keep so level-headed? Is it because you work all the time? Is it to do with your mother?"

His body went stiff and formal. "I work all the time because she wants to be out." "Who?"

"My mother," he said.

"Out of what?"

"Her form."

"Right," I took a drink, "you're sounding a bit like a crazy artist to me here Jacques."

He nodded in agreement, unperturbed. I didn't know what to say, so I said, "they really are all of your mother?"

"Mostly, but a few are of women I don't know. Their faces just come to me, and I sculpt them, release them from their form as well," he said.

"Well, they're wonderful, whoever 'they' might be. And however insane you might be. So, what's the deal, do you release them through your sculpture?"

"Yes," he said, and I sensed that he didn't want to explain it further.

"Huh," I thought for a second or two. "That's an interesting idea and kind of related to why I'm here actually. Listen, I need a favour."

Jacques looked up with interest, "anything, name it," he said.

"I'd like you to carve me two tiny, finger-sized women," I said. I figured two would allow me to make a mistake with one. I had this crazy disfiguring idea that could go horribly kitsch, voodoo wrong, but it was worth a try.

"Of course, are they for your boxes?"

"One is."

"And the other? If I can be so bold as to ask?

"I'm not sure. It's just that, well, the mind responds to an imagined event just the same as it responds to an actual event. Did you know that? The trick is to get the mind working beyond its reason. I'm hoping that this box or, at least, the ability to talk about it, might set something in motion, but it's a long shot and about as sensitive as a tongue in a jar of burrs."

"Right. When do you need them?"

"Over the next couple of days. Can you do that?"

"Sure. Any special features?"

"Long hair and if you could make her singing that would be great."

"Ah, is it for Elora, the singing woman? The one with the busted eye?"

"What do you know about her?" I was taken aback.

"It was just a guess. I heard her singing beside the river and she seemed impenetrably tragic and in need of a talisman." There was something in his voice, his face that made me nervous.

"Let me give you some advice, you stay away from her, I don't really care what you do with yourself, but I am the one and only person in this stupid town that doesn't. You, we, in fact, are under surveillance. Elora is married to the sheriff, Arlo, you've never met him and you don't want to, trust me. He is a horrible man."

"The kind of man beats his wife," Jacques said and stared past the window to the breastplate hanging on the tree. I looked over and saw the wooden face of Elora. It was too late. He had already carved her face and he couldn't look me in the eye. She was living inside his garden, inside the wood, and I realized too late, inside his mind.

"Yes, and the kind of man that will think nothing of killing you," I said, and put my cup in the sink. "Don't make me worry about you Mr. Beaumont," I said, feigning a light heartedness that I did not feel.

Around 10 p.m., there was a small rap on my door. I opened it. The lightning bugs set off the locusts' alarm, chimes on the breeze, and the smell of dirt and split wood. Jacques stood with the two carvings held out in his hand. They were the image of Elora.

"Could I see her photo box?"

I showed it to him. From the shards I snagged a bit of fabric, he touched it and raised his eyebrows in question.

"She's a talented seamstress," I said.

I'd painted parts of the photographs with purples and greens. "The colors of a bruise," he said, and I nodded. "What about the yellowing? The beginning of the end of pain, where is that?"

"I'm hoping that is what the other sculpture will represent. Shall we see if she fits?" I took one of the women and stuck her inside the beaker. The waves came up to her chest.

"Perfect," said Jacques. "She's perfect." And I knew he was talking about the real woman.

After he left, I went out into the yard and waited in the soft apprehension of shadow, where the sky ensues evergreen and the moon lays broken across the river. I needed to feel unenclosed.

Whatever is happening has already begun, I felt, so be it, and looked up at the stars, there was no harm in asking for guidance. "Help her," I said to no one, to everyone, to everything. "Help them both."

Elora Winter

The following evening, I poured the sleeping powders in the scotch and waited. Arlo came in through the back door and I could tell by the way he struggled with his boots that he'd already been drinking. We had had another argument and things had gotten rough. He needed courage to see me, I thought, and I was right, for when he saw me sitting at the kitchen table he said, "Oh baby, just look at you."

He knelt down beside me. "I'm so sorry. I could just kill myself. This whole thing is crazy. This situation, you know, it damn near makes me crazy," he put his hand on my knee. It was the same story, same song and dance, same patter, only this time, I had a possible way out.

"That mine?" he nodded at the scotch. "Yeah," I said, and handed it to him.

"I don't know what I've done," he said, and took a swig, "to deserve a woman like you. I love you Elora, you know that don't you?"

I nodded and stood. I'd heard it all before. "You hungry?"

"Starving. I'm so sorry, baby," he said, and necked the rest of the glass. "What's for dinner?"

"Pot roast." I took it out of the oven.

"Smells good." He sat down and I dished him up a big helping.

We ate in silence and when he'd finished, he wiped his mouth with a napkin and said, "I think I'll just go lie down on the sofa for a little bit. It's been a hell'o'va long day."

I nodded and started tidying up the dinner plates.

He was snoring within a few minutes. I went into the living room, stood over him and watched him until I was certain he wasn't going to wake up, then I grabbed my coat and softly stepped out into the night.

The land was spread like a palm before me, a hand waiting to snap shut and for once, I thought, I might be able to escape its grip. It was only a matter of time, I told myself as I walked along the river towards Birdie's. Time waited inside me like air in a bottle, invisible to the naked eye and heard only when breathed into, when turned into music.

When circumstance fast-forwards the heart, the age of the body becomes irrelevant, but there was a time when I'd been young, when I had yet to be weather-beaten, had not yet found my place inside of peace or denial and believed that the order of things could change with little sacrifice. The want of youth is as merciless as the regret of age, both injuries, one the sharp stab of impatience and the other, a slow leak. When I was young, I spoke like diving. My conversations went like this:

"Daddy, I can sing," I said.

"You get that from your mother. She could sing."

"I'd like to be a singer, Daddy."

"She could bring down the angels above with her voice, that woman, she could make you cry."

"I'd like to study music at college next year."

"I remember a time in Boston. We were dirt poor. Your mother said she'd had enough of living on love and potatoes. She said, 'Tonight we'll eat steaks,' then got up, walked out the door, and stormed down the stairs. Just like that. With that wild look in her eyes, she'd get when she fixed her mind on something. I just let her go. I thought, what now? But the next thing I heard was her sweet voice rising from the busy street below, rising up to the open window and resting right there on the windowsill like a spring robin. I kid you not. It wasn't even two seconds, and I heard the first coin drop. That night we had enough money for two steaks and some greens. Lord we feasted like we'd never done before. Decided right then and there to move out to the land of the plenty."

"But Daddy ..."

"Just stop right there Elora, there's no sense romanticizing about the impossible. You just pull your head out of those clouds and be happy with the life the good Lord gave you. It ain't a bad one. You hear me? It ain't bad."

Birdie Dubois

I had no idea that she'd come on the night I finished her photo box. Fate is damn coincidental if you ask me. I keep thinking back to things, said or done, and linking them in ways that felt forewarning, but that's what people do after the fact. I was surprised to see her though. I had just lit the wick of a glass hurricane lamp. My mother kept a few around the house. We both liked their glow and primal flickering. It was like reaching back through time towards a memory I felt at ease with but couldn't quite grasp. I remember my mother saying that a hurricane lamp made her feel like a captain's wife, noble and capable of waiting out a storm. Again, coincidence.

Also, Stan had called, out of the blue, from a payphone. Just to see how you're recovering, he said, but I could hear sadness in his voice. I asked him if he would be able to check in on Elora if she agreed to use my apartment as a safe house. Of course, he agreed, but I could tell he was worried about me and, to be frank, I let him be. Why should I have to put his mind at ease? The plan was that he would phone me every Tuesday. I played it cool and said, whatever you want, but my heart was doing somersaults.

Through the open windows I could smell and hear the pageantry of the night, and then hesitant footsteps on the path that led to the house. Jacques? I went to the door and opened it. Elora's face was wet and crazed. She didn't say hello, she just walked straight in, sat on the sofa, and with great care, folded her hands in her lap. Her eye was as mean as a canker sore and her nose was starting to scab. I moved the hurricane lamp to the coffee table beside her and she glistened with moisture.

"Elora," I said, and she turned her face away, the lamp outlined her sharp profile. "I am so glad you came. Are you here to leave him? I mean, is that what you want?"

"I do. It's just. Difficult."

"I imagine it is. You're very brave to have come in the first place."

"It feels dishonest. But, I have to do something."

I said nothing and put my hand on her shoulder, she flinched, then relaxed into my palm.

"Let me get you a drink? A hot tea or a glass of wine?"

"Wine please," she said, and I got up and went into the kitchen.

"You have every reason to be nervous. I don't blame you one iota."

"No, but I blame myself, otherwise it would never have come to this."

"What do you blame yourself for?" I handed her the wine, she took it and I sat down across from her.

"I don't know. Being empty, I guess, emptiness."

"We all empty out sometimes, Elora. We'd become stagnant otherwise, and stagnant water can turn to poison. What you fill yourself with is important."

"But I've tried, I've tried to fill myself with goodness, happiness," her face began to crumple. "You don't know how I've tried."

"No, I don't, but listen, let's not make this so huge, it becomes scary," I could feel her retreating. "You're here now. It's good to just chat."

I left the sentence hanging in the air. I didn't want to scare her. We sat in silence. She took a drink of wine. "This is nice, thanks," she said.

"I brought it from Chicago. I was saving it for when I had company."

"Is that what you call me? Company?" she laughed.

"I think you're as good as it's going to get," I said and we both laughed, too loud, I thought she might cry, so I said quickly, "I have something to show you, but it might make you uncomfortable." She watched me with curiosity as I took her box from the table and handed it to her, "what is this?" she asked.

"It's what I do, my art practice is to make photo boxes and I made this one for you."

She examined it. I couldn't tell if she like it or not.

"Listen, I have an idea. Just hear me out, okay? It might sound a bit strange, but I was thinking that we should have a ritual, where we use her, you know, as a sacred symbol."

She nervously handed me back the photo box, "what do you mean?"

"I'm not talking about bleeding goats or virgins or anything, relax, I just mean using poetry, prayer, and symbolism to spark a change for you," I tipped the beaker upside down and the woman fell into my palm. "Let's use her as a symbol, pure and simple," I gave Elora the figure.

"Okay," Elora took another big gulp of wine. "So, what exactly do you want me to do with it?"

"Do you trust me?"

"I think so. Yes, yes I do."

"Good. I'm going to count backwards from ten, and when I reach one, you will be in a state of relaxation, like a trance or a dream." As I spoke the words my voice softened and lowered. I had learned hypnotism from my mother. She used it on her patients. "You do not have to do anything against your will, but the words I use, and the ritual you perform, will remain inside your mind, where you can access them instantly for strength," I began counting.

Elora closed her eyes. Her face was almost wet with moisture as though she'd been swimming through the lamplight.

"Hold the image of yourself and think of it as the symbol it is. Now think of your past as a map and begin to unroll it until it extends all the way to your childhood. Look at it. It's like a long inscribed road with fields and timber and valleys and the Mississippi. See the town square, the red barns, the church, and the park with the swings, the school. Everything is there. Can you see it? Wonderful. Now, light up the people and events that have caused you pain. Make their lights bright and visible. Take your time. And when you're ready, raise them above the map, so that they're floating. Let each one rise, tell them goodbye and let them enter your symbol. Fill that symbol with all your pain, your anger, your loss, your fear. Is it completely full? Is it shining with light? Good. Now, turn it off. Turn the light off. Snuff out every little glimmer, until it's dark and dead, like a stiff corpse in your hands. Now we are going to walk outside and bury it because that woman is dead, gone. Are you ready?"

I took my satchel from a hook and opened the door to a vivid night. Elora followed me. The lamp lit the cobwebs on the grass. We walked to the riverside. Elora cradled the symbol like an infant in her palm. I knelt and took a trowel from my satchel.

"Look at the river," I said. "The river is constantly reshaping the banks that define it. People can do that too. We can reshape the way we hold ourselves to enhance the way we flow. Stop blocking yourself, Elora, and take the trowel, dig a hole and bury her."

Elora dug a deep hole.

She placed the woman inside and covered her completely. She wiped her hands on her thighs and sat facing at the river. Her eyes were closed.

"The pain does not own you anymore. It does not control you anymore. It has no power over you. It's gone. You destroyed it. You will replace your pain with your own strength. You will become strong because you are the one that shines now. You are the one full of light. Now, when I finish counting forward, you will reach full consciousness where you'll feel stronger and more able to manage your life."

I counted her back to consciousness and after a few moments of silence, I placed the other small woman inside a geode I'd placed in my satchel and handed it to Elora.

"Open it," I said.

Elora opened it and found another tiny carved woman inside a bed of crystals.

"That's the new you," I said, and took her hand. "From now on, remember, no matter what happens, that's you."

Elora began to cry.

Now, you can think whatever you want about our ritual, but I'm telling you, it was the beginning of the end and it felt that way. We felt connected. I don't know what came over me or why I decided to perform it or, even, why I had a geode in my satchel and knew to ask Jacques to carve two women. At the time I'd asked him, I thought it was because I sensibly wanted a spare, but sitting there on the riverbank, holding Elora, I felt as if I'd known this was how it would develop all along. As if I had divined it, and, like I said, the art knows before you do, art is prophetic. I should have paid closer attention.

Jacques Beaumont

When he arrived in Callisto, he stood on the threshold of a curtainless room, watched the sunlight slant across the floor in a way that seemed cathedral like and pious, and thought, everything will change. He was hesitant to walk through the door. Marge busied herself with removing dustsheets. The 'studio' was the size of a small farmhouse and perfect.

"Can you play?" she asked when she reached the piano.

"Yes, my mother taught me," he said.

"I always wanted to myself, never had the time. Well, it will be a comfort for you to have it here," she said, and took a key from her pocket. "This is to the front door and this here's my number," she wrote it on scrap paper and put it on the refrigerator. "If you need anything, just phone me first, okay? Phone me before you phone anybody else."

She looked out the window at a van coming down the lane.

"That'll be Jimmy the Mail Man. He's an ass, but it's tolerable because he's always on time. Are you expecting something?"

"Just some things from Canada," he said.

"No kidding, well, Christ, here we go. There's no time like the present I suppose, just keep your head down and be polite. I gotta go. I'll be back tomorrow with a dustpan and a mop," she said, and walked out the door.

"Thanks again," he called after her, and she waved without turning around.

The house was incredibly quiet after she left. She was like a mini tornado. He unwrapped the bread she left on the table, broke off a bit, put it in his mouth and spat it out again. It tasted like salt and detergent. Detergent. He could use some detergent. He was ripe with sweat. Jimmy knocked on the door. After this, he thought, I will bathe and sleep. When he opened the door Jimmy was obviously shocked.

"Who are you?" Jimmy asked, and Jacques felt a punch of confrontation. Marge hadn't been wrong.

"Jacques Beaumont. Who are you?"

"You're Jacques Beaumont?"

"Yes. Is that a problem?"

"Nope. Just a surprise is all. We thought you was French."

"I am," Jacques said, and Jimmy laughed.

"No, you ain't. Look. I got your stuff in back, five boxes, right?"

"That's right. Let me give you a hand."

"I reckon you can manage," he said, as he opened the rear door to his van.

Jacques carried each box to the porch while Jimmy sat in his van. His arm hung out the window, bent like a tanned chicken wing. The skin above his shirtsleeve was white.

"You done yet?" Jimmy hollered over as Jacques put down the last box.

"Yep, that's everything," Jacques nodded, "thanks, and nice to meet you."

Jimmy started the van and drove off.

Jacques unloaded the five boxes and placed them in the corner of the living room. He opened one and took out his blanket and pillow. Upstairs the bedroom had slanted ceilings and a view of the river. A path as straight as a seam ploughed its way to the water's edge. He lay down on the bed and fell asleep. He dreamt he was walking along the path and the ground behind him was unfastening.

Marge arrived the following morning as promised. She brought a ladder, some cleaning supplies, a Sears catalogue, and Birdie, who refused to stay put. He was happy to see her, as he'd spoken to her the previous night, and her company was preferable to Marge's. She had seemed so pleasant in her letters but in person he found her a bit harsh. The phone was working, so Jacques ordered a few essentials, while Marge polished and tuned the piano.

Birdie took a small bundle of sage from her bag, lit it until it was smoking, and then walked around each room muttering a low chant. Jacques cleaned the windows and removed a bird's nest from the fireplace.

"I'm going to light a fire with the rest of this," Birdie waved the sage in the air. "Just to clear your flue."

Jacques nodded. He was cleaning the baseboards and layers of dust came off like fur. He thought of Callisto and his mother and walked outside to collect some kindling. The land was bone dry, but he could sense fertility underneath the dirt.

"We're in a drought now," Marge had told him, "but usually this soil is so fertile you can bury spit in the ground and a mouth will rise up singing. Veins to roots overnight."

He thought about green blood. He took a deep breath and felt dirt clinging to his nostrils. Everything was subdued by a hot fume, the sky, the ground, the glare encasing the trees, the rolling flash on the river. The colours here did not come in big blocks, but as flashes, orange on a pheasant's wing, the rush of a red wing, pink smears in the clouds. Back home in the mountains the snow would still be blanketing his mother. He didn't feel like thinking. He walked to the side of the river. The water slapped like syrup against the bank. He could even hear this swishing from his bedroom window. It was everywhere. He plugged his ears and heard his own heart swish, his dark reflection on the water, behind his eyes, waiting for him. There was nothing he could have done. He unplugged his ears and the tall grass hissed with insects. The sound was a kind of radiance, a drum, and he listened to it until his mother disappeared.

Boxelder bugs clung to the screen door and dropped like black and orange peas when he slammed it shut. The floors glistened with Pine Sol. There were little bouquets of herbs in each of the corners and geodes on every windowsill.

"Well, I'm off," said Marge, removing her marigold gloves, "I'll be back first thing with groceries. I stuck a casserole and some other bits and bobs in the fridge. See you later. You get on back to the house and put that leg up young lady," she said to Birdie.

"I will, don't you worry, and thanks Marge."

Jacques handed Birdie the sticks he'd collected. She was sitting on the floor beside the fire grill. "Do you need help? I feel a bit bad with you on the floor like that," he said.

She waved him away, made a tent above the sage, and struck a match.

"You ever seen a geode?"

"Is that what this is?" Jacques picked one up and glittered it in the sunlight.

"Yep. This area's covered with them. They look like normal rocks until you crack them open and find they are full of crystals. I've known a lot of people like that," she said.

"So have I," he said.

"You'll be fine, you know," she blew on the fire. "It'll all be worth it, just wait, even if it takes a good long while, it'll be worth it all."

"I don't know what you mean," he said, a little startled that he'd been so transparent.

"I know you're running from something. I have a sixth sense for these things. You don't have to tell me what it is, but," Jacques stopped her.

"I'm here because I lost someone I loved," he said.

"I'm sorry to hear that," Birdie said.

"I needed to be somewhere else and the name Callisto means something to me. Well, to my family. It's kind of a code, I guess."

"Callisto. Ursa Major. Now let me think. You all part bear or something?" Birdie said, and Jacques laughed, her accuracy was incredible.

"That's about right. Now, let me think. With your sage and intuition, are you part witch or something?" Jacques said, and it was Birdie's turn to laugh.

"Touché," she said. "But seriously, this isn't Canada. You're a generation removed from Klan activities, so I mean it when I say, be careful."

"If it's so backwater, then why are you here?" He asked.

"I'm here because I was born here, plus, I'm working," she said.

"I'm here to work too," he said.

"Okay, so, tell me about your work."

"What do you want to know?"

"The sculptures you unpacked and put in the window were quite interesting – what are they, like, amoebas?"

"Sort of, actually, they're prompts of pure emotion. They show me how light moves around different solid shapes."

"Ahhh. I get that. Words are prompts for me. Poetry. So you sculpt to shed light on something, what, like an idea or ... ?"

"It's more about shining light into something,"

"For clarity?"

"For actuality."

"Right, turning art into life, abstract into form."

"Yes," he said, "that's it exactly."

"Well, Jacques Beaumont, I think we'll get along just fine."

He was numb for days, too numb to dream, to create, to resurrect. He mended and painted the house. He planted a garden and ordered a shipment of logs. He went around touching things, stones, flowers, doorknobs, and asking for forgiveness.

Marge brought him groceries and he cooked and ate his meals in silence. He walked through the night until he was tired enough to sleep. It was as if his dreams wanted him alive before they'd enter him. They waited until he could feel again, until his awareness was sharpened by grief, each hair on his body like a small steel receptor ready to dig the dream in, so that when it arrived it stayed with him always, always the same dream:

He's watching a rabbit twitching in a field. A black dog jumps from the woods. It chases the rabbit around and around him in circles. He can't run away. He can't move. He looks down. Two mouths have swallowed his feet and are slowly chomping up his legs. The dog finally catches the rabbit and drops it at his side. He looks again. It's not the rabbit at all, but a hand with stars for knuckles, spit laced, and gnawed.

Elora Winter

Days passed and Birdie's words were a current inside me. During the day I did not sing. Daylight was like a licked finger and thumb that extinguished me and inside of its hours I became unidentifiable to myself, as if I'd been sucked dry, a raisin, a shrunken head, but with a mouth that formed words, with arms and legs that followed instructions.

I stood in front of the mirror and touched the skin healing on my face. Sweat made it sting, but it remained unbroken. My face had gone from broken to unbroken. Once again, I looked like the sheriff's wife and people could treat me with as much indifference as a tin of pineapple or Spam. I perpetuated their indifference by wearing a public face that was both agreeable and undemanding; a pretty mask that worked in a way similar to how birdsong disguises the cruelty of wilderness.

People felt safe around me, so I was able to keep myself hidden, and those in hiding know how to listen and the more I listened, the more I understood that the skin was often a rug that character was swept under, like dirt. The skin, the body, was immaterial. When I dared to believe in anything, I believed in music, and Jacques kept arriving in song.

It was hot in the car, even with the windows down; it was like breathing though a steamy washcloth. Arlo made me wear stockings to church.

"Ladies wear stockings," he said.

We laid towels across the vinyl seats so the back of our legs wouldn't burn. My towel was wet with sweat. Arlo draped a towel over the steering wheel and started the car. I stuck my head out of the window and the breeze was like the harassing breath of some animal. My face had all but healed. As soon as we reached Highway One the dust stopped.

"Thank goodness for that," Arlo said. "It'll be good you getting out and seeing folks. They have been asking how you were," he put his hand on my knee and patted it.

Highway One was a paved road that shot straight through the heart of Callisto, splitting the two halves of the town like an apple on either side of its asphalt. A finger snap of white wooden houses, enclosed by river and prairie, snugly tucked inside the clapping blue waves and flowering virile grasses that kept Callisto hidden, mirage like amid a feverish green.

Unparalleled freedoms existed inside such seclusion, but dwelled as all freedoms dwell, inside their own shape of entrapment, so Highway One was a necessary emblem for the mind as well as a convenience for the body. It was a way out just in case one wanted to use it.

Arlo preferred the back roads; the intertwined dirt paths that he'd helped to carve and level. The dusty and insensible tentacles that lead to ponds, to cabins, to shacks, to overgrown groves, fields, homesteads, to the river, to nowhere, and dead ends. Taking Highway One was a Sunday exception, because Arlo washed the car on Sundays and wanted to keep it as clean as possible for church. "Cleanliness is next to Godliness," he would say.

Every Sunday there was a moment of breathlessness as soon as the wheels touched the highway's spine. A moment where the uneven jerk and pop kick of gravel became a purr, smooth and tranquil. It made leaving seem easy. A simple course of action, like licking an ice cube back to water, a steady and balanced movement inside which time would alter the entire consistency, the entire nature of the thing, of me. It seemed so easy that I imagined myself jumping from the car, running all the way to the interstate, and hitching a ride to Chicago. My mind caught in the whirl of motion and dreaming.

Then the sight of the white cloud-popping steeple and Arlo slowing the car as he pulled into the parking lot and the white wooden church, square and stout with three stained-glass windows that ran along either side. The shape of the windows mimicked the steeple, arrows pointing up; pointing in the direction death will take you if you'd enter. The front door was a simple unpainted oak and above it a round stained-glass window, blue with a white dove holding an olive branch in its beak. We walked beneath it. We were always early.

I stood there trying to smile. I was too hot inside my knee-length skirt, my long-sleeved shirt, and stockings. I straightened my spine uncomfortably. Everyone seemed to move in slow motion, as if they had each been bitten by a poisonous spider, and the heat was turning their insides to liquid. I imagined them all melting, dolloping through the cracks in the floorboards like mercury.

The sun streamed through the windows, a torch behind a slice of coloured Swiss cheese, I felt dizzy. Rainbow prisms shifted across wooden pews and the white walls, and I felt as though I were inside a kaleidoscope. It spun. I spun. The edges blurred and rounded, spinning, spinning, then black. I fainted. I collapsed like a person without bones, no person at all, a doll that fell and fell through a black gelatinous dream.

It was the dream of a play already in motion. Where I was a single drop of water that began to vigorously multiply, three of me, then five hundred, sixty thousand of me split, divided, and filled like a cloud, until it became a forceful grey throttle and released. I dropped, crisp through the sky, a glass arrow headed for the earth's throat. A million of me followed, mirrored droplets, inside each one the watery reflection of my face, ten million faces, twenty million faces, plummeted and smacked and folded through the musky sucking mouths of soil. Rain, and with it, erosion. Fragments of me pushed as one, all of my faces carved, forged, split rock, and push towards the churning deep and blue.

Then. A slap, not hard but intending. My eyes opened. Above me their damp faces relaxed and softened from worry.

"It's okay, folks," Arlo said. "It's just the heat. She's just fainted from the heat." He held a damp dish towel against my forehead.

I felt sick.

"I feel sick," I said, and they backed away not wanting vomit on their Sunday shoes.

I was woozy.

"I need some air," I said, and they backed further away allowing me girth to rise.

Arlo helped me. "Steady," he said, "steeeeady now."

As though I were a horse he was leading into a stable. "Steady, girl, steady."

I pushed his hand away. "Just give me a moment."

I walked towards the door. The dove in the window glared at me; its yellow eye seared a hole in my forehead, while behind me the reverend clapped his hands.

"Show's over people, let's return to our pews quickly, quickly now."

The organ began to play and I could hear Arlo's laugh. He was happy. It had gone well, I had performed, clearly, I'd been unwell, and he had gotten away with it. Maybe they thought I was pregnant. He was already talking to someone about fishing. I opened the door and stepped out into a colourless womb of dust. A veneer of dust covered over everything like camouflage. A tree was not a tree, but dust in the shape of a tree. The bank was a brick square of dust. I wanted to hide as well, so walked across Highway One and into a deep ditch, where I laid down and waited for the dust to cover me.

Then Jacques.

Jacques stood above me, looking down with curiosity and not judgment. Neither one of us were startled.

"There you are," he said, and with one hand helped me up to standing. In his other hand he carried a bunch of purple clover.

"It's for salad later," he said.

Hair, black. Eyes, black. His body was large and strong against the sun, his body sharpened the sun. Jacques.

"Your face has healed," he said, bent down and touched my temple with his thumb. "Are you alright?"

What could I say? He was open and frank. "Sometimes," I said. "Not really," I turned away. "No."

"Come on," he took my hand, "I've something to show you."

We walked through the field together. Grey clouds umbrella above us and raindrops began to bounce off the dry earth like clear rubber pebbles, an instant shattering of bullets. Thunder cracked and opened a waterfall, at once, we were washed, baptized. We began as a flood at the drought's end. It was like this: I wanted to sing, then I met Jacques and there was song, wretched song.

The fresh rain mixed with sweat in the folds of my skin. It caught in the hair on my lip and slid into my mouth like hot tears. I could feel dripping everywhere and mud, slick and gritty between my toes, filled my shoes. I stopped to tie my hair into a knot on top of my head. I stared at his hands, wrinkling with rain; I could not meet his eyes, but sensed him looking, thinking. We sloshed down the weed-worn track and all the way to the studio. The storm was loud and crackling. He motioned for me to follow him around the back. I could see the river was dimpled like wet grey silk. We stood under a canopy of maple leaves. The raindrops fell heavy and irregular against our heads, against the wind chimes. In the watery blur I could see smudges of red and yellow vegetable and berries. I could smell onions.

"Wait here," he told me. His feet smacked against puddles until he disappeared. The rain let up a little and the sky lightened.

I noticed I wasn't alone. Wooden sculptures of women were everywhere, watching, enclosing, a small army of goddesses in every size and shape. Some were tucked away, others were standing or lying on the ground, some were hidden in bushes, among the branches and the rhubarb, one was on top of the house, in every corner, carved women. Some were useful, were benches, chairs, one beside the back door had outstretched arms and hooks for fingers. Some were pregnant, were one-eyed, or half-fish, half-bird, half-wolf, or were half-buried. None looked finished. They were all crude and hovering with the sense of the unmade. I shut my eyes. The noise they made combined like a murmur, no voice singled out, no one thing heard or identified, no song.

"Ready," he said. He was holding a carving the size of a breastplate.

It was a large single wing with my face chiselled in the centre. In it, my eyes were closed, and my mouth was open. In it, I was singing. I felt speechless.

"Do you like it?" He smiled a white crescent.

"Yes."

"I heard you. The other night by the river. No, wait, don't get embarrassed. I understand it, where it comes from, that feeling of being out of control of your body. I know it."

"I knew someone was there," I said. "I was afraid."

"I know," he said. "I was too."

"Of what?"

"Can I?"

He didn't wait for me to answer, he untied the knot and my wet hair fell and smacked against my shoulder. It was a sound that stopped everything. Like a gunshot, a child's cry, a turning doorknob, water. He brought his mouth to mine. I felt them watching, trees trapped inside bodies designed by his hands alone, and turned away. They desired him, I could feel it, they craved him, and I felt as though they were closing in, from the beginning, felt doomed by his sculptures. I knew they wanted to be human.

I pulled away. "I can't."

I ran back through the field and rain poured from the sky. The exhausted earth lifted and opened in a hazel gratitude. What had been dry was filling, feeding again. Lightning and thunder in the sky and inside my chest. Dust settled and the world seemed green with possibility. Outside the church, children were dancing in puddles and a hot vapor rose from the reawakened ground. I stood beside the car in the parking lot and let the rain pelt down upon me. I wished it were acid. I wished it could melt my skin and make me someone new, someone that could walk away from my life and into another, without fear or guilt. I took the small woman from my pocket and held on to her.

The church bell rang. In minutes the parishioners would run from the door to their cars. How could I re-enter my life? I touched my lips. He had already washed away. We are still thrown, I thought, even the dead, even me, live inside an impulse we had imagined was impossible. The galaxy still explodes above us, redefining, reconfiguring the course of things. I want to be new, I lifted my face to the rain, make me new, I prayed to the sky.

"Have you lost your mind?" Mean eyes unlocked the car and opened the door. "Get in the goddamn car and use the towel. People are staring. Jesus, woman," he said.

Inside the car it was silent and warm fluid drained from my ears as if they'd burst. Arlo drove. I could tell he was searching for words. His hands wrung the steering wheel.

"I don't know what's gotten into you. Half the time I come home to find you staring at the river, or a tree, or space like you're in a coma or something. Now this, standing in the rain, catching your death, in front of Christ and everybody. Don't you have no pride, no sense? I know things aren't always good between us, but that's just folks, that's just marriage, rough and smooth, but goddammit, Elora, you have me at my wit's end acting like a crazy woman," he paused.

I watched raindrops slide down the window. He parked the car in our drive, turned the ignition off, and looked at me.

"I know I shouldn't drink so much, but I gotta lot to deal with, keeping the law and, well, coping with you. You ain't an easy wife, Elora. This ain't an easy life. A man has things he wants, a good and sane wife, a family, sons. Half the time you don't even give me a proper dinner. I'm not complaining, do you hear me complaining? I know you got things on your mind, but I want you to know that behind every action there is a reason. I love you though," he turned my head to face him, "with all I put up with you gotta know that."

The rain did not stop, it didn't even slow down, so that what was moist and alert began to droop, saturated and oppressed against the bloated ground. It collected in the wires of the screen windows like cells of a dragonfly wing when magnified. Like loneliness, I thought of things that fly and die within one season of Jacques, sweeping in, and then, suddenly visible. To see my face in a wing. To feel captured, and let go, at once. Soon the soil will swallow no more and the fields will swell until they spill over. Like me, I thought. Tonight, as soon as Arlo has left for his card game, I'll walk to the river. Close to him, I'll test providence.

Jacques Beaumont

Jacques stood at his bedroom window with the lights out. He could just see Elora beside the water's edge. Thinking about her was like driving through a storm. It took concentration. Few things arrested him in such a way. He made the decision to see what would happen if he drove through to the other side, walked down the stairs, and waited for her with the front door open. He could see that she was holding the small woman he'd carved for Birdie.

"That's the second carving I've made of you," he called out, and she stopped on the path. "Did it work?"

"I don't know," she said, and walked towards him. "I'm sorry I left the other day."

"Don't be. It's okay. Everything will be okay." She sighed heavily.

"'That world inside your sigh, knows no home,'" he quoted.

"Who said that?"

"I can't remember, somebody, maybe me," he said, and she smiled.

"That's better. Hey, why don't you come over tomorrow and I'll introduce you to my sculptures. Who knows? Maybe you'll make some new friends."

"Wooden friends," she said.

"The very best kind. They know how to keep your secrets."

Birdie Dubois

It started off with little things you see, tiny erosions of humanity, like he'd go into Rosa's café and she'd pick up the phone and ring somebody so she could ignore him for as long as possible, hoping he'd just leave. Or he'd go into the grocery store or the drugstore or the library and looks would be given and soon enough a clerk would pretend to stock shelves in every area that he'd enter. I guess they thought he'd steal something. By the time the incident at the happened the whole damn town already suspected him of crimes they couldn't articulate, so to blame him for that just felt like placing the missing words in a sentence that has already been spoken.

I made a photo box for the incident in an old gun case. On the outside of the case, I painted the many tiny ears and long spirals of wind that carried letters that didn't make sensical sentences or words, apart from Guilty and Accused and Immoral. Those were the words everyone was saying. I kept hearing those words spoken inside of absurd sentences. Those were the words they fit into everything, even if they had to bend the sentence around a falsification. On the top of the gun case, where the handle was, I painted a large mouth and the wind spilled from its opening.

Look, I can't claim to know anything about being black, but living and creating with Jacques taught me an awful lot about being white. Things I never thought to think of before. Like how I can go anywhere, be a presence in any public place or knock on any door, how I can say anything, basically just live and communicate and function and I don't have to have one single excuse, my white skin is reason enough for me to enter and be wherever I am. My white skin is my alibi. That just wasn't true for Jacques. Everywhere he went people asked questions. Even if those questions were just asked with eyes, think about how it would feel to sense that type of observation. Think about the oppression of having to feel like you were expected to explain every damn movement and interaction. Not everyone treated him this way, but enough that it was unnerving. I tell you I'd crack. I don't know anybody that wouldn't. It's outrageous.

The thing about Jacques was that he didn't grow up here, so this feeling of infringement wasn't ingrained or tread into his everyday existence from day one, it wasn't a part of his demeanour, nor should it have been, but that made him stand out. He didn't understand it, which meant he didn't bend to the ridiculous unspoken norms of racist culture. I was proud of him and respected his confident stature. He had the air of someone who possessed unique knowledge beyond the confines of accepted society, which, of course, was true, and it gave him a strong atmosphere that he was unaware of. He'd grown up in the back woods of Canada and when he saw people at all, they were natives or recluses, so they were unbothered by his presence. That wasn't the case in Callisto. He was noticed. That's the other thing I learned about being white. It makes you invisible in a way you never value until you've spent time with someone who is watched. Dissected even.

We went to Memorial Park for a picnic. Jacques wanted to see the stone carving of Winfield Scott and we both felt like we needed to get out of our surroundings. We were good friends by then and could work together in silence. It was on one of the first cooler days in late August, so the park was full of picnickers. We sat beneath the statue and ate our sandwiches. Nobody spoke to us but that wasn't surprising, as we were locked in conversation, until Jacques took out his sketchbook and began drawing. It was fascinating to watch him work. He circled around the statue, touched it, even smelled it, and drew while standing or walking back and forth. After he'd finished, he sat back down, and I cut into the apple pie he'd made earlier. I gave him a piece on a napkin.

"Honestly, I've never seen an artist so mobile before. I'm tired just watching you," I said.

"Well, I'm creating stationary presences and I don't want them to feel stagnant."

"Okay, makes sense, I'm a lazy artist all the same. Can I see what aerobic drawing looks like?" I asked, and he handed me his sketchbook.

There were three, maybe four, lines on each page.

"I hope you don't mind my saying, but these don't look anything like the statue," I said.

"I wasn't drawing the statue," he said, mouthful of pie, "I was drawing the drift lines, that's what I call them, the places where the statue feels rootless and, therefore, active."

"So, you weren't drawing what you saw?"

"No, I was drawing what I felt when I looked. It's not an emotional feeling, just a sense of how the work exists in its space, that's the relationship I'm interested in."

"Because a large sculpture is fixed?"

"Yeah, it's not like a painting or photograph that can be moved around, rehoused, rediscovered, so reinvented. It would take a crane and a very important reason to move this statue."

"Or an earthquake," I said, "would you like to create something this permanent?"

He thought about this for a moment, while I took the opportunity to finish my pie, then he said something I'll never forget: "The impermanence, the erosion, is what I love about working with wood, but I don't yet know the long-term effects this erosion will have on the lives my work has resurrected. It's not a question of wanting to create something permanent, rather, that I might need to create something permanent, and I don't want it to be inert."

It amazes me how he was always honest and transparent about his ability, like it was hidden in the open, yet because of its improbability, it took me a long time to understand exactly what he was talking about.

The following day, two police officers came to my door, asked for Jacques, and accused him of "defacing the statue of General Scott who had defeated Black Hawk on that very spot." A red X had been spray painted across the monument's chest. They claimed it was a blatant act of anti-Americanism. I thought to myself, well, one genocide after another, but kept my mouth shut for Jacques. Of course, I defended him and was a witness to his innocence. Actually, I told them, a red X across the chest of a revolutionary general could mean a lot of things. They knew that we'd come to the park together and left together, that his alibi was solid in a court of law, that they could never prosecute, but they harassed him anyway. In part, to rough him up, which they did, but mostly, to show their power. To feel their power. When they left, he said something that broke my heart, he said, trying to make light of the situation, "well, that's the first time they've ever used my name. I guess we're getting somewhere."

He found the fact that they never used his name the most insulting aspect of all. It didn't necessarily matter to him if he was disliked, particularly since his likeability had nothing to do with his character, so seemed pointless. It's contemptible how skin can become a defining aspect of character. And, when it's brought to your attention, it is not a unique response, especially amongst authority. Think of the Irish, the Turks, the Jews, the Gypsies, the Russians, the Muslims, the Mexicans, the Immigrants. Those that are demonized are nameless. It is a way of stripping a person or a group of their basic humanity, by not recognizing them as individuals it becomes far easier to persecute them as a group. To be nameless is to be inhuman, unborn, and objectified. To name someone is to take them into your consciousness.

But understand this. There was a time when you just couldn't even have these conversations. That I, as a woman, could even confront Arlo with accusations made me feel emboldened somehow and safe from repercussion. I took this as a sign of social progress, which was naive of me and, I see now, such naivety was a privilege, but I truly thought that I could just display my artwork and there would be little consequence.

I removed the foam from the gun case and placed two photos I'd taken at Monument Park. The case was meant to be positioned on its end so that it resembled a hinged frame. On the top I wrote "Alibi" in white sharpie. One photograph was of a white man, standing near the statue, who has nothing in his awareness but the serenity of the clouds, the birds flying overhead, the trees, peace. On the other side of the case is a photo of Jacques, a black man surrounded, suffocated even, by words depicting a consciousness full of excuses that justified his being in the park. He does not notice the birds, the clouds, the trees, because he can't ignore the people. What I wanted the case to impart was that even when there is no actual act of blatant racism, it's living under this form of constant scrutiny that is an infringement of freedom.

I grasped this a little bit because I'd purposely benefitted from my white and female invisibility. It allowed me to reach the frontline of photojournalism. What could a white woman do that was incriminating? A hell of a lot as it turns out. At the time, I was always covering riots or protests and not just for women's rights either, for everybody, human rights. Though I could reach the frontline, my view was seldom taken seriously, until I turned it into art. We had that in common, Jacques and I, we felt that art was a way to magnify humanity. The thing is, you can't allow injustice to proliferate in one area just because it doesn't seem to infringe on you specifically. It's all interrelated. An act of racism, misogyny, or homophobia is a trespass on the whole of humanity because it devalues us all.

What I know for certain is that creating my alibi box made me consider my role in society with an honesty and a clarity that I hadn't realized I'd been missing. That's what art does, that's its gift. I planned to display the box in the library and hoped that the experience of viewing it, witnessing it, would produce the same effect for others. And it had an effect all right, just not the one I wanted.

Jacques Beaumont

Arlo left for work and Elora went to Jacques's studio, past the sculptures and up the porch steps with muddy calves. She knocked on the door.

"You came," he said, as he opened the door. "Come on in, I'm making breakfast."

She was breathless and her hair stuck to her face in lashes. The large windows in the living room cast rain-speckled shadows on the floor. She stepped from square to square and followed him into the kitchen. Her socks left wet marks that absorbed unnoticed. Jacques was making eggs and coffee. He put a large dollop of honey into his coffee and stirred it.

"I eat everything with honey now. The flowers are different here and the honey tastes like sun," he took a sip and flipped his egg. "Are you hungry?"

"A little," she said, "I can't stay long."

"Well, I'm delighted you're here at all, so I'll take what I can get," he placed eggs and toast on the table. "Sit and eat, please," and pulled out her chair.

"I probably shouldn't be here," she said as she sat down.

"But you are. So maybe you should just enjoy yourself," he handed her a fork and sat down in front of her.

For a while, they ate together in silence, then she asked, "Why are you here? I mean, of all the places, why here?"

"My father tracked a bear that he had named Callisto. He was obsessed with her and after my mother died it just seemed symbolic that I'd have a cousin in a town named after my father's bear. I guess I'm a sucker for symbolism. Plus, I needed a change of scene, you know, something else to look at."

"I understand that. People always say you shouldn't run away from your problems, but I don't believe that at all, I think it's therapeutic. A different view gives you a different view, right? But I'm not sure our Callisto offers the most interesting outlook," she said, and finished eating.

"Well, Birdie's here and she is becoming a good friend and is definitely interesting, to say the least. And now I'm getting to know you. It seems to me that at least two interesting people live here. Plus, this studio's perfect. But tell me, if you could run, if you could give yourself a different view, what would that look like?"

"A city, I suppose, or mountains," she said.

"Mountains huh? Well, Pine Creek, where I'm from, has plenty of those. Maybe we should swap houses for a while?"

"Now that's something I wouldn't wish on anybody. But this place, now, this place," she stood and touched the walls softly, "I don't know how to explain it, it's strange, like I've been here before or imagined it or something. Stepping inside felt a bit like a dream, no, that's trite, it felt like the sense I get, that slowing down sense I get, when I know a song is developing. Do you understand what I mean?"

"I do. Everything ferments into a container of silence ... "

"That suddenly opens..." "And reveals the words or images you were looking for."

"Yes. This place feels like that container."

"Perhaps it is," he said, "or perhaps we're imagining it because we want it to be, either way, it's real."

What difference does it make to the condition of the mind if a place is real or imagined? Remembering is a form of imagining that fastens the mind to a place, and real or unreal, it's the place that matters. The place is where the identification is made. When Elora walked into Jacques's house, she identified with it immediately. It was in part the image of her personal landscape. The image of her escape, of her as free.

"Had you seen it, like in a picture or something, before you came here?" Elora asked.

"No, but I knew it was empty, big, and isolated." Like you, he thought, "I knew it had a view of the river and I understand that scale of lonely."

She noticed the words "lonely" and "understand" in the same sentence.

"So, you're an artist." A statement, not a question, she had seen his sculptures of course, but wanted to legitimize him. "I'd like to see more of your artwork."

"Of course, follow me, it only seems fair, after all I have listened to your voice and I must say that you, too, are an artist," he led Elora to the back door.

She stopped and hid. Birdie was sitting in one of the Adirondack chairs beside the river.

"We'll have to wait," she said.

"I know Birdie wouldn't say a word," he said.

"Don't be so sure," she said. "I should leave as soon as she's gone."

She looked though the side window. Outside, his sculptures bloated with water. He had positioned one next to the windowpane, and Elora stood in the hallway and looked at her. The grain had begun to split like a hoof up the centre of her body, she had no arms, just a neck and head like a clothespin.

"It's like she's peeking in." Elora drew a circle in her breath mark on the window.

"I know," he said. "I quite like that, but I can move her if it bothers you."

"No. It's fine. It's just, different, that's all. I should go," she said, and glanced to where Birdie was sitting.

"Different good or different bad?"

"Jacques, what do you know about me?"

"I know you're less, far less, than you should be," he said.

"And you know about my husband, Arlo?"

"Yes," he said. "But that doesn't bother me."

"Why?"

"Do you want the truth?"

She nodded, yes.

"Because I imagine that the part of you that married Arlo is the part of yourself that you don't love, but want to heal," he took her hand. "That's not the part of you that I'm interested in. I want to know the woman that I heard singing, the woman that Arlo doesn't recognize and perhaps, even fears," he said.

They stood in the darkness of the hallway. "That's why I carved you, twice. My specialty is to resurrect life and, believe me, there are as many ways to live as there are to die."

He was a sculptor. He brought things to life. He could carve a woman's body from a dead tree. He could carve a rosebud from a dead tree, a cathedral, a rabbit, a soldier, a wand, but he chose her. He led her into the light of the studio and pulled her close.

"How long will you stay?" She lay against his chest, his heart in her ear. When the emotions came, they arrived like a herd.

"I don't know. As long as it takes, I guess."

"As long as it takes for what?"

"To finish them, release them, and feel the need to leave."

"Your sculptures? What will you do with them?"

"Leave them. They belong here."

"But they're yours," she said.

"They're nobody's, casings. They're practice."

She opened her mouth to speak, but he put his finger over her lips and slowly unbuttoned her shirt. She was stunned. It was as though she were someone else, had entered another's body. She let him undress her until she sat naked in the late morning light.

He lifted her arm above her head and traced the slope beginning at her wrist and curving all the way to her hip bone. He lifted her hair and placed his finger on the bone behind her ear, moved it across her hairline, then down to the end of her spine, and around to the front of her waist to her navel. He circled her navel three times, then moved his finger up, and traced each rib. From there to her breasts, he circled the girth of each breast before he traced her collarbone, her neck and jaw line, then shoulder, he drew a circle on her shoulder before he moved his finger down the outside of her arm, past her elbow to her hands, he spread and moved between each finger. Then he did the same between each of her toes and circled her anklebone, traced up to her knee, circled, circled then lifted her leg, and pushed her gently back. His finger drew circles on the thin skin behind her knee before it traced down to the soft underside of her thigh and down, down.

The heart's fabric is the filament of dreams. He pulled at the very seams of her, pinpricked and unravelled her until she stepped out of her skin and into mid-air. She could see where she wanted to land. She could see who she could become. He tucked his sculptures like artefacts into the foil of his person, where they stayed with him persistently, like faith or guilt. So that, for him, the act of creating was a form of tracking, tracking his secrets, claimed and unclaimed, following footprints and branches as broken as dreams, until he met a pair of eyes. Until he saw himself. Meeting her was standing unafraid in the middle of his wood, where all of his animals lived, some peace-making, some deadly, but all of them ravenous. The idea of loving her was like entering the incalculable fold of time and eating through layer after layer of sediment, becoming, inhuman with the power to save.

"I sometimes imagine myself as water," he whispered as his finger entered and traced the inside of her.

"I look at the log I'm about to carve and imagine myself as water and the log thriving once more from my nourishment," he circled her.

"This is what I need. To give life again by taking the decayed away, weakness away, to be the hands that offer reincarnation. That resurrect another form, another you," his finger moved in deep circles.

She could not speak.

"Yes," he laid his body on top of hers, "what I want," he kissed her open mouth, breathed each word down her throat, and one by one they entered her.

"What I want (inhale) is to (inhale) wake (inhale) you."

Elora Winter

It was foolish to fall in love with a man who could envision himself as water. For such a thing could never be held completely, instead longed to hollow caverns, forge with rivers, and respond to the tender dry slurping of roots. The thing we most need to contain, to live and churn under the moon, enters, shapes, and slips away. Sometimes she could see him clearly. She could see his watery body shoot like a transparent bullet, through trees, through her, sculpting rings, small historical sentences of antiquity, he was the ringmaster. That is what he was. The ringmaster.

Birdie Dubois

As promised, Stan called every Tuesday from a payphone. Melissa had lost the baby by then and was desperately suspicious. In fairness, Stan was just lonely. We had been friends as well as lovers, after all, and he simply wanted a break from her intensity. He said, "I just miss laughing, you know, like proper laughing?"

I invited him down. I said, "Just tell her you're on a course, some kind of self-improvement BS she'll believe. We'll do nothing but laugh, I swear." And, sure enough, the next time she had a weekend full of rehearsals, he told her he was attending a cookery course in Indianapolis. He arrived with two cabbages and insisted on doing all of the cooking, so it wasn't a "total lie." I asked Jacques if he wanted to join us for dinner and he helped me move the table out onto the porch. I set it with mismatched crockery, cosmos in a vase, and a large clay jug full of sangria when I heard a car coming down the gravel.

It was Arlo and when he knocked on my door, I was scared to death it was about Elora, as I'd often seen her sneaking into Jacques's studio, so when he said he'd come over to personally ask me to take my alibi box out of the library, I laughed with relief. It made him angry.

"Birdie, folks like you always want a revolution. First your parents, now you. The apple don't fall far from the tree."

"What kind of revolution do you think I'm trying to start by insisting that we all respect one another? That's no revolution, that's just human decency. That man is worthy of your regard."

"Only I decide who's worthy of my respect. I'll give you that he ain't done nothing wrong that I know about, I'll give you that, but his fate is tied to those that have."

"You mean to other African Americans."

"I mean it's my civic duty as an officer of the law and as a concerned citizen to keep an eye on any new man in town."

"Civic duty my ass."

"You know, a lot of folks around here used to call your parents communists, back in the day, and I always defended you because I respected your daddy and, boy, could he grow a tasty tomato. But I wonder now, with all your protesting and art and judging the mouth you have on you, I wonder if the time will come when I have to shut it up."

And he pinched my cheeks with his thumb and forefinger, brought my face to his own mouth, and kissed me with a forceful tongue. I slapped his arm away and spat as he tipped his hat to me and walked back to his car.

I controlled my trembling until he slowly drove away.

An hour or so later, Stan arrived, and I was still quite shaken. He noticed straight away. He walked up the steps and gave me a hug,

"How are you Keeter? You're walking without a crutch?"

"Show's how long you've been missing. I've been crutch less for weeks," I said.

"What's wrong?"

"I had a visit from Arlo," I said.

"Who Rosco Peeko, the town Sherriff?"

"A lot has happened recently," I said.

"Okay, take me to the kitchen and tell me all about it."

Stan poured me a glass of wine and set about making dinner while I told him about the Arlo, Jacques, and Elora saga.

"You see, I didn't mean to start an out and out war with my alibi box. It is not that I am only an advocate for black liberation, but that I could see that black liberation, just like women's liberation, or any damn liberation meant human liberation. You can't discriminate against one group of people and believe there is freedom for any or all others because the mere act of discrimination is a soul shackle. So in that way, I was hoping for and working for and creating for the unbinding of people. I know it sounds grandiose but I still believe that humanity can cut itself lose from the chains of its narrative. God, it is so good to be able to talk to you," I said.

"I know, I've missed this too," he seasoned the beef on the skillet and turned down the flame. "So, are you saying that you think words are responsible? Narrative?"

"No, I think words shape everything, but the responsibility is ours. I just don't know what to do. On one hand, I'm pleased the box caused such a ruckus. On the other, I fear for Elora, especially now that she seems to be involved with Jacques. He is my cousin after all, and while I don't agree with adultery, I disagree more with abuse," he put his arm around me.

"Hey, it sounds like you have done everything you can do for her," he said, "you offered her your apartment, you tried to raise racism awareness, you're allowing Jacques to stay, you preformed a ritual ... "

"Oh, yeah, like that worked ... "

"Well, it seems to me it did."

"I wouldn't call having an affair with Jacques a solution."

"You can put the process in motion Keet, but you don't know the path it will take. You know that. Stop worrying about other people's reactions," he said.

"But that's what I do! Plus, there is a part of me that just wants her to be happy. You didn't know her. She, well, she was quiet then, I guess she still is, but she used to make her own clothes, a talented seamstress really, had a preference for polka dots for some unknown reason. I guess you could say that she wasn't someone you'd appreciate straight away. I think that was part of her charm, you know, how she grew on you. She wasn't immediately gorgeous or immediately friendly. But then, you'd notice something, like how she'd listen and remember what you'd said. It's hard to think of an example because it was ingrained but she'd do things like once she saw a thimble with a tiny little hand-painted bumblebee on it and she bought it for me. I was just starting to create my boxes then. I basically just put poems or photographs in old crates. But I had mentioned in our photography class that I was creating a box for a poem I wrote about usefulness, so it was perfect on many levels, which she only knew because she'd listen to me describe it. She just put it on my worktable when I was out. I must have been at lunch or something. The point is that she didn't care about receiving the credit for it, you know, she just did things like that for no other reason than kindness. I didn't realize how rare it was then, but now that I'm older, I realize that true generosity hardly ever happens at all. The world is self-serving. That is in part where her beauty came from, like a well or a spring, that and her black hair. She looks a bit like a pixie, very chiselled, you know? Oh and her hands. She had beautiful hands. They, like the rest of her, weren't delicate, they were large and slender and perfectly shaped. All in all, she's a sculptor's dream so it's no wonder that Jacques has fallen for her. Once, when we were having one of our evening chats, I remember him saying, he was reading The Odyssey for the third time and it was that part where they are all choosing wives from King what's-his-name's veiled daughters, and we were sitting by the river shelling walnuts from those trees over there in the grove, and I was telling him to be careful with Elora. And I said, how do you think it will end? And, Jacques picked up my purple-stained hands and said, "I'd only need to see a single pinkie finger to know the rest of her was perfect," then he brought my little finger to his mouth and gave it a friendly kiss.

"Don't worry Birdie, I think it will end with an ending." So what am I supposed to make of that?"

"Nothing, you're supposed to let it be," said Stan, "and breathe."

"I'm sorry," I said.

"For what?"

"I'm rambling on and on when all you wanted to do was laugh," I said, and there was a knock on the door. It was Jacques.

"He's punctual," said Stan, and I kissed him on the cheek. "Let's have fun," I said. "Pull up a chair," I called from the kitchen window, "we'll be out in a sec."

I held the door open for Stan who was carrying a large dish of stew, "He's made you a traditional polish stew. Bigos, it's delicious. The cabbage is from our community garden in Chicago."

"You made this man bring you cabbage?"

"I know. I'm devoted to a Pole, what can I say, you become particular about cabbage."

"And the sangria?"

"Eh, Stan's not the only man I've loved." I poured three glasses. "Stan, Jacques, Jacques, Stan," I said.

"Great to meet you," said Jacques.

"Likewise," said Stan.

"To international relations," I raised my glass, "and my personal role in preserving the variety of the cauldron," I said, and we drank. "Please, tuck in and help yourself."

"Thanks, this looks amazing, seriously, until recently, I've been living on canned soup. Did you make this bread?" said Jacques.

"Guilty," I said, "I'm not just a cabbage snob, I'm a bread snob."

"That's the French in you."

"Absolutely," said Stan. "And you? Any food pretentiousness hanging from your family tree?"

"Living in rural Canada? Um, venison maybe, just joking, no, not really, although I miss fresh fish," said Jacques.

"He's growing his own vegetables," I told Stan, who treated his own vegetable patch as though it were an ailing relative, which sparked a half-hour conversation about compost, that I, thankfully, wasn't privy to.

I was pleased that they were getting along so well. And, although I missed easy conversation, Chicago, and Stan, I knew that I wasn't ready to go back. Later, we walked down to the grass and around the house. We sat in the Ariondack chairs facing the river under the shade of a tall maple. I'd moved them there the other day to watch the birds dipping across the water. The evening chorus was at its finale and the crests of river went from silver to pink.

"I'd forgotten how much I love it here. The city does that you know? It's almost like I've had a cork yanked from me and I've gone into overflow," I said, and Stan raised his eyebrows. "Okay, bad analogy, focus less on the cork and more on the overflow, what I'm saying is that I think I'll stay here until Christmas. I can't explain it but there seems to be more for me to do here. Unfinished business. Jacques, you, too, are welcome to stay. In fact, I'd be pleased if you did."

Jacques Beaumont

Weeks passed, and although Jacques carved his mother, she never resurfaced. He tried carving her in every possible way. Perhaps she wanted to die. Perhaps she'd given him Elora instead. Elora had become the focus of his carving, his living resurrection. She was visiting him regularly now and he could think of nothing he wanted to sculpt more than her form.

Sometimes his gift felt like a dream, and he had to test that it was real. He rigged a few traps behind the shed. On the second night he caught a fox. It was dead by the time he found it, which was fortunate, as he'd always harboured a soft spot for the creatures. It was cruel to catch it, but he needed to be sure of his gift. He released its floppy neck, took it inside, and laid it out near the fire. The evenings were cold now and his hands would cramp in the air. He wanted this carving to be accurate. He placed a small dish of milk next to its head so it could drink when it awoke. It took one attempt. He placed the sculpture on the hearth, opened the front door, and watched the fox skitter out into the mud-coloured evening.

A large thump hit the window behind him, and he walked into the living room where the collision of the kestrel was powdered across the glass in a delicate sketch. As though the bird had hit the window at such a speed that its ghost had been knocked from its body and captured on the glass. He opened the window and looked out. The bird with the broken neck lay at the base of the house. He picked it up and held it. His mother was near, her presence perfumed around him, and it struck him that without his thoughts, this bird would carry no meaning, his mother would remain dead. Only ideas give significance to forms and light. He stared at the bird until its name vanished, then he laid the bird out on the table and began to chisel a piece of chestnut. All the while, he felt certain his mother was blowing into the kestrel as though it were a feathered bellows.

Inside each of us lurks the thing we did not choose, he thought, but what is chosen for us. One day a catalyst for it appears. One day, death. One day, love. Art. And then, you begin.

Birdie Dubois

Jacques and I had the bond of being young and creating together. Sometimes, during our talks, it felt like we were paving the way for something, some new form of thinking, it felt like we were making our own movement and there was a sense of our time being archived, remembered in the fabric of the place.

It was one of the reasons why Arlo's cruelty was so jarring. To understand Arlo, you must understand how he'd loved Elora since we were all kids. He was fascinated by her and didn't care that she was younger. He used to follow her around all doe eyed. Once, after church, he picked her a bunch of clover and when he handed it to her, she just ate the top of it off like a goat, then spat them out. She told him she'd never accept anything from a person that could harm a poor soul like Lenny Collins.

When I asked her about it later, she told me that she'd caught Arlo holding Lenny's finger over an alter candle. She'd found out Arlo had money on it that Lenny wouldn't scream in church, fearing God's wrath more than Arlo's, I guess. Lenny was a simpleton that Arlo constantly tortured. And I actually mean tortured. Arlo used to pin him down and take a sickle to his hair whenever it got below his ears. Lenny's parents were simpletons as well and he wasn't well looked after. So, Arlo would take an old farming sickle and grab Lenny by the cuff. "Time for your haircut boy. Can't be having a half-wit hippie roaming 'round." He often nicked Lenny's ear and once cut a slice of it clean off. As soon as Elora took to defending Lenny, Arlo changed his tune and eventually began defending Lenny himself. After that, Lenny worshiped the ground Arlo walked on and followed his every command. In fact, now, Lenny was the main person trying to bring Arlo's killer to justice. When everybody else thought it was just an unfortunate accident, Lenny was certain Arlo was murdered. Devotion like that has a scary element to it, you know? That's why we were all so shocked that Elora could marry someone like Arlo. She was once a quiet force.

Arlo used to do the yard work for most of the town when he was a teenager. I guess that's where his fixation on Elora first began. Elora's father paid Arlo to mow and look after things around their house, he certainly wasn't able to do it and Elora, well, she was busy attending everything else, the cleaning, the cooking, plus her studies. Mr. Winter wasn't a drunk to begin with, it just sort of snuck up on him, as I imagine these things do, after his wife died in childbirth. People helped out when Elora was young, but it became difficult when Mr. Winter became more and more reclusive as the liquor took hold. After a while, all people could do was treat her and speak about her father as though he were the man he used to be. That seemed like a kind enough action and it worked I guess, it worked to make her a sort of town child. Everyone took it upon themselves to look after her.

Not just that they could collectively raise her, yes, there was that, but it was deeper somehow. The collective feeling was one of dignified sorrow. Half the women in the town were married to alcoholics. So, it was felt that Elora had to learn too soon the hardship of adulthood. I remember hearing two women talking about it and making the comment, "poor thing, having to pretend this early." And it was true; she pretended everything was fine, just fine, so she never got the chance to be innocent and believe her life could be different. The belief in the possibility of change is something to be savoured as a young person, you know, it's vital.

The Sculptor - Gret Heffernan

I'm not saying her situation was entirely unique, I mean, I think many young people are born without the luxury of innocence. The type of innocence that is free from adult burden is Western romanticism. The majority of the world's young people, mere children by our standards, are managing adult roles admirably.

But, with Elora, she handled it so, well, gracefully, I guess that's the word I'm looking for, she was an example in grace and this made her a kind of beacon that was untouchable. It didn't hurt that she was beautiful and angelic with long wavy black hair. So when her father died and she married Arlo, it felt as though a tragic end was inevitable.

Once when I was coming home from school, I saw Arlo's mower parked outside Elora's house and I caught him spying on her. I can't explain how predatory it looked. As though he were hunting. There is possession and there is possession you know? I think he felt that she could save him from his despicable self, elevate him somehow.

I remember hearing this story about a tribe in the West Indies that used to bleed their beautiful and vivacious young so that the elders could drink their blood and purify themselves. The Rampersiad. They kept the blood for various physiognomies in femur bone vials. Archaeologists found a cave that was like an apothecary with little paintings above each jar to advertise each characteristic. I can't remember if I read it or heard it, but anyway, Arlo came to mind, and I've never forgotten the near perfect analogy.

By that, I mean he'd drink them all, but also, mostly, I'm talking about blood, about the belief that there is such a thing as pure blood, and the devotion to this belief that is as socially destructive and severe as bleeding a child. But most of the town held this particular type of devotion. That's what you must understand. Their prejudice wasn't just a dislike or even base hatred, it was a type of bespoke religious biology. In their heads, it was a kind of predestined biology.

So, when she fell in love with a black man she, to put it mildly, fell from grace.

In the end, Elora wasn't just killed by Arlo, she was killed by everyone.

Elora Winter

Jacques. Every second. Jacques. I spend afternoons in the garden. His skin still inside my fingernails, I long for soil, to dig and plant. It is too late for flowers, so I plant bulbs and the idea of things growing beneath the surface, the idea of flakes of him feeding the spring, these thoughts have no data, these thoughts develop as instruments develop the first time they're played. Which is to say that they ripen into the music they were born to create.

I enter the house and wash my muddy hands in the sink. Arlo, comes up behind me and sticks his finger inside a black bubble. He smells of beer and stomach acid. He pushes his cold hand up my shirt and presses his pelvis into my thigh. I can feel his holster against my leg.

"I thought you were going to go fishing," I said.

"I like watching you in the garden," he whispers in my ear, and pulls my head backwards so that he can kiss me on the mouth. Compared to Jacques everything about him, his skin, his tongue, his movements, is sloppy and rough.

I force myself to turn and face him, but he stops me, reaching around my waist and lifts my skirt. I let him. I am not his. What he takes is mere fluid, tears, blood. Salt. His violence is not the violence of evolution, but of the underdeveloped and crude. Outside of myself, of his invasion, I am developing and the world all around me is embryonic. It is the place where birds defy the ground. Where I am sky.

For me it was a time when things were made, not destroyed. After Arlo left, I sat on the porch and watched the leaves red as blood fall, singularly, like pinpricked drops filling the garden one by one. There was life developing inside of me. I unwrapped the ideas I'd bandaged, my memories, so that light could get through and grow. I could feel the growing, growing.

The following day at his house.

"Do you think she saw me?" I asked. Birdie had been to visit.

"Yes, but she'll keep it secret," he said and put his arm around me. He smelt of soil.

"What did she want anyway?"

"Nothing much. I think she just stopped by to say hello. Are you hungry? Because I'm starving."

"I could eat. Are you sure she won't say anything?" I put my arms underneath his chest and hugged him with my cheek against his back.

I knew I ought to visit Birdie and explain my relationship with Jacques but admitting it to another person made the danger of what I was doing seem real. I wasn't ready to deal with that yet.

"One hundred percent sure. Do you have time for a sandwich? I made some bread."

"I think so, a quick one."

"I wish you didn't have to go."

"I know, so do I."

"Just a minute," he ran outside quickly and came back with a fistful of basil. "Cheese, tomato, and basil perfection."

He put the basil to his nose and breathed deeply. His expression was one that I had never seen and that's how it was between us. New and intense but limited because of my predicament.

I sat down at the table and bit into the sandwich. Jacques took a pitcher from the refrigerator and poured two glasses of iced tea. He raised his glass.

"To us," he said.

"To us," I took a drink. "Tell me something."

"Something?"

"About yourself, your past," I took another bite.

"Like what?"

"Like, I don't know, anything, like why do you have silver polished spoons, yet only two shirts?"

"You want to know about my cutlery?"

"Nobody uses the word 'cutlery' here," I said.

"I'm not from here," he said.

"I know. I love that. But it doesn't answer my question. I feel like there are so many things I don't know about you," I wasn't ready to tell him that I was pregnant, not yet, not until I was sure, but I felt the need to unearth remnants from his past.

"The story of my cutlery is a marvellous tale actually. It's deserving of an ode. Ode to the Beaumont Cutlery," he said, and raised his sandwich like a sword.

"See? This is what I mean. You avoid my questions about your past."

"I'm not sure what you're truly asking, and besides, you might not like what you hear."

"Of course I will. I just want a bit of history. A bit of, I don't know, understanding."

"Okay. See this spoon? I once found it poking out of the garden like a sliver carrot."

"I'm serious."

"So am I."

"Why do I love you?"

"Because I am mysterious and leave you full of wonder? Come here," he pulled my arm, I got up and sat on his lap. "Be patient with me."

"I have to go," I said. "Arlo will be back soon," I stood to leave but he didn't let go of my arm.

"I'm sorry," he explained. "The spoon was my mother's. She buried the cutlery in the garden when she was losing her mind. It's hard for me to talk about my parents. They were, distant. Preoccupied. Now, they're dead and I'm trying to move forward."

"So the sculptures," I said. "So that explains the things you can give life to."

"You have no idea," he said.

"Maybe not. But I'd like to."

"Stay the night," he said. "Let me show you."

"You know I can't do that. What about Arlo?"

"He's not invited."

"Don't joke. I'm serious, Jacques."

"So am I. You want me to open up to you, but I only see you in stolen moments, trust takes time, it's mutual," he said.

"I know. I'm just scared," I said.

"So, why don't you let me handle him?"

"No! Promise you won't. It will make things worse. Look, I'm sure there is something that I can do. Just let me figure it out, okay?"

Jacques Beaumont

After Elora left, Jacques sat at the kitchen table and picked up the spoon. It was true. He had found it poking out of his garden like a silver carrot. His mother had emptied the contents of the utensil's drawer onto the floor. He remembered that everything had crashed but the cutlery. It was missing.

Jacques and his father had been sitting in the living room. Jacques was reading and his father was looking at his maps. She had taken a handful of flour down from the cupboard and started sifting it onto the floor like hen seed.

"What are you doing?" Jacques said.

"Catching footprints. Someone's stolen our silver," she said, and looked up as though she'd actually seen someone.

She leapt towards the corner and her flour-covered fingers ripped apart the air. Mathis stood up and took a deep breath. He grabbed her by the shoulders and wrapped his arms around her as she lurched towards the invisible thief. Jacques had tried not to look at her, but she was glowing irresistibly. She always shined during a fit, as if she'd been scrubbed clean.

"I need your help," Mathis said. "Grab her legs and let's lift her to bed."

Jacques bent down to take her legs and she kicked him square in the eye. "Jesus Christ!"

"That's right! Shout! It's good to shout!"

Jacques and his father began screaming and Nora joined them. The three of them screamed until their heads ached, then they flopped down on the kitchen floor like panting dogs. He remembered how the flour had stuck to their nose hairs.

"He stole my silverware from France," Nora whispered to Mathis. "Kill him."

"Okay, Nora, I will," Mathis said.

He stroked her short hair. It had grown quite a bit and her scars were nearly covered. She fell asleep with her head in his lap.

"What will we do?" Jacques asked.

"Find it," said his father.

"That's not what I mean," Jacques said.

"I know. Help me get her up."

They carried her to bed. His father's grip was emblazoned on her flour-dusted arms. She was as thin as a wishbone under the sheets. Jacques remembered her peaceful face and how they had stood watching her.

"I don't think it will be long," Mathis put his hand on Jacques's back. "Come on. Let's find that cutlery," he said.

They searched everywhere for the spoons. In the larder, in pots and pans, linens, under loose floorboards, in the woodshed, the commode, everywhere, when Jacques finally remembered that he'd seen her, days earlier, scoop away a bald patch of snow from the vegetable patch. She had poured a kettle full of boiled water over the uncovered ground.

They boiled the kettle, grabbed a shovel, and stepped out into the cold night. He'd seen her standing underneath the charms she'd made to keep the birds away. The charms hung as still as wooden icicles. Sure enough, as the hot water melted the soil, they could see little shiny handles like silver carrots poking through the ground.

They collected the cutlery without saying a word and walked inside. Jacques's hands were so cold that they burned when the warm air hit them, he stood thawing for a moment by the fire, while the sensation of pins and needles spread across his body. His father wiped the cutlery clean of mud, polished each one slowly, thoughtfully.

"When I showed your mother these, she just stared at them. They were like shiny jewels to her. It physically pained her that I ate with them. Once I came home to find the house decorated with cutlery. I have to admit it was beautiful the way they sparkled, I laughed and laughed, sure my father was turning over in his grave at the thought of cutlery on the mantelpiece or hanging from the doorframe. You see, your mother and I are similar creatures; we share the same curious eyesight. We both can find magic and lustre in what others find ordinary. I love her for that, for many reasons, but most of all for that. I'm telling you this because it's how I want you to think of her, treat her. Even when I'm gone. Do you understand?"

The following morning his father blew into his hot cup of coffee and closed his eyes to its steam. The logs cracked and burned steadily, and the room was silent, but for their little sips. They did not look at one another when they heard her feet slap across the floor, the water pour into the bowl, her hands gather it and splash it across her face. He had tried to think of something else, tried to think of a happy time, and remembered as a child her strapping him across her back like a snug little cub and the three of them snowshoeing through winter mornings. He remembered his parents' holding hands and the snow falling, like powdered sugar, dusting over them all. When she entered the room her hairline and eyelashes were still damp.

"Morning, well, this is certainly a day for porridge," she said cheerfully, and filled a pot with water. She opened a drawer, "Ah, my silver, I've been wondering where it got to."

Jacques thought of Elora and his mother and love. He made a pouch with his shirt by lifting the end hem and scooped up the cutlery from the drawer. He walked around decorating the house, forks on the mantel, spoons on the windowsills beside the geodes and knives on the bookcase. He put them wherever the sun shone, so that the light would have something to strike as it moved around the house. He thought of light like this, as a solid thing, as a block that he could press a shape inside.

He had learned to manipulate light from his father. To his father, light was something to hold, direct, and capture, but to him it was a life force to break and redirect. He had taken life, had broken light, and placed his shadow, as the image of himself, in front of her stream, however frail, however weak, like a blockade, he had made the final decision and it filled him.

He could bring the shadows back.

He looked around the room. Everything had a reflective quality, the geodes, the cutlery, even the piano bounced, and outside, the river, brown and muscular, reflective, yet moving as though something were thrashing underneath and he understood its violence. It was as thoughtless and shaping as the light. It was not the violence of war, but the relentlessness that poisons the marrow enough to fight. This he was trying to mould. This he was trying to cut into. One snap of peaceful transcendence, one snap of an independent world.

The source of radiance is often hidden. Was Elora this source for him? They certainly kept one another hidden. Their relationship revolved around the fear of truth, rather than its embrace. There was something that he couldn't reach. A meaning that seemed to constrict every time he came close to touching it, the worm of his childhood, small as a blood vessel, which used to vanish inside the coral whenever his hand drew near. It kept him from telling Elora about his ability to resurrect. She approached singing in the same way he approached sculpture. At first, he believed that this would allow her to understand his gift, but the truth was that her singing produced nothing physical. He could create life from death and that fact would always separate them, but he wanted to tell her about his mother.

Did that mean that he loved her?

It wasn't love in the way that he had anticipated love. Yes, the lust was there, yes, the heat and excitement, but perhaps he just wanted somebody, anybody beside him. Somebody he didn't have to explain things to, who hadn't the courage to ask and delve. No, courage is not the right word. She had courage. He couldn't deny her that. She was risking everything for him and yet, there was something else. It was as if she had a vested interest in keeping him only the man of her perception. He had to be the right type of saviour, the bad prince, but a prince, nonetheless. She would never leave Arlo for a murderer. Is that what he was? No. He couldn't have saved her. He had done his mother a service. Would Elora, or anyone for that matter, see his actions as benevolent?

It was better not to ask, not to risk breaking the illusion that served them both. He had told her the truth about the spoon, she could have pushed open the answer, but had decided not to, he felt, so that he remained safe inside her need to keep him perfect. There is nothing luminous about a man with faults that he can control.

In truth, he was a dry rock, and her devotion, her body, was like the water that made him glisten. He was ideal for her. The only flaws she saw in him were the ones he could not change. And as for him, he needed someone to hide inside, love like a blanket to a prisoner. They were each other's perfect escape. At first, he welcomed her desire, of course he did, he was starving and she longed to be devoured. He wanted someone to touch without cutting and we are drawn to people with ideas as big as our own. It was hand-in-glove chemistry, but now? Now she was trying to make him real, and reality suffocated him. Inside reality he found no air. He had come to believe that air was something he needed to create.

He was ashamed to admit it, but the sense of relief he felt after his mother had died was enormous. Her life had become a jaw that snapped around him, and then it was over, and he was floating, momentarily in his own air lifting off the ground like a dragonfly unclenched and let loose. He was beginning to feel free. It was shameful. It was so unlike him. Actually, that's a lie. It was just like him. He despised neediness, weakness. It made him feel as though he was shrinking.

He didn't want to lie himself into another life that's wrong. But how to know?

He'd always felt as though he'd been stuck inside the wrong body, the wrong mind, with his own flickering nature too buried to excavate. Thinking of her felt like choking on the dirt of himself. It's far better just to carve new figures, new bodies, chiselled out of his own rock self. Sometimes he wondered if he might just find one that resembles the actual him. He doesn't mean this in a sentimental way. A piece of wood with his face trapped inside it eager to revitalize into something else. He's talking about the flow and stacking of atoms here. He's talking about sculpture as exploitation of space, where he would assume the space that was meant for him. The shape that fits. When he disposed of his mother's body, he felt atoms buzzing around the emptiness like flies ready to reconfigure.

How could he tell Elora about his gift? Would she understand? If he loved her then surely it would be something he would want to share with her, right? He was afraid that it would always divide them, and she would grow to resent what she couldn't possibly relate to.

His time now, in simple terms, is the occupancy of collage, what to keep, what to take away, what to hold, what to push, what he allows to harden. That's one of the reasons he finds sculpture so seductive, for no matter how flawless the image, the wood will always succumb to forces beyond his control. She will never be what he expects. Like love. Love is also the beginning of erosion, in terms of the perfect self, but think of the beautiful shapes erosion has created. It's why he likes to keep himself fluid, lava like, it lets him carve the space around himself in the hope that one day he will crystallize into a shape he has created, then erode.

Jacques went to CC's first thing in the morning. From the moment he stepped foot in Callisto, he felt noticed and watched, as though a crow were following him. She was right. If they stayed together, they couldn't stay here. Perhaps they could run away to Chicago or some other wilderness? Maybe she could give him whatever it was that he needed? He was stuck between picturing his life with and without her.

Marge constantly came over with extras, meat mostly, and with his garden, it had been enough to keep him from town. He hadn't prepared for this type of exposure, but couldn't turn around for home now, as he felt that would raise suspicion. For what? He wondered.

The door chimed when Jacques opened it and right away he saw CC chewing on a toothpick with his arms folded over his chest.

"Well now, it's our own bonafide Frenchman come out of hiding."

"Hiding? I'm not hiding."

"That's what we thought. We thought you was hiding yourself or something from us."

"No. Just working, that's all."

"That's what I hear. I hear you're an artist. Some kinda wood maverick, but hell, even a working man's gotta eat."

"Well, Marge does most of the shopping and I have a garden."

"Must be one helluva garden. I had heard Birdie's been helping you out as well. She's madder than a hornet near lemonade."

"She's been really kind actually."

"She's a witch you know. Got to watch out for witches."

"I don't know anything about that."

"Doubt you'd say if you did."

"Maybe we should start over. My names Jacques Beaumont," he went to stick out his hand, but CC waved him away.

"I know your name, son."

There was the usual stuff on the shelves and Jacques put tins, toilet paper, meat, milk, and eggs into his basket. He was desperate to get out of there. A young girl with Lucy written on her name tag stood behind the counter and rang up his purchases. She went to bag his groceries when CC cleared his throat to get her attention. She looked up at him, he shook his head no and she handed the paper bag to Jacques with eyes full of apology. He bagged his groceries and walked towards the door.

"Nice to meet you," he said to CC.

"Yep," CC kept his arms folded across his chest as Jacques balanced the bag on his hip and opened the door.

Pig, Jacques thought as he stepped out onto the sidewalk. The bag wasn't heavy, but it was cumbersome, and he wished he hadn't bought the biggest pack of toilet paper. The day was warming up and he had a long walk home.

He walked down Main Street. A few of the shop fronts had been recently painted. Rosa's Café had a green and white awing. On the window was a painted wreath of red roses and Arlo's face looked through it straight at Jacques. He was sitting in his usual place buttering his toast, watching the small world. He saw Birdie's Toyota roll to a stop and hoot the horn at Jacques. "Never let a good-looking man walk when you can give him a ride," she winked.

He laughed and approached her window. "Don't you ever stop?"

"Lord no," she said. "I have to remain deserving of my reputation. Moral disgust is my disguise. Now, get in."

"A businesswoman through and through," he said, as he opened the door and arranged his bag of groceries. "Thanks. I'm not sure how I would have managed this," he nodded towards the toilet paper.

"Shit always gets in the way," she said and laughed hysterically at her own stupid joke.

"What in the world are you doing in town anyway?" She looked accusingly at his groceries.

"I could ask the same about you," he said.

"Yep, you could, and I've been at the bank, but it's different because I'm not sleeping with anybody's wife."

"Yet."

"I'm serious here, Jacques."

"Right. You caught me."

He rested his forehead on the glass. Silos scattered across the green fields like pieces from a wreck. He pictured a machine world above the clouds aborting the broken parts of itself, heavy things falling from the sky.

"They can't do anything to me," he said, finally.

"You're a damn fool. Their granddaddies could have had you arrested just for walking Main Street and you don't think that's bred in? They are just waiting for an angle and if you weren't rich and connected, they'd have run you out by now. Listen. You're lucky. You want to sculpt, so sculpt, and stay out of sight and mind if you want my two cents," she stopped for a breath.

"Do I have a choice?"

"Not unless you like walking. If you want another two cents, cool it with Elora, I mean it, I feel it, let her down gently, but let her down. It will only end badly. Arlo will kill you both."

"What if I told you I loved her?"

"Love's a fluid thing, Jacques, especially when lives are at stake. But if that's the case, you need to disappear. And quick," she said.

"Elora wants to us to run away to Chicago."

"Well, if you're gonna run, you better run further than Chicago, think Mexico, think someplace where they'll never find you, because if you take his wife, and they find you, you'll live together for eternity."

He said nothing. The sound of the road pinched him like a tight belt. She pulled up to the house and he could barely breathe.

"Don't tell me if you take off. Just go. The least amount of lying I have to do the more convincing I am. Listen, I know it's hard. I'm in a tricky love triangle myself, truth be told," Birdie said.

"Wow, with your character I would never have guessed it," he joked.

"Okay, I deserved that. He's coming around tomorrow night. Why don't you join us for dinner? Take your mind off things. He is a fabulous cook, among other things," she said and smiled.

"Can I bring a date?"

"That depends, yes if she's wooden. No, if she isn't."

Elora Winter

As it turned out, I didn't have to resort to tricking Arlo. Fate intervened.

The phone rang just as I was setting the table. I could hear Arlo's voice go soft and quiet. "That so, well, that's a shame, yep, yep, I'll be there, see what I can do."

"Honey, bad news," he said, putting on his boots. "I've gotta go to Alabama for a few days."

"Alabama? Why?"

"Well, an ol' brother of mine has gone and got himself in a spot of trouble ..."

"A brother?"

"A friend Elora, don't interrupt me, a friend that's like a brother, anyways, I got an understanding of prison, being an officer and all, so his family called on me to help ease the situation."

"He's in prison?"

"Yep, well, the judges don't always see the right side of the law, but, don't you worry about that, don't you worry about anything cuz I'll be back in two days, three tops."

Act normal. Act normal, I repeated to myself. "Can't you eat first? No sense driving on an empty stomach," I put a bit of chicken on his plate.

"Well, this is nice, real nice, I just love you fussin' over me."

As soon as he was gone, I ran all the way to Jacques.

Birdie Dubois

Borders mean that the "ordinary" of one place does not have to be accepted as the "ordinary" of the greater world. Borders create the mental frame-work of a group, a community. Fanaticism, racism, all the terrible "ism's" that happen through slight shifts in what is deemed as ordinary. Like buying milk or posting a letter or walking down the street or taking a bus. A community where gossip alongside unspoken decrees of birth right condemn the ordinary rights of a law-abiding human is a community that is no longer stable. His presence brought a shift in the balance of ordinariness. I don't know how else to say it. It went from fireflies to pitchforks overnight.

And it was down to gossip. It always is, because if it was down to philosophy, to folks being rational, it simply wouldn't have happened. It seems the largest tragedies have provincial beginnings. Remember the penniless prophet who preached unconditional love over Roman law and gathered a loyal following? Prejudice is a jealous dog guarding its owner's idea of their position in the world. And to let that dog roam freely you've got to overturn what is deemed as ordinary and, very often, righteous, in the world. The very best way to do that is by utilizing inexact gossip about the positions that people fear losing the most and then offering them a reason for their fear that, crucially, does not require internal reflection or responsibility. Gossip has brought communities together since the beginning of humanity. Usually, it's about someone from within the group, but when it's about someone from outside the sphere, from a whole other experience, it validates and unites the group experience, which is all they know about what it means to be human, as the one true experience, thereby rendering the other person as inhuman.

But I think the idea of Jacques had morphed into something more than inhuman by the time they killed him, because when people commit horrendous acts of cruelty against other humans it's because a group consciousness has become its own allegorical dog. And the only way a dog ever gets past its master's hatred, for hatred in this circumstance is a master, is to fight and kill. So, it wasn't Jacques that was inhuman, it was the opposite, like I said in the beginning, all the wolves surrounding him that were unearthly.

That evening, Elora's last, I had spent the day walking the abandoned train lines. Pre-highway, when this town was thriving, there was more than one train line that freighted goods from steamboats to the remainder of America. Nettle and dock between the tracks. Crab apple and boxelder trees along the furrow that eventually gave way to wide fields of soybean or wilding grasses. I was looking for rail spikes, and found a few, for a photo box I was contemplating. But also, I'd taken to exploring the environment of my childhood, and writing down the memories I'd had of being young and alone.

When night fell, I returned home and sat on my porch watching the day draw itself into evening. There was a weeping in the smoky sky, a spasm of red and orange, my heart, my stomach, told me that something was about to go wrong. Across the field, I could see the shadowy figures of Jacques's wooden idols. This was normally the time that Jacques would arrive, and we would talk about our days. The warm light of his windows cascaded to what appeared to be another sculpture standing beside the river, when it moved, I saw that it was Elora creeping up to the back of the house and knocking on the door.

Jacques opened it and she blazed inside his grip. Enough was enough. I stood, walked inside, and began preparing the invocation.

I am not powerful enough to identify myself as a witch, but I have rituals of my own that help reinforce my understanding of connectivity. The ideas and events of a period are related, even when they seem not to be, and creating art is the greatest way to influence this connectivity, though it can take a long time. So, preparing rituals, using symbolism and meditation are, for me, quick means of influence. I wrote a prayer, took the small figure from Elora's box, and wrapped her inside it. For what? For safety. How did I know she'd need it? How does anyone explain a premonition?

Elora Winter

Our lovemaking was always for the world and against it.

A juxtaposition that was ravishing because it felt like a salvaging necessary to rebuild ourselves. It was eternal because, in a way, it felt for everyone. For all of us standing in the same house and looking out of separate windows, wondering why or how life had become something that we hadn't expected or even wanted. And then, turning to find that the answer was in a human. It seemed like a worldly gift, and I opened in love to shape a new physiology.

Jacques kissed my neck. Loons and fireflies.

"I can't believe you are here," he said. "What happened?"

"Arlo got a phone call. Something about helping out a family in Alabama. I don't know. My heart was beating so fast, I just tried not to scream with happiness. I could hardly listen; I just know he'll be gone for two nights. Two whole glorious nights! Can you believe it? God," I said and looked up at the stars, "it's such a beautiful evening."

"Yes, it's the perfect evening for a concert," Jacques said, and kissed me again. "Come on. Everything will listen."

So we set about preparing.

Clues of the rain's battering remained in frogs, fallen crops, fat creeks, and mosquitoes, and the sulphurous smell of hot decay rose from the prairie's humid bottom. The grasses were straight spines of lime green that twitched against one another.

I stepped down from the porch and into the field towards a patch of thistles. I could just see their tall purple heads spiked against the night sky like bee stings. I loved the pride of a thistle, how it could be both hard and soft at the same time, like the face of a porcupine or the gloss of polished metal.

"Elora," he called, running to catch me, "you'll need these," and he placed a pair of garden gloves into my hands, then bent down, broke the flowered head off a bit of white clover, popped it into my mouth, and walked away. Everything he did was sensual. I chewed the flowers' sweet gum all the way to the thistles, then squat between the grasses and bent the base of a thick stem until it snapped, releasing its sticky milk. I brought its gentle speared flower up to my face and felt a tremendous sense of relevance that I wanted to remain, to live, a rightness, the ant crawling up my arm, the heat releasing from the prairie's marsh like a velvety lotion upon my bare legs, the moon in the sky, everything in its rightful, wilful place. And although I felt this way, I also understood that the child inside me was a small presence. I would have to wait to tell Jacques, for I couldn't bare it if I lost our baby and broke both our hearts.

I gathered the thistles together and walked back to the house. I placed them in a jug and put the jug on the piano. One by one, Jacques was hauling his carvings into the back garden. He placed them in rows.

"Looks good," he said, appearing once more from behind the house. Under his arm was the wooden figure of a woman with fish scales for skin, her closed eyes and mouth were shaped like crescents.

"I'll wheel the piano out in a minute," he said, placing the figure in the yard next to a plump naked woman with a featureless face and a wreath around her neck. "After we eat."

Earlier in the day he had pulled from his garden carrots and onions and put them in a large terracotta pot with a chicken and some garlic. It had roasted all afternoon and filled the house with a delicious smell. He had picked a big handful of spinach, runner beans, some tomatoes, and coriander, cut them up and stuck them in a bowl. His rhubarb was ripe and delicious, he chopped it up and baked a cake for dessert.

"Can you take the cake out of the oven?" he called from inside his work shed and emerged with a large rectangular block of wood. I saw the beginning chisel marks of legs and what looked like a tail.

"No need for her to miss out on tonight's festivities just because she's in the womb," he smiled and caressed her, then stood her beside the figure of one whose arms were left as branches. His wooden audience was in place.

Jacques moved a small end table out onto the porch. He placed a piece of cut chicken on each plate and a helping of spinach salad. He poured two glasses of wine. I stuck a fork in the cake cooling on the countertop. It was clean when I pulled it out.

"Come out here and sit down," he said from the door. When I stepped outside I stood still for a moment, paralyzed by the view ahead of me. He had placed each woman side by side facing the porch, so that there were three long lines in the yard looking like twenty wooden soldiers. An audience of warfare goddesses and behind them a wave of black and a fractured moon.

The sculptor removes. He takes one thing and makes it another by eliminating what he deems as unnecessary. He manipulates space, and it is true, there were things he chipped from me that I did not need, that I was better off without, such as the presumption that human beings are any more divine than other forms of life. Yes, we are the thinking creatures, the planning creatures, but what of the instincts we have lost and suffused?

This is what he gave me.

The removal of calculation and the introduction to instinct, which gives way to the soul, just as the chiselled piece of wood reveals the curvature of a neck, and an air that swirls like a lick inside it. Spending time with him was like blowing away sand and uncovering a body hidden beneath. The soul preserves, waits for you to find it, and waits for you to engage.

"Tonight we'll give them a show they won't forget," he said, taking a bite of chicken. "This is delicious. If I do say so myself."

"What songs will we sing?"

"Any that come."

"Inventive singing. My favourite. I feel sorry for our audience though," I said.

"They'll love it, they've served their purpose anyway and deserve a party," he said, and put down his fork.

"What does that mean?"

"It means I've done all I can for them and you're the only figure I want to carve now," he got up and wheeled the piano out onto the porch.

We sat together on the bench; single chords struck the dark like random splashes. A prairie night is a riot to the unaccustomed ear; you must adjust your breath to hear through its clamour, slow your breath to hear music. It gives nothing away and forces you to pay attention.

"Are you ready?" he said.

"Yes," I said, "actually there is a song I'm working on. The one you heard me singing, it's like a ghostly ballad about the place of my grandmother's birth. It's this little place in Ireland, Passage East, and she used to tell me stories about a harpy that supposedly lived in the sand dunes. It's not finished though."

"Well, let's finish it," he said.

"And, how do you propose I do that?"

"Just stand up and open your mouth," he said, "I'll play the sounds to follow you."

The porch felt like a stage. Above me the clear night loomed in waiting and the stars, a million animal eyes shining against a black as far-reaching and meditative as a deep sleep, and the carved women ahead of me, softened by their shadows, pearl like, waiting for me to begin, so I opened my mouth and nothing. Nothing. I opened it again, left it open, until a sound swirled up the back of my throat and fizzled its way out like a dying firecracker, a struggle.

Jacques struck a piano chord, I followed it, breathed the sound in and out until it became an incantation. And the atmosphere began to give back, oscillated between my voice and the air's own wide bellow, we played, catch and throw, catch and throw, until the words:

> Heart that's flayed, open ribcage
> The coast she cries her loss
> Close your eyes should she surprise
> Her form an albatross.
>
> Shriek of luck, your sight she'll pluck
> Collect with which to find
> The soul she lost, the fury it cost
> The world she wants to blind.

It was not as before, no bone fork in my throat, no thunderous musical revelation, but rather an eager partnership between the air and voice, like the steady tension that vibrates between would-be lovers, and each thing bounced on this taut thread compelling me to sing its human name, so that I stepped out and sang every part unto me, and every part came alive and the night, a stirred dust, collected in my droplets of wet eyes, tongue, lungs. The tanginess of time, the taste of mould and rust, particles rose up and settled, coating both colossal and microscopic, each arched blade of wheat and each burst of pollen, the curve of every petal, and the angled pockets where leaf grows outwards from limb and the sky, a black drum pounding. It activated everything. Everything. Shifted. Electrified. Hummed.

I called their names, their own essence – mosquito, mothwing, cricketcry, ragweed, cornhusk, riverslurp, thistle.

I called myself, I called our child, I called him, playing behind me his collection of notes that flowed and scattered like wildebeests, heading towards his carvings, his women, our audience, I sang them alive for him like a gift.

Their anxious figures, tenderized by their shadows, chewable, no longer wood, but meat and flesh. One by one. I called them out of themselves – names, pure syllables, they rose with bones of air, straight into his heart of lush, lush unearthing, of discovery, they walked, I walked, calm as a believer approaching a terrific storm, that power. We ate every drop of stew, ate every crumb of cake, drank every drop of wine, and then one another. Thank you. Thank you. Thank you. I whispered. Then later –

"I love you," I said. "Let's run away together."

"Where do you want to go?"

"Anywhere. We'll grow together, move together, change together. I'll follow you."

"Are you sure? Whatever the cost? Whatever the sacrifice?"

"Yes," I said.

"The song you sang, the ballad, who is it about?"

"I'm not sure. It seems to be about someone I know but only in memory or dream. I don't fully understand where it's coming from, but I sense it needs to arrive. Does that make sense?"

"Perfect sense," he said and kissed the top of my hair.

In the middle of the night, I woke. His arms around me, his mouth, his weight, the weight of a loan, then sleep, his shadowed face turned from me. His cheekbone lightened with blue light, on it were two pockmarks, like craters in the moon. He was like the moon, that close to the body. That far away.

It is remarkable how the heart can become the sum of a life and the body just a way to feed it. Touching him was like placing my hand through a cool running stream to grab a piece of gold I'd seen sparkling there, elemental, elemental to a fault, not a love a human can sustain, not a love that can want, but must remain as is. This is the deception, and yes, when I met him, my truth split and revealed only the brightest half of itself, like iron before it cools into a gray shape, and this was the truth we lived in, formless and molten. I could not ask anything of him, no detail that would place him inside of a shape, no clues, nothing to hold, there was only now, he'd say. But what he meant was, that with no hint to a past there can be no indication of a future, for one needs the other to see. I thought this was artistic, adventurous even, and at first, could not recognize its cowardice, for a life will always find someone to take responsibility for its existence. That is what lives do.

For him to remain molten, I had to become the shape of his steel but first to melt, the embrace, the melting, the time spent in my liquid state, when any form seemed possible, any carving, any casting, any shape, and so, I was content to just flow around him like water in a bottle, to run off his body of ideas like a fast-moving drip.

Even my fear of Arlo was diminishing. I now lived in a place beyond his control where my body could create a new life. Little soul, I whispered to it daily, stay with me. I wanted to tell Jacques, but couldn't, as though voicing the words would make me lose the baby. Also, there was still a distance about him, as though he inhabited a space, he had not shown me.

It was the way Jacques spoke of the present that made it pliable and unlocked from the past or the future. His disguise was freedom, like a religion; so holy he guarded it to the point of devastation. But too often devastation is mistaken for revelation. I felt guilty for wanting anything solid, so guilty I spoke only of things no human could catch. Stars. Songs. Plants. Time. Impossible things. Impossible when you realize that nothing indefinitely needs you.

A child matures with or without you, love lives with or without you, and hate, nothing needs you, nothing but your own will to create a miniscule space for throwing life into, a hole in the ground, a net in a tree, hands leaking water, but sometimes, sometimes you get the sensation that there is more than survival, and a collection of disappearing firsts. Yes. Sometimes you feel a pattern flash inside of you with no memory behind it, no future ahead of it, just a perfect moment wanting nothing more than to live itself out, and you think, this is mine, mine alone. Singing inside the night's intimacy was such a moment for me.

Only these flashes, these instants can be kept; no person, but there was once one I would have died for; no idea, but there were many that I dreamt; no song, but there was once one that'd been sung; no thistle, but I had once held one in my hand.

Somewhere I knew this, somewhere I knew that ownership was not a concept nature recognized, and had I thought about it, I might have been able to retrieve this inborn knowledge. Perhaps then, I could have swelled with the peace that comes from allowing each moment to be just what it is: a moment among a series of moments among lifetimes, were it not for the terrible power of desire. Of human want. Terrible the way the most cherished things are terrible; terrible the way all that is worth living for is also terrible – because as soon as it enters us it becomes human and to be human is, inevitably, to end.

Callisto, Illinois

It was sunrise when Elora got home. He had parked around the back. The prisoner had been stabbed in his cell, so Arlo had stayed with the family long enough to offer condolences, then drove back through the night. He was waiting in the dark house, beside the shutters and their ladders of light. When she opened the door, he grabbed her by the neck and the geode she'd been holding crashed against the floor. The small woman fell out of it.

"What the hell is this?" he kicked the carving with his foot.

She couldn't answer. She couldn't breathe. He recognized the carving as one of Jacques's.

"A nigger whore? Is that what you are? A nigger whore?"

He tightened his hands around her neck. She kicked and scraped against the wall until she stopped. He let her body collapse onto the floor like a marionette. He wiped his hands on his uniform.

He stepped over her and picked up the carving from the floor. The rims of his eyes were red with hate. He put the carving in his shirt pocket and poured himself a whiskey. He sat down on a chair and looked at her. Shit, he thought and grabbed a kitchen towel and dropped it over her face. He couldn't have her looking at him, not when he needed to think.

He walked to the garage, flicked off the security light, and scanned the room. He'd take her to the river. He took the tarpaulin off his fishing boat. She'd fit under it nicely and the town knows how much he loves fishing, so nobody would think it strange. He'd leave in the evening, after work.

He took his wallet from his back pocket, removed an old slip of paper from behind his driving license, read the telephone number, and dialled.

"It's me," he said and cleared his throat. "I'm sorry to wake you, but now I'm the one needing assistance. Can you get a group together by tomorrow night?"

There was a silence while he listened to the person speaking on the other line.

"That's right. Well, you know I can't be involved. You'll find him at the old Dubois place, he's living in their converted barn, Beaumont's his name. And Harold?"

He poured himself some more whiskey. "I'm asking you to get old-fashioned."

Jacques Beaumont

Flora had left before sunrise. His craving for her that night had been ravenous. She was like a trunk he wanted to cut open, thrust open, and with his tongue like a chisel, he severed her and severed her, until she was small enough to swallow with one bite. All day, her scent coated his hands and arms as he carved. If he could have chewed the wood, he would have, it was his first real sculpture and it was of her. But there was something missing. Something retrieved and of the earth, he knew it, and so, the river stones. He needed stones for the eyes, perfect polished river stones.

He went to the river and dug through the mud, he felt the soil and thought of her body. The trees cracked in the wind, black branches on black water, he looked and saw her pretty mouth gasping beside him.

A fish, he thought, a mermaid, crawling up the riverbank towards him. Her name did not arrive, and he stepped out of himself and into someone he recognized as dangerous.

He held the stones in his hands, one on each palm – eyes – he had always thought of his hands as eyes. He could see with them. Like a gift, they had led him to her. Her eyes were flat black. He winked his hands at her. He noticed red marks were already around her throat. She lifted her head towards him, and he felt it was a sign. He carefully placed the stones in his pockets and his hands and fingers along the marks, like letters, inside the script provided. It was perfect. Now she would be able to understand him, to know his gift.

"I'll bring you back," he whispered into her wet ear. "And I'll love you. This way, we can both escape," he said, and squeezed until he felt her leave.

It was delicate. There was nothing thunderous. It was like easing a cork from a bottle, she just went pop, and it was over, done, drinkable. The air was drinkable, and he tipped his head back and guzzled it all, drank until he bloated with unearthly desire. I can bring her back, he thought, and with his fingers brushed her hair clean of sticks and pine needles, before he folded her into the river, and the river took her, soft as a tissue. He fingered the stones in his pocket and felt free. Both of them. Free.

Birdie Dubois

I threw a cardigan over my dressing gown and slipped my feet into my work boots. Earlier, I'd been walking the train tracks, looking for bolts, spikes, or fastening iron, when I saw Arlo's truck, and hid. My guess was that he was night fishing. His trailer and boat were attached, and I thought he'd drive past into the bay. But he stopped near the small timber, reversed in, lowered his boat into the water, got out of the cab, and fiddled around in the boat for ten minutes or so. He had on waders, and he walked behind the boat, messing with something underneath the tarpaulin. It was strange that he hadn't removed the tarp, stranger still that he risked getting his trailer stuck, then he drove away. I noticed he went the opposite direction to Callisto.

The whole witnessing gave me the shivers. My mind had felt as twisted and cramped as an octopus inside a small cave. The moonlight was pulling me out of myself with a beckoning. The sounds outside were like lamentations and I knew that my restlessness had meaning behind it.

I walked alongside the river towards the timber. Jacques's lights were out, and his goddesses were all standing together like a mythological army. I held my breath as I walked past them. I was heading towards a copse of pines just beyond Jacques's house. The trees led all the way into town, black evergreen wings like a gathering of dark angels penetrated the sky.

I had seen a nighthawk there last year, nighthawks were two boomerangs tied together with a body and nearly soundless, but for their insect diving. The air whirled off them as though they were small steel aircraft. It's been a good year for mosquitoes and there was a pool of water near the copse. I stopped and listened for the plummet of wings, for a clue. The grass was wet and buggy. I should have worn tall socks. I scanned the trees through my binoculars.

Nothing. Nothing in the air. Everything was still, too still. I scanned the river.

It looked as though a log had caught itself on a slab of rock that jutted from the bank. I walked closer. The river was somnolent and trapped sound against her reservoir. I watched the water cover and uncover, cover and uncover the hand as though it were a water lily, splayed and out of grasp. The white root of an arm descended towards a head of hair that danced, almost separately, from the body that tapped against the rock, until it unlocked and was carried away in a swirl.

At first, I denied what I had seen. That is what the mind does to protect itself. It seemed too graceful to be tragic. The way the body had moved appeared deliberate and alive. Elora. I ran to the side of the rock. There was nothing. No torn cloth, no blood, just a spin of motion in the water hitting the bank. I closed my eyes and squeezed them until I saw red shapes. No, I thought, no, but there it was, resting on the needled floor among the pinecones. The tiny carved woman. I picked it up and wrapped my hand around its shape as thin as a finger. I let out one cry and ran.

I pounded on Jacques's door. He opened his bedroom window and peered down.

"Are you alone?" I asked him. He couldn't see my face, but my voice must have sounded cracked and raspy.

"Yes," he said, and I burst into tears. He ran down the stairs.

"Hey, hey, hey," he said, as he led me by the shoulders through the front door. The river woman was lying down on the sofa; the dark stones were set into her hollow eye sockets. She was the size of a torso. He picked her up and gently placed her on the floor. I could hear him talking to her in soothing tones. He stroked her forehead. Her face looked like Elora.

"Her eyes are drying," he said, and motioned for me to sit down. "Birdie, breathe, whatever it is, trust me, it will be fine, just breathe," and he took a deep breath to show me how. I followed suit, the two of us sat in silence taking and releasing breaths until I took his hand and kissed his palm.

"Listen to me because there isn't much time. Arlo has killed Elora. I saw her body in the river. You will be next or get the blame. I found this," I showed him the tiny woman. It was clutched, indented into my palm. He took it and rolled it around in his hand as though it were an object of infinite mystery.

"This must be her gift to me," he said, and looked over at the carving with love.

"What?! No! You are not hearing me. I know it's a sudden and terrible thing, but you need to listen! Elora is dead!"

"No, Birdie," he said soothingly, and took my hand. "She's not."

"She is!" I snatched my hand back and slapped him across the face. "Wake up! She's dead and you will be next! Arlo will kill you. I'm telling you this because I want you to live."

"You're right. I need to live," he looked again at his carving. "It's important that I live."

"Yes," I said, and started, once more, to cry. "I am so sorry. I never should have asked you to get involved, to carve for me. I will die with this sorrow, this guilt, I will die with it. But you don't need to. You can go. You can erase. The sun will be up soon. Pack a bag and I'll drive you to St. Louis. Take a train to anywhere and never come back."

That's what I'll do, he thought, I'll ride trains, I'll carve, I'll be free, but when he opened his mouth he said, "Elora."

"You will find someone else. You're young, believe me."

"I carved this for her," he knelt beside the carving on the floor. "I can't believe it, but it's true. She led me to her, to my carving," he had the eyes of a fanatic, rollicking, black dots inside of whitecaps. "It's the first one that's ever been real. I can't leave her."

"Elora or the sculpture?" I looked at the figure lying on the ground. The river's water had soaked a stain around her eyes. He had put the stones in wet, I thought, as though the woman were crying.

"If you stay here you will die," I said, sat beside him and took his hands in mine. "You will never sculpt again. Bring her with you."

His face was more alive than anything I had ever seen. Translucent.

It was its own planet.

"You're right. I'll bring her to me," he said, and stroked the grain of her cheek. "I have that power."

"Okay," I said. "Okay, but we need to leave. I'll bring the car around. You pack."

I drove him to St Louis where he caught the Burlington Northern Railway up to Chicago and then on to Canada. They drove through the final colours of the night with the windows down to drown out the silence. The city seemed to calcify against the horizon. Jacques had rolled up his window and motioned for me to do the same, I did, and the molecules between them turned to gel. He pushed, slow and difficult, he pushed his hand through the space and stopped, fingers spread, in front of my face.

"See this hand," his eyes, his voice both calm and wild. "It can do anything. I can bring her back, but she will need to recover."

"Who?"

Jacques gave me a hard stare before he spoke. "When you see her, tell her to find me. Make sure she comes for me Birdie. The best way for her to recover is to create something phenomenal. A song or whatever it may be. I'll do my best to fill her, but I might not be able to do it all on my own. I'll need her to work on her cognizance, you understand?"

"I understand Jacques, it's you that doesn't. She's dead. I'm so sorry to have to keep saying this, but I saw her," I said, my voice cracking. Was this really true? Had I seen her? His insistence was making me second guess myself.

"I know this is challenging and I have no right to ask for your help, but I need you to keep your mind open, okay? Open and ready to accept the unimaginable. The success of her conversion depends on this, on your guidance, because I can't be there. I wish, more than anything that I could, but I can't, so I must rely on you. It will make sense soon, I promise."

I dropped him off at the train station. He looked exuberant. I remember thinking that. He's exuberant and lifted. Everywhere I looked the city was steaming, grey. He passed through the concrete swift as a bird's shadow and disappeared. On the drive home his shape remained in the seat beside me like the presence of a dream. I realized I was trying not to think, that thinking made me shake. What did he mean? Worse yet, who was he?

I drove into the metallic morning. The sky's blur like my mind. Gravel.

A junior officer by the name of Morris was waiting for me on the porch. He held out my post. It felt remarkable that ordinary things remained. I stirred myself into character.

"Can I help you?" I unlocked the front door.

"Where you been?" he asked me.

"Visiting my friends Stan and Melissa. Not that it's any of your business, but she's just had a baby," that was something Arlo would believe when he reported back to him. "Why can't babies ever be born at a reasonable hour? Anyway, to what do I owe the pleasure?" I asked.

Inside parts of me were breaking away and whirling, a pile of leaves left for the wind. Be done, I thought, I need sleep.

"Well, you missed one hell of a show."

"Yeah? Arlo doing the whiskey dance at the tap again?" Throw them off the scent with humour, I thought. Sleep, sleep, I needed.

"This is serious Birdie, serious. Seems your lodger was a full-blooded dark horse. He killed Elora Donnelly and then himself."

"What?" I breathed out surprise I didn't have to fake. I leaned on the porch railing and swalled back the bile collecting in my mouth. How could they think that Jacques had killed himself? "No. Are you sure, is this, is it real?" I touched his shoulder and he flinched away.

"As real as anything. I'm here to report to his next of kin, that being you, that they've found his body about an hour ago up near the station in Moline. Seems he jumped in front of a train."

"No," I stared past him at the feather-white clouds, the words spoken out loud crashed against the bits of me hanging in the blue. "That can't be true. It can't be. It's impossible, I know it's impossible." I sat down on the porch chair.

"I'm sorry Birdie. Arlo found him himself and sent him back up north," he didn't even feign sympathy. Was it true?

"To Canada? But you just said that I'm his next of kin, surely, I should be the one to, I don't know, identify him or?"

"Well, I don't suppose Arlo cared about that much at the time. In any case, it's with the Canadian authorities by now, across the border. I doubt there'd be much to identify, some say he wasn't completely dead when Arlo found him, but you didn't hear that from me."

"And Elora?"

"Her clothes washed up a few miles downstream and Arlo called off the search. It's hard as hell to trawl the Missis. You can do it but it sure costs taxpayers a lot of money. Not to mention risking our men.

If the river's got her she could be in Louisiana by now. He refuses a funeral for her though, can't blame him, she's got no folks to protest. Fish food, that's what he calls her now, but hell, you can't blame him."

I closed my eyes and took a deep breath. "God help us," I said to the sky.

"Seems to me he already did," said Morris.

Jacques Beaumont

Jacques took the train. He placed her gently in the seat beside him, his gift from the river, he'd take her home to Canada. He was worried he couldn't completely turn her. After her initial awakening, she had remained caught inside death, a butterfly beneath glass, and he feared that she might never return. He spent the train journey etching her an inverted leaf dress and long sinews of river hair. The veins in the leaf simulated the veins of the body, and the stem was a chain of tiny pearls that wrapped around her throat like a necklace. Then he had an idea, a premonition, a life inside a life.

He carved a baby in her arms and her essence flickered, transitorily, like how a butterfly, waiting, still as death, will unexpectedly beat against the window. He knew that he could raise her. That it would take multiple sculptures, like it had with his mother, and this knowledge was like a window behind his eyes, which he opened, and felt the filamental interconnectedness of everything spread like a frost beneath his eyelids. So, although her rebirth was fleeting, ephemeral, he knew her resurrection had begun and any future sculptures he would create were ways of developing her and colouring her in. He was certain that she was out there and he's drawing her, carving her towards him.

The stars were silver filings in the night. Chips from something hard and cold, metal or bone. The motion bump, the flash along the track, a nerve along a spine, and the houses dissolved, her soft face with its windows dissolved into the water, fading, shading the wind, her body drawn with charcoal on his, then gone.

He felt her scattered.

She came to him as an after-image, as though he'd been staring at something illuminated, then closed his eyes and waited for the retinal image to appear.

He felt her in the silver filings.

The other bodies and his, a magnet, they flung against. Coating him, sharp foil digging in a shard of shine until he felt like someone new, someone heavenly, all at once, alive.

He wrapped his arms around the carving and propelled life through his skin, gentle and chilling, he brought Elora forward.

Mathis Beaumont

Mathis had followed her trail, claw raked of twisted bush and littered with fresh scat. The air was thick with the smell of digested fish and hung like a canopy of moisture above him. His skin chewed with insect bites. Moss hung in green cloaks from the trees. He followed the trail her enormous stomach had rolled through the pine needles towards a keyhole of light. She was staggering. She bashed against branches. He looked up and saw the mountain gnarl the sky. Splintered teeth on soft grey flesh. He was gaining elevation and the sodden air began to crystallize and break from heavy to fresh. Snow was on its way. He turned around and looked behind him. The way back was a dense darkness. He looked forward and the keyhole glowed. He was clumsy and weak as he stumbled through it.

Her cave was as small and black as a nostril.

He entered the smell of rotting death, and there she was, a breathless boulder. Dreams die when they are caught, he thought, die, and become reality. He touched her scared face, her dry black nose. Her soft ears and the hump of her silver back.

He lay down beside her because he could. He curled up next to her body, stiff under its fur. He had sensed she was tired and old. Snow slanted in the moonlight. He watched it fill the mouth of the cave. He could die if he wanted to, but he didn't, more than anything, he wanted to live.

He had his knife. He could make a fire. He had his camera. He brought the thick pad of her paw around his shoulder. She was as heavy as a nightmare. His head was against her throat, her chest, and he imagined a heartbeat there, at last, he had her warmth. He picked some soil from her black claws and scratched it into his own fingernails.

He had food. She would feed him. His substance.

I'll be full of you when I come down off this mountain, he thought, and slept.

He can't remember the words his mama had used, but words are mere exactitude, and it was apparent that during her sessions, the quiver around the letters was the frequency meant for the gods. So, the sounds come to him, and because they are formless vibrations, they rattle him until his bones let loose and he shakes down to molecules, to dust.

"It's just a body, son," she used to say.

"Tell me what you want," she'd stroke his hair, "Mama speaks to Gods." And the sounds would begin. The tremors of candlelight combining atmospheres and unhinging realms.

"You can't come back from this. You can't return to the unknowing." It was true. He couldn't. There is a spell inside language that binds us to our ancestry, which has little to do with the words being said, rather the evocation of atmosphere that sound provokes. Ordinary things, boiled potatoes, and laundry days, when spoken in native tongue conjure landscapes and place and ghosts.

The dead live there.

And the people that we've been and killed to survive or willed to keep living. The dreams that manifested or died and the lies that truth revealed or buried. Laughter. Everyone's. What we remember isn't accurate because it's selected, but the way it shapes us is as real as anything we could touch.

Mathis thinks of this often and it's as though the different stages of himself were stacked and his mind, a borehole, tunnels through them all and his artwork, the echo through the tunnel.

Still.

He cannot speak of Callisto with a foreign tongue. She is native to him as though he was a terrain removed from the earth and singularly his own, without memory or place or utterance, unhuman yet human, like pre-birth. She runs up and down his tunnel.

She is a separate dimension.

The door had been left unlocked. He shoved it open, stepped into the house and inhaled an emptiness so thick it felt embraceable. He wrapped his mind around the knowledge that Nora must be dead, that his son, Jacques, was gone, but alive. He walked to the window. Webs against his brutish hands and grime thick as snot on a tongue. He rubbed it against his sleeve, opened the view.

Jacques was out there. Dark green pines needled the clouds and bruised them like fruit. He knew Jacques wasn't dead. Knew it like a sleeping person knows when another is pressed against their back. That warm connection, he let it sink peace into his bones. My tired, dreaming bones, like old planks, he thought, turned, and saw the encyclopaedia open on the table.

Beside the red circle, lay the letter from Marge.

Mathis put his finger on the town Callisto. So, this is how she'd return? He'd leave after he had rested. He'd follow his son. Track the bear.

Callisto, Illinois

It was early morning when Mathis arrived. He'd walked all night along the river. His skin was sodden and his feet were wet, wrinkled inside his boots. His son had not been difficult to track.

On the train he tried to think of something to say. Something that would bring the months back, but that which must be defended slips into insecurity, and Mathis was a stubborn man who wanted to believe in himself. There was nothing to photograph, so he whittled instead. He looked up at Jacques's house. The lights were out. He looked towards the garden. The sculptures lay before him like a mirage. They took his breath away. He walked through them. I'm inside a half-human game of chess, he thought, weaving in and out of the pieces, watching dew roll down their faces, their bodies, like tears. He helped one that had fallen to her feet. There was nothing skilled or smooth about Jacques's carvings. They looked painful and frenzied, like animal claws with human intention.

They looked like Nora. What had happened to Nora? Mathis knew that Jacques was trying to make peace with himself.

Mathis understood that monster. How it can rip out of you. He touched the sculptures, mournfully, as though they were victims, then left them and walked around to the front of the house.

The door was open, and he stepped inside. There were two coffee cups on the table. He picked up a geode from a windowsill and walked upstairs. The only bedroom had crumpled sheets. He touched the mattress, and it was cold. From the window he watched the river. It was pewter coloured and moved like a long jerking machine.

He walked down the stairs. His hand ran along the banister. There were little maple leaves carved into it as though it were a tunnel of wind. Jacques had chiselled maple leaves everywhere, on doorframes, window frames, and baseboards as though he needed wind. Impermanence, thought Mathis, and touched a chord on the piano. The room pulsated the sound.

He took the carved figure he'd made of Callisto and twisted off her head. From his breast pocket, he took the small shell he'd found all those years ago in the forest, placed it into her hollow torso, and popped her head back in place. She was the size of an arm and he stood her between the coffee cups. Jacques would remember their tradition. He'd know that carving Callisto would mean the hunt was over.

He'll come back home when he's ready, he thought, or perhaps he won't, perhaps he can't forgive me, but then, he thought of the encyclopaedia laid out on the table. The map to Callisto, Illinois seemed to be proof that he hadn't given up. Mathis felt hopeful as he left, the air invigorated him, and his steps were light as he walked to the road. He'd walk to town and inquire about renting a room. He didn't want Jacques to feel obliged to let him stay, as he knew their relationship was tenuous and would take time to rekindle. Now, with Callisto and Nora gone, he had all the time necessary.

A truck bumped down the path and kicked up dust. It stopped a few feet in front of him and he could see it was full of heavy men. Harold squeezed out from behind the wheel. His hat shaded his eyes and a rod of fear shot down Mathis's spine.

"Mr. Beaumont?" He said. "Yes."

"I see you've had a shave."

The observation was disarming, and Mathis stood wondering what it meant, and had he not been so surprised he might have run. "Well, now," the man chuckled, "ain't that appropriate."

Harold walked back to the car. The window was rolled down, he leaned forward and placed his elbows on the doorframe and spoke to the men.

"That's him," he said. "Let's get it done and dusted."

The men looked at one another, jumped out of the car and ran around to the trunk. Harold walked back to Mathis and grabbed him by his backpack.

Mathis shouted and struggled to break free.

"Only take a minute. Now hush," said Harold.

The men returned carrying tools and before Mathis could say or do anything a shovel smacked his temple. He saw a slit of weak blue, then his eyes, round as two worlds, closed.

"Take him down the road, boys. Not next to the car," said Harold, and he followed as they dragged Mathis by the legs. "Here'll do," he said, and they stopped and circled around Mathis.

Arlo parked his car a hundred feet down the road and walked towards the tools rising and falling. Small splats of blood flicked through the air like ladybirds. It was as though they were mining the body. As though they were searching for some wealth to keep. Some did. Some kept mementos. It's what the old timers used to do too. That wasn't so long ago. Arlo remembers clearing his Granddaddy's attic and unwrapping a foot, bone sawed at the ankle. His father walked up behind him.

"Well, I'll be goddammed, you know what that is? That's a hanging memento. You didn't hear it from me, but they all did it. That ol' coot, keeping his handiwork after all these years," he let out a snort of laughter. "Now I shouldn't say that. Not these days. These days are different," he winked and ruffled Arlo's hair.

Arlo remembered light coming through the old slat boards and his father's smile. Sure, some said he was as crazy as a bull in heat, but Arlo had always found him loving in a hardened way. "Get me one of them fingers," Arlo shouted as soon as he was in earshot, his hands still resting in his pockets. He's a sentimental man. He looked towards the river at the distant tree copse were he had left Elora. Now why didn't he think to keep a bit of her as a momento? Even though it chagrined his heart knowing she was with that nigger, even though, he knew he'd miss her little ways. Her eyes had been calf like. They'd been together years, not donkeys' years, but, hell, years all the same.

"Brother," Harold nodded at Arlo and Arlo nodded back.

"Let's wrap it up now," Harold said. He threw them the burlap sack he'd taken from the trunk. "Fill her up," he said, and walked over to join Arlo. "You gonna tell me what this is all about?"

"It's 'bout Elora," he spat chewing tobacco on the ground and didn't meet Harold's eyes. A train rattled by, slow and steady.

"It ain't a thing a man wants the courts to deal with," he said.

"Nope, not these days," Harold said. "Well, I'd say you got your justice. Looks like a train wreck."

"I 'preciate it. And you know I owe you one, so."

"Yep, will do."

A few of the miners stuck bits of chipped bones like diamonds into their pockets. They took the shovel and scooped steaming piles of gravel and body into the sack. They wiped their hands on their wet jeans. They wiped their tools in the grass and kicked bits of gristle from the road where the animals could easily feed. They stood, catching their breath, beside the bleeding sack.

"Meant to have a heavy rain tonight," said Arlo. "Perfect timing. It's good to get old-fashioned every once in a while," he patted the finger in his pocket. "Gives folks a sense of place. Now I don't need to tell you that this never happened. I may be the law, but I'm also just one man, and I thank you from the bottom of my heart. My Elora thanks you too. God rest her soul."

They all bowed their heads at the mention of her name. Beside them clouds of red continued to bloom across the sack. Arlo watched it with the serenity of one watching the sunrise. Later, he'd stick a brick in the bottom of that sack and throw it in the river.

Elora Winter

I woke. Mud and wet reeds against my face, green, brown, black, I breathed the violent, lung-scraping breath of one cutting through the surface alive. But I am dead, I thought, for there was no feeling in my body, as though I'd been hammered out and cauterized by my own skin. My body blackened without its rush of life and jetsam of fluids and dialogue. A dearth remained in a way that a canyon is still a living thing but carved by forces now absent and from my canyoned mouth sounds lifted and fell, not like birds, but the idea of them collapsing mid-air and in pain. From this, my new form rose, disguised by the familiarity of my previous crust, but inside, I whistled with a clean emptiness and the only heat in me was the brilliance of memory. Hands. I looked at them, touched my face, my arms, everything.

It was the opposite of feeling. The opposite of being infested, but the swarming, the thronging inside the marrow was the same. A cut so deep it was numbing, and my job was to realize the pain.

The river dried on my hair and skin. With each step, the ground crumpled, then rebuilt around me, as though I were walking on feathers, billows of white burst through the black, alive as any animal. Using my body was like being in a blizzard, for I had an idea of where things should be; houses, memory, people, thoughts, but my vision could only see white. I managed to stand, bones and muscles stacked into place. I walked through the whiteout. Beyond the whirling boundary, I could hear the mob of sculptures waiting for me to enter their domain. They knew I was blind and they scythed me with their stammers, hisses, and wooden hands. I had received the life they had wanted. I went past their groping towards Birdie's and fell on the grass. The night was quiet in the way that prowling is quiet. I had to tell my body how to lift and move. The blood rushed to my ears; each beat of my heart was a collapse into my new skin.

This is me. I am this thing. Alive. I remembered his words - I can bring you back. I can bring you back.

Nothing pronounceable would ever have meaning again.

Birdie Dubois

It was as though I'd awoken to a blanket of snow. That quiet covering with a few scratches inside it magnified by silence. A knocking. A raccoon, I thought; no. Footsteps. My mind, an unspooled cloth, quickly gathered itself to attention and waited. I could hear the snap of embers from the fire in the grate downstairs. I could hear a hand grab the bannister of the porch and climb the steps. I could hear the gentle knock on the door.

Was it Arlo? Jacques?

I rose and put on my dressing gown. In its pocket I placed the switchblade I kept in my bedside cabinet. The throat, I thought, if it's Arlo, I'll go for the throat. I knew I could not ordinarily outrun him but was betting on the fact that he was blind drunk, so put on my shoes and grabbed my car keys. I took a deep breath and opened the door. I looked out into the darkness.

"Hello?"

I squinted but could see nothing beyond a sky the colour of old iron, ditches.

"Anyone there?" I asked, but I knew the answer. The answer came to me all at once, the presence of her stuck to my soul, my eyes, like a cornea. Elora. The night was brimming with her, tidal with her. The darkness rearranged in greenish-blue globules as though it were constructed of gelatine. Streamers of dull light and shadows rolled inside it.

"Elora?"

No, she's out of my hands now, I thought, I rationalized, she's gone, just the spirit going to its house.

There was a puddle of river water on the porch. No, I thought, she's dead. I had seen her with my own two eyes. Hadn't I? There are many reasons for a porch to be wet, I thought to myself, closed the door, and bolted the lock.

You've had a fright, I rationalized, everything is difficult and confusing right now. You've been injured and that's why you need to keep yourself together, you just keep yourself strong, I lectured myself as I walked up the stairs, climbed under the covers and turned off the bedside light.

I lay there, eyes open in the darkness, something outside felt insoluble and not in a human, logical way. It encircled around the house like a memory. Nothing matters that isn't also invisible, I thought, and looked at the window. Love, belief, passion, death, dreams, hate: our lives are totems marked by invisible labours.

The curtains were pulled shut, but I felt certain, more certain than anything, that someone stood behind them. Elora's blue watery face flashed in my imagination. It took all my courage to rise and walk to the window. Let's be done with it, I thought, and quickly opened the curtains. Nothing, no face in the glass, just a small circle of condensation where one had been. I watched the breath vanish, and the obscurity beyond, but no one rose from it, nothing met me but my own terror.

Sleep came in fits. I dreamed I had entered Jacques's garden. It was not quite dark. The firs serrated the sky. The stars were cold and lay across the river's long, broken sways. The back door was open, and the kitchen light shone in a long rectangle that lit up Jacques's statues. I saw an axe stuck in one. I was too afraid to call out. There was the silence that falls after struggle.

I followed the flattened grass to the river and before I registered Elora's body, I stood confused at the water, tapping against her still hand. In my dream, I put my hand into the water and when I touched the fingertips of Elora, they moved, so I grabbed her arm and pulled her from the river. Elora vomited up water from her blue lips. She grunted like a heifer and the ground went warm and sticky.

The scene acquired me, dispelled my retina of its screams, and insulated me enough to be capable of action. I fell at Elora's side; her lips were still warm and a weak breath bubbled out of her mouth while I caressed her forehead. There was blood everywhere, but mostly, I noticed, on her legs.

A child, I thought. "Forgive me," I whispered, and opened Elora's legs. The baby's head was crowning. "Dear God," I said. Elora drew a single, horrible breath and then her whole body contorted and pushed the baby into the river's mud and my waiting hands. It was not like any other infant I had ever seen. Skin like the purse of a mermaid. Heart like the shark's shadow swimming within. Above me the stars rotated in a quick circuit. What I held was not human. I put the child in Elora's hands and they both dived into the river.

When I woke up, I was wet with sweat and panting. It was early dawn, but I did not go back to sleep, instead, I walked downstairs and made coffee. Across the garden, a light was on in the studio, and I sipped my coffee wondering if I should just pack my bags and drive to Chicago. I watched the presence of the light as it dimmed with the arrival of dawn. I knew someone was inside because I'd made a point to shut off the lights before I drove Jacques to St. Louis. Any way you looked at it, a run in with whoever might be in that studio did not bode well and I was scared. Yet, sometimes, you have to enforce upon yourself a radical will and walk through spaces you never knew were doors. It felt like such a time, so I stayed.

I have yet to comprehend the facts that follow, yet to rationalize them in my human mind, so the best thing to do is just to state what happened. I went to the studio and found Elora sitting naked on the piano bench holding a carving of a bear in her hands. Her body was translucent blue like a newborn chick's. The veins splintered across her like cracks, her bruises like the inside of mussel shells, and tight red strips that ticker-taped around her neck. She did not seem cold. Her eyes were filmy. Imagine seeds inside a watery pulp. She watched me, in active examination, for I felt a rod of misery plunge into my chest and search my insides.

She's alive, I thought, but how? I'd seen her dead.

I sat down beside her and struck a piano key. I let the sound reverberate and expand into nothing before I hit another. Nothing from her. I felt the emptied sounds gathering in the corner like small beings, spiders. They sat there releasing notes into Elora's vast anguish until I spoke.

"How did you survive?"

Elora remained silent. She turned her head and looked out the window at the river. I could not comprehend how she had lived. I had seen her float away, but she must have crawled out, she must have pulled herself out of the water. I tried to imagine the strength it would take to do that. How had Jacques known she'd survive? Perhaps he'd realized the power of Elora's will, perhaps I'd underestimated her. When something happens outside of the mind's experience, we pretend it doesn't exist or we rationalize it into something normal. She must have come up for air, I rationalized. She must have caught on a log or something and floated above the water. All the same, Jacques's words haunted me - I can bring her back. I have that power.

"You can't stay here," I said.

I rose and walked up the stairs.

In Jacques's bedroom I found a sheet, so carried it down and wrapped it around Elora. Either way, she has beaten the odds, I thought, and she needs me. I looked closely at the small round of her stomach. Her skin was still grey from the water.

"You're pregnant," I said, and Elora nodded. "Come on," I said, "you're coming with me," and I helped her to her feet.

"Help me through them," Elora said and closed her eyes.

"Through who?"

"Them," Elora pointed to the sculptures on the lawn. "They want me."

"Okay," I said, "Okay, you've been traumatized, but we have that baby to think about now. That little one is our main concern. Come on, I'll help you."

Elora Winter

I hobbled through the grass as though my legs were disjointed and held my hands against my ears. The world past my eyelids was florescent. The den of insects in the river's weeds. The suspicions of birds. The mind – could I call it mine? – racked, like sheet metal music and the slow slew of sunlight against the sculptures as though each beam were a laser. I could hear them burning, hot and disfiguring.

How could I live like this? How could I not?

Birdie led me up to the spare bedroom and tucked me into bed.

"He's done this to me," I told her, and she removed a tendril of hair from my face and sat down. My mind was a dark station where memories of that night peeked around corners and through windows.

"I know," Birdie said. Did she know I was talking about Jacques and not Arlo? Did I want her to know? "But I'm here and you are staying with me. You're safe with me. No one knows you're here, so no one can hurt you. They, maybe you already know this, but the truth is, they all think you're dead."

"I'm not dead."

"Obviously," said Birdie as she pulled up the quilt up to my chin.

Jacques peeked through my mind's window, his white teeth, his hands, as real as anything.

"Is he?"

Birdie Dubois

I took a deep breath. "The honest answer is that I don't know. I took him to the railroad station, but when I got back, Jimmy told me that Arlo had found him dead, which probably means that Arlo killed him," I stopped myself from saying, "too," for the woman was here, right in front of my eyes, alive and talking.

"He knew. He must have. He knew they were coming for him, and he carved this for me," Elora placed the wooden bear in my hands as though it were an infant. We looked out the window at his garden. I saw red and yellow leaves cascading through woodenheads, wheaten light braided in the river. It was real. He was telling the truth.

"He created people," Elora said. "It wasn't a metaphor."

"Well, he certainly created one," I said, and looked at Elora's stomach.

"Tell me, when you took him to the station, did he mention me? Did he know I'd survive?"

"Yes," it was the question I dreaded, "he said to tell you to create something phenomenal, then find him. He said that is how you would recover. He wanted me to make sure you found him."

"So he knew I would be alive," Elora said.

"Maybe. I can't make sense of it, but one thing is for certain, you have to let him go now. Most likely, Arlo killed him, Elora, and if he finds out you're alive, he will kill you too. You have to think of your baby."

"Yes," she said, and pressed her head into the pillow and closed her eyes.

"That's it, sleep," I said, and stroked her hair. "You need to rest."

While Elora was sleeping, I performed a binding ceremony for the tiny carved woman. I cleansed a cloth in the river and wrapped it around the figure like a bandage, preventing the carving from causing more harm. I buried it in the ground before the first freeze.

To be honest, I'm not sure what would have happened if I didn't have practical jobs to do. Preparing for the baby and caring for Elora took all my reserve, which was a blessing, because I couldn't face the questions producing artwork would inspire. My photo boxes were willingly thrust aside. I simply tended Elora. Every day I brought a spoon to her lips. It was only a small thing inside of an enormous one, a campfire inside a forest, but I tended her all the same, kept her spirit alive and burning. My actions were mindless. I washed, I cooked, I lied when I was in town, I lied to Marge, I lied to myself, I read her stomach stories. In the evenings I made sure that I was so tired I collapsed into dreamless sleep. Pushing down Jacques's words of premonition, pushing away my uncertainties, my grief, was exhausting. I knew two solid things – Elora was lost. She needed me to find her.

Elora Winter

I believed in nothing but holes. Nothing was certain but the holes that woke me, that whistled me to sleep, until whole days became whole nights marking weeks, where each one was indistinguishable from the next, which was the exact opposite of our beginning where every second glared against me like sunlight on metal.

I sat growing our child and remembering it all, his knuckle calluses, the pen in his shirt pocket, wood shavings stuck to his bare feet, a piece of loose hair on a plaid shirtsleeve. The sickness of Arlo. I was unable to feel and could only observe each dazzling trace of my past life, as they spilled into one another, grinding away, gnawing away at my heart like acid, a billion microscopic mouths working, working me back to nothing. Teeth.

Birdie Dubois

The autumn was mild, and I was thankful. I cooked for Elora, kept her warm and gave her clothes to fit her growing stomach. Snow fell and melted over Jacques's wooden army. The whole scandal became folklore and Arlo, "poor Arlo" he was now called, had a freezer full of casseroles and a parlour full of church ladies. I said nothing. I seethed in my torment. The anger in me crashed like thunder in a jar. Elora also said nothing. She didn't speak. She just ate when I made her and lay in bed. At last, when her belly was swollen enough to pop, she broke her silence.

"Bury them," she told me one winter morning. "His women. I can't have them out there. Speaking to me, calling for me, please, just get rid of them."

It was the end of November, the baby was due any day now, and the ground was frozen. How could I bury an army of women?

I rang Stan and asked him to come and help me. I was making his favourite rhubarb pie when I heard his van come down the drive and park outside. I walked out onto the porch drying my hands on a dishtowel when he opened the door and smiled at me.

"Your undertaker has arrived, madam," he said and I've never loved him more.

"Thanks for coming," I said.

"It's not often you ask for something," he held my shoulders and studied me, "what the hell is going on?"

"Come in and eat pie while I talk you through it all," I said.

"Now that's an offer I don't often get," he said.

"You don't know what I'm going to tell you yet," I put the coffee on and cut him a slice of pie. I explained everything that had happened, from Elora's assumed death to her asking me to get rid of the sculptures.

"There is no way I can bury them," I said.

"Why don't we drift them down the Missis? Let her polish them back to something decent," Stan said, putting his clean pie plate in the sink. "It near breaks my heart to see trunks all cut up like that. Burying them would be difficult, plus it seems a bit cruel, you know, a trench of bodies in the ground."

"Actually, putting them in the river sounds like a good and soothing idea," I said.

We set to work, releasing each one into the black river like a silver fish. I thought of Elora rolling down the river, saw her snag and catch on the debris, saw her hair billow underwater like some soft-tentacled urchin attached to a pale rock. I sat down on the grass. My whole body was outlined in sweat and my insides were full of mucus and sick. Stan sat down beside me.

"This feels crazy, Keet," he said.

"I know," I let my head fall against his shoulder.

"You look tired. Why don't you come back to the city for a while? Huh? No questions asked," he put his arm around my shoulders.

"I'd love to Stan, but, again, I can't."

"Come on, It'd be good for you. Get the brawl in your blood. We'll listen to music. We'll dance and eat ribs."

"What about Melissa?"

"Melissa's gone half the time anyway. She has the lead role in something or other," he said.

"Wow, it sounds like you really pay attention."

"I try to be involved, to listen, but running a diner on your own is difficult and, seriously, sometimes I just want to kick back and have a beer after closing. You could have your job back?"

"As enticing as you make that sound, honestly, I can't. I'm looking after Elora. She needs me."

"So do I, and what's she got that I don't?" He nudged her side.

"A baby in her belly."

"Damn, she has me there."

"Only in event and not in looks," I laughed and rubbed his ever-growing Buddha belly.

"Oh yeah? Well I'll have you know that I'm working on the perfect 7lb 5oz little monster in here for us Keeter! It takes time and dedication to make a love baby," he said, and massaged the sides of his stomach.

I pretended to punch him in the stomach.

"Now that's the fightin' bird I like to see," he rose and helped me to my feet. "How many of these broads do we have left? Let's get the job done," he said, picked up a sculpture and carried her to the shore. "Off you go, my beauty."

We worked in silence, slipping them into the water, and when we were finished, we stood watching them bob up and down like a fleet of wrecked figureheads, rolling, rolling back to the sea.

Callisto, Illinois

If his sculptures could speak, they would say:

We took to the wind like wooden birds, we wanted to lie down and anchor beside him. He had found us tangled and overgrown, limbs shrieking in the night. We were already falling when he caught us, a hook in the belly of a rolling log; it was just in time, just in time. We thanked God. When he began carving his vision, we let him, grateful for touch. During the stages of becoming, we grew confident and whispered our desires like spells, please, please make me a woman, a crane, an angel, a mermaid, a horse, ibis, ibis. And he listened. Chiselled us out like blown eggs. In the beginning we were as full as we'd ever been. He seemed a life giver. The gift of rebirth. Then the air began to circle us like it'd move around a cave, chilling and hollow, and we knew we were nothing, nothing, but drafts.

Elora Winter

I lay in bed and listened. I could hear them speaking, Birdie and Stan, but more than that, I could hear the sculptures release themselves like burning coals to the water, there was relief as their murmuring stopped. I imagined their bodies eroding back to nothing, their cuts smooth and worn away until they were unrecognizable.

On the nightstand the carved image of a bear looked over at me peacefully. He'd left it on the table as a gift. He had told me that his father had tracked and photographed a single bear for twenty years. Callisto was his obsession. Perhaps that's what the carving meant? Perhaps he was telling me that I had become his animal? I am, I thought, I am his obsession. He can't be dead. We will find one another again, I thought, and the first wave of pain hit, I screamed like I belonged to it, wanted it.

I heard feet running up the stairs.

I sat on the edge of the bed. Still. My heart hung from my ribcage like a single talon holds a falcon to a cliff. The voice was a whistle that rolled through a canyon, a hiss. The voice distant and muffled. Elora, Elora. A scream underwater. Can you hear me? It's Birdie. A scream inside a gloved hand.

She touched my arm, skin on skin like red steel on a pale petal, Elora. Her voice breaks through. Elora, the baby is coming. A siren. So loud it blurred.

The pain left me breathless. The sheets were wet, and I imagined the water soaking though the bed. It calmed me, I took little breaths, saw the water spilling through the floorboards and the downstairs ceiling, leaking through the living room, the basement, past the cracks in the cement, and into the deep tissue of soil. It soaked all the way to the centre of the earth where it began to boil.

I heard boiling. Sheets ripping. I breathed into the sounds and the pain travelled through me and broke like bubbles through the searing. Birdie was there. Her voice was a smooth chant, but there are no words for life pushing through you, no words for the beginning of life.

There is air only, breath only, and the awe at what we are up against. It is stunning that humans have survived despite such traumatic and frail beginnings. Tiny beings of instinct, little sensory organs, sprinting out towards the light, she flew like a wet bird, a girl. We are a hungry species, from the second we are born, we spend our lives wanting and needing nourishment, changing only what feeds us. Our hunger is desperate.

She was stillborn. Her name was Lorelei Beaumont.

Clouds layered the sun. It glowed like a white mouth through muslin.

That was just it. She was still born.

He used to use an imaginary chisel and cut into my body. Naked in bed. He told me he was leaving his design. That's what he's done, he's turned me. Into something lifeless of his own making.

It was as though I had aborted a dream I'd once had, and it changed me, how could it not? I had carried death inside of my body and through the sheer force of will, had released its form, but not all of it. Part of it stayed with me, as though my cave had been a room our child had smudged its handprints across, death had left its imprint and for a while it looked as though I, or whoever I'd become, was not returning from this earthly hollow.

The Sculptor - Gret Heffernan

All dreams are placed somewhere, in love, in action, in drink, in seas of regret, I built mine like a stone tower around myself, and from the top, I watched. In waiting, I placed my dreams in waiting for the return of feeling. There was nothing and everything that I wanted.

And so, the absence of life became one.

Elora Winter

I sat in the chair and watched the prairie, the river. All day, every day. All week, every week. I could see the exact spot where they had buried the child. Mine. Ours. The small, perfect mound of earth, and I imagined myself trading places with our daughter. Imagined myself as a curled foetus in the tall grass, red, raw, and infected. It seemed so desperate and extreme. Imagining myself this way had an intrusive violence to it, as though I were a stranger standing in the shadow of a lit house. The allure of the ugly and disapproved. In my mind I gently poked this image of myself with a stick like she was an injured animal.

If Jacques were still alive and I found him, could he bring Lorelei back? A child without sensation is no child at all. My grief was a feeling that took place outside of my current body and inside the memory of my former self. I knew how to grieve, but felt no pang of emotion, and it was the sense of nothingness that kept me a nonbeing. To not exist, yet to have a memory of the way one exists, requires a torturous adjustment. What would a child resurrected into oblivion eventually become?

What had I become?

With an examining reverence I considered the way the earth redigests itself. The methods of disease and infestation the earth had created to redigest us, to change the form of our bodies, our minds.

And, perhaps, our souls.

I considered the things that burrow and eat flesh and the ways to hollow a person, to decompose a psyche, decompose a body, so that it returns to the earth to feed what is new. I am new. Somewhere, perhaps, my child is new. There is something so gorgeously economical, gorgeously practical, about the way each thing dies, even a mind, after it leaves, still eats from somewhere, feeds something. We consume ourselves and through our demise we make way for something better, greater, so that nothing is ultimately wasted.

But time.

It passed and I filled it with ideas, pictures, of myself, which I cut from scratch after scratch and rip until I was sure I couldn't feel it anymore. Until I was sure that I'd begun building some sort of clockwork heart to claim. One that might grow and function.

Birdie Dubois

"She stares," I said to Stan, during our Tuesday talk.

"Stares at what?"

"Anything and everything, she just stares, and stares and doesn't speak," I said.

"Best get her a camera then," said Stan, always practical.

"A camera for what?"

"People need to find a reason for odd behaviour," said Stan. "That woman needs to be around people. She needs to see there is life out there, ready for the plucking, and there is no place so full of life as Chicago. But we can't have her walking around the city staring at everybody like a damn zombie, can we? Get her a camera, an excuse, teach her how to use it, and get her up here."

"Stan, you are a genius."

I went out and bought her a Kodak Retina "I" Type 118 camera that afternoon. I placed it on the armrest of Elora's chair.

"If you're gonna stare, use this," I said, as I sat down beside her.

Elora looked up. I suspected that a part of her adjustment meant that her ability to concentrate had changed, as though she could see things that others could not, which made her stare openly at the world. Well, the world outside her window. It was a type of exposed grief.

"I figured you needed tools. Like a mask," I said.

It could have been anything. A violin. Knitting needles. Binoculars. But a camera seemed the perfect accompaniment to Elora's stare.

"I can't sing," Elora said. "I've tried and I can't."

"Because it sounds bad or because you haven't the heart to?"

"Both," said Elora.

"Well, I'm sorry about that. I know you loved singing, but there are many ways to release. Use this camera as a temporary release. Just until you get your voice back," I said.

"I won't get my voice back," Elora said. "This is my voice now."

"Well," I patted Elora's shoulder. "You can do the singing yourself or you can make things sing, your choice." Elora took the camera in her hands and held it up like a weapon, a gun. I got up and went into the kitchen. We'll see what comes of it, I thought to myself.

Elora Winter

This mouth is not my mouth. This tongue is not my tongue. These vocal cords are not mine, yet I belong to them. Maybe this, I took the camera into my hands and remembered how Jacques had once showed me a photograph his father had taken of an osprey. The bird dipped into a slim rift beside the ocean and was slanted with its wings fully spread. The camera angle was perfect and portrayed the bird as a bridge with one wingtip appearing to touch the cliff edge, the other, a wave, fixed and breaking all at once.

"Look here," Jacques had said and pointed to what looked like a smudge.

"What is that?"

"It's the reason I love this photograph. Look closely."

"A shadow?"

"Yes, another bird's shadow. See the spread of wings? It can't be the same bird."

"I do, that's amazing," I traced my finger over the imprint.

"You never know what you'll capture when you cut a slice of time."

The following morning, I woke up and walked outside with my camera. The first snow of the season was wet and sluiced the morning. The river diminished inside the white and Jacques had been gone for months, for a lifetime, forever, an hour.

In my hands I held a machine. It wasn't so dissimilar to me. It could lay up the images of time but could not live it.

I heard a gunshot, hid behind a tree, and saw, ten feet in front of me, a goose fall heavy as a weight from the sky. Its wings were still spread in flight, its neck was twisted, its wet eyes were black, and its beak was open in shock. Blood poured from its upper chest.

Right away I saw the potential and used my foot to move the red into a circular pattern so that it resembled a sun with splattered rays setting into the feathered head.

Seconds after I'd taken the photograph, a dog arrived, snatched up the bird with its spitty jaws, then disappeared, tail wagging, over the hill. I looked down at the stain the blood had left in the snow and saw more shapes in it, a mask, a crystal algae.

Death is when a thing changes shape. That is all.

I stared at it for a long while without feeling anything and thought of myself as a bird locked in a block of ice. A small body locked in a dead cold, blue and foggy, with only a pair of black eyes looking out, unblinking and afraid of overheating, of melting and releasing a tiny bird's frantic heart.

Birdie built me a small darkroom in the closet of the spare room. She taught me everything she knew about taking photographs and developing them. She gave me an egg timer, a thermometer, and a book that described how to mix the chemicals and unload the canister onto the reel. I practiced each step in the light a dozen times before I felt comfortable attempting to do the same in the dark. When I turned out the lights, my other senses took over, and I found that my hands, though unsteady at first, eventually understood how to work the equipment. Once the lid of the developing tank was secure and the chemicals were at the correct temperature, I started pouring the mixtures into the tank and timing my agitations on the film. I rinsed the chemicals from the film for ten minutes, then, holding my breath, unscrewed the developing tank and unrolled a row of ghosts.

The perfect imperfection revealed itself. The film hadn't completely developed and had a granular washed-out effect. Dark blood pockmarked the snow. The goose's body appeared weightless against the white, as though it could be brushed away, only the blood showed gravity. It was exactly what I wanted to capture. A way to mark time as manufactured by me, staged by me. The camera was a box of emotions that didn't require a claim. I was attached. Connection was my new form of love.

I started orchestrating my photographs. It gave me control, as though I were designing a montage of deliberate representation. It also acted as a reference library for feeling. The goose on the snow explains how the brutality of survival can diminish light. I could rationalize this as truth, but could not experience it as emotion, like a mirror I began to see myself through the lens.

My orchestrations themselves were small still lives. The parts of recent activity that represented vanishing. Birdie's reading glasses left on the table and shot throughout the day at different intervals, so the thin wire shadows suggested time. Discarded shoes. Open drawers. A hand towel with wet patches on it. A pile of cut fingernails. Like a study of the mundane and routine, but inside each photo, I placed the small, thumb-sized paper crane, as a way to honour the goose.

Its grounding had given me flight.

I tried to make absolute sense of my being, for up until that point, and sometimes even before the river, I had been parading myself as real. In many ways I began to understand how the two women I'd been were counterparts of one another. I walked and breathed and made all the correct sounds, but always, my internal rhythm was a beat off, a pulse late, deeper, sonorous. Like an echo that bounced off my loss and along my days. But the camera was my own timepiece, no chance circumstance, no misgivings, the shutter snap was the second between my sound and the outside.

I used the lens to capture my subject's interior through my eyes as though I were a conductor, and like water conducting electricity, it gave me a surge. In the way that singing had once given me a surge. Not an ocean, a river, or a stream, but more like a photographic lake, inert and unmoving, a reflection of what a human should be. Somewhere along the line, my stillness was replaced by a numbness that's remained frozen for a long time. When I skate along my photographic history I always arrive at the goose. A strange thing to spark the light of consciousness. As strange as a fire inside an igloo and as life preserving.

It was, in essence, a way to live.

Birdie Dubois

I had been at the shops. Afterwards, I found myself driving to Memorial Park. I thought I'd go for a walk, but I just sat in the car. It was hard to cope with how normal everyone was acting. Hard to cope with how they just returned to their lives. I know that the real tragedy of death is how ruthlessly time carries on. But the legitimacy of Jacques's death remained unanswered, and it made me furious that nobody cared, nobody raised the subject, in fact, I sensed the town felt an overriding feeling that justice had been done. I was stuck. I couldn't start ringing alarm bells until I'd made sure that Elora was safe. My inaction was Elora's protection. And, she wasn't ready to leave, though her behaviour was becoming more and more erratic. I feared for her sanity, and I was right to for that afternoon when I arrived home I found the front door slightly open. A heat was coming from inside where Elora sat meticulously cutting out the pages of a bible with an Exacto knife. Her face, her neck, wet with sweat. It wasn't normal.

A book on origami lay open by her side and she was folding an army of scripted animals that she hung, one by one, from the room's ceiling with string and masking tape. Crease, turn, crease, turn, crease, paper punch hole, tie string, stand on chair and hang. It was a slow process, a methodical process that left her entranced and exuberant. I watched her for a few minutes and she didn't notice me at all.

"What in the world are you doing?" I finally asked, as I hung up my coat. I stuck a lump of fried chicken wrapped in foil in the refrigerator.

"Can't you tell?" Elora looked up in surprise. "I'm creating a fortress." Her eyes were arrested with shine, and I knew she'd tipped off-balance again. Here we go, I thought, how could I handle this?

I slumped down in the chair beside the fire. I felt tired and weary and unable to cope with another one of Elora's bizarre episodes. I had learned to keep my heart and head out of such behaviour and just play along.

"What kind of a fortress?"

"A stronghold. It's for our own protection."

"Protection from what?"

Funny that she'd been thinking about protection as well.

She didn't answer. "First, I'm going to secure the ceiling in the living room, then the kitchen and my bedrooms. Is that the right order? I wonder about the order."

"I'm sure it is. There is chicken in the fridge if you get hungry," I got up, took a beer from the refrigerator, and went upstairs to have a bath.

It was difficult sharing my space with someone after all these years of living alone, especially someone that was crazy and possibly, even, undead. Over the months I had often spoken of moving back to Chicago, but Elora refuses to leave her child's grave and I feel the matter is too fragile to push. It was fine if I could keep Elora hidden. At the moment that didn't seem to be much of a problem as only Jimmy visited me, and Elora only left the house at unsociable hours, but she was testing boundaries, and becoming unpredictable.

By the time I had finished my bath, Elora had folded and transformed religion into wilderness, into wings and fangs and freedom, so that an overhead jungle of biblical defence swayed from the ceiling of the living room.

Elora was lying on her back beside the fire photographing her floating zoo. She put the camera down when she saw me.

"Soldiers," she pointed up at the cranes.

I watched her creations hang in their suspended universe, each one, a still little death.

"That's enough," I said, and began opening windows. With a frosty roar their bodies rustled and cracked at the wind's touch, paper wings hit paper paws, smacked paper necks, twisting and struggling, harnessed, and caught. I'm not sure what came over me, but I wanted the madness over. I wanted my life back.

I grabbed a broom and with sweeping arm movements, mowed through the lettered animals. Their delicate bodies tore and fell in pieces to the floor.

Fell around Elora. She did not rush to save them, instead, laid expressionless as I cleared each room, sweeping bundle after bundle into the fire without her protest. The flames rose with hot ferocity and when I had finished, Elora sat by the hearth and watched the fire eat. The hairs on her cheeks, her eyelids, reddened and singed, her skin was hot, yet she stayed, watching through the unforgiving night and into the morning long after the embers had turned black and gone cold.

I slept on the sofa that night to keep an eye on her, and in the morning, I found Elora still on the floor. Her hair hung in sweaty coils down her back, a brown wool blanket wrapped around her bony shoulders. Defeated, deflated, a cavity, a stone cellar caving in. Heartache throttled the throat of her dejection. She was skin disguising a worm-infested fruit, heartache had eaten through her, and in her hands, she held the smudged paper crane. She was rubbing it between her forefinger and thumb. She didn't look at me. She stared at the cold coals.

"They were clouds on the ceiling. You burnt the clouds," she said, took her camera, and photographed the embers. I hate to admit it, but something inside me felt victorious.

The "crane incident," as I like to refer to it, broke the back of Elora's silent mourning. After that, Elora went around stomping and smacking her limbs as though she hadn't felt them before, as though she were beating the life back into herself. She spent hours arranging rocks, thimbles, hairs plucked from her head, screws, orange peel, and anything else she could find to pattern into a still life. A small table in front of her window was the stage for her photoscapes. Once they were arranged, she would wait patiently for the perfect shadows to appear, then press the shutter down. It was still odd and slightly worrisome but better than the depression of before.

Marge delivered a large box of film and chemicals. I was happy to keep Elora supplied with photography materials, as strange as her themes were, they seemed to be healing her. At least she was talking now, I thought, as I opened the door for Marge. Elora was upstairs with the window open, hoping for the winter wind to ruffle some feathers she was attempting to photograph. She was under strict instructions to be quiet and to hide if she heard someone walking up the stairs. Still, it felt extremely risky, and I was desperate for Marge to leave as soon as she walked in. It didn't help that Marge seemed to be scrutinizing my actions as well as every damn thing in the house.

"Why are there two plates and one casserole dish in the sink? Have you had company?" She asked, while taking the liberty to make herself a cup of tea.

"No. I just ate the casserole over two days. Why are you giving me the ninth degree?"

"I'm not. I'm just observant is all," she said.

Since when, I thought, but said, "How is you sister doing?" I knew that would occupy her mind.

"Oh she's fine as long as she's complaining. I never heard a person complain so much about surviving. Speaking of which, have you heard the latest and greatest about that man?"

"Which man?"

"The coloured one," she said. I was shocked.

"You mean Jacques?"

"Of course I mean Jacques," she said.

"Then why didn't you just say his name?"

"I don't know, I feel funny talking about the dead, I guess, but that's just it, he might not be," she said.

I could feel the walls tighten, could feel Elora listening, "What do you mean?" I asked.

"Well, Gladys told me that somebody from Canada has been poking around the police department asking questions," she said.

"What kind of questions?"

"Like, where is his body and who actually sent it to Canada, which, of course, was Arlo," she said.

"You mean his body never arrived in Canada?"

"It appears not. Apparently, you can't just ship a body to Canada. I guess it makes sense when you think about it, but that's just what Arlo said he did, so we believed him. But, you see, what happened was, Jimmy got a parcel, tools or something, for Jacques and he took it to Betty, the clerk at the police department."

"Why didn't he give it to me?"

"That's exactly what I asked, but Betty said that it needed to be signed for by Jacques. It had photographs from his father or for his father or something, but it was for an important magazine, so Jimmy took it to Betty so that she could ring the proper authorities in Canada. Arlo wasn't in the office at the time and after lots of toing and froing with phone calls, it turns out that he..."

"Jacques..."

"Yes, had never been registered as dead. I guess his family were notified and so they've been calling around asking questions. You really know nothing?"

"Honestly, nothing."

"Then, I don't mean to sound rude or anything, but why on earth are you still here?"

"Oh," the question took me aback, "for the same reason I came in the first place, to work, you know, have peace and quiet."

"I would have thought their deaths would have disturbed your sense of peace," she said.

"Well, it has, I mean it did, I don't know, maybe you're right Marge," I said.

"Of course, I'm right. You should skidaddle on back to Chicago, it's downright morbid round here," she said. "I might move to Florida. My sister and I are looking at a timeshare."

"What about Arlo? What's this mean for him? Is somebody investigating his involvement?"

"Why? If he lied about finding Jacques, which it seems as though he did, he only did so to save face. I know he's dreadful but can you blame him? If anything, they should be investigating the whereabouts of that nigg," she stopped herself and looked directly at me, "that man and arresting his sorry ass for murder because there's one person that we know is well and truly dead and that's Elora. God rest her soul. I can't believe I was so wrong about him."

Elora Winter

I sat on the top step and listened to her. Nigger is a terrible, grisly word that demands excuse. It was the sting of hearing this word rather than its actual intention that surprised me. Its crash in the air followed by a bang, the sound but not the intent that caught me. That's how they saw him. That's all they saw. A story about a dead nigger, not a name, not a man, a lover, a creator. My Jacques.

I held the carved bear. I could almost feel him alive, and something else, something weighted, a look of distance I'd seen in his eyes, not a look of malice exactly, but the remote coldness of one who had been left behind, back-wood eyes, I thought, wasteland eyes. We shared this now. I realized it was a way of feeling. We both shared the unforgiving gaze of the exiled; a bloodline burned by circumstance that left a smell about the place like hair burning against hide. I caught this scent, like a hunter, I smelled our hearts, flayed victims, the pungent meat of terrible love and prejudice. The unknown truth was a rope that bound us together and at the same time pulled us apart; it was a noose.

I placed the bear in the middle of the feathers, waited for the wind and took the photograph.

Birdie Dubois

"Meatloaf tonight," I shouted up the stairs, with more enthusiasm than I felt.

Marge had left me exhausted. Could Jacques still be alive? Should I tell Elora, or had she already heard? What then?

"Come on out," I said. "You're not going to make me climb the stairs for nothing are you? Come on now, Elora, I know you're still alive because you ate the sandwich I left you."

No answer. Dammit all to hell, I thought as I climbed the stairs, she's probably in there holding that stupid bear. My leg was better, but it was still mildly painful to put weight on it.

I'd just got off the phone with Stan. "She says she's feeling him, feeling Jacques, that she's feeling he's alive, like a goddam diving rod or something," I'd told him. "It is enough to break your heart. She spent months sitting in that chair, staring towards the field where her baby was buried. Remember the little thing, terrible, like a stone with a skin covering. Poor, desperate girl, she cried so hard the world cracked and dropped her into the pit of herself, but now, shit, she's nuts. I'm all for creative madness, you know me, but she's screwing screws into mud pies and photographing them with that bear and an origami crane. Now what on earth is that about?"

I knocked on Elora's door. "Can I come in?"

"Yes," Elora said. Sure enough she was holding the bear, still wearing her unwashed dressing gown.

"Christ, you look like a ghost," I put my arm around her shoulders. "And smell like a dog."

"I've been working," Elora explained.

"Yeah? Well, I haven't and it's time I did."

I looked at Elora's table full of mud and objects. Feathers were poked into the mud so that they stood upright, and the bear was positioned behind them as if he were peeking behind trees. I sighed. Symbols, it all boiled down to symbols, sometimes I knew what they meant, other times they were completely obscure. Elora's belonged to the obscure camp, but at least she was using them. There was healing, and as I've said a thousand time, there is healing inside symbols.

"Take my hand," I said, and led her to the bathroom. "Have a shower and then come down for some meatloaf. It will do you wonders."

A half an hour later, Elora entered the kitchen fresh from her shower. Her shampoo mixed with the smell of onions and garlic.

"I started sautéing without you. Here, sit down and dice this pepper," I told Elora, and began rummaging through the cupboards for flour and spices.

"Good," I said. "Now put everything in this bowl and squeeze the mince between your fingers until it's blended. Therapeutic, isn't it?"

We moulded the meat into a bread pan and placed it inside the oven. The methodology behind cooking has always eased me, not that I'm any good at it, but focusing on the sequence of one ingredient following another until reaching a stage of completion is strangely calming, plus it brought a bit of order into the house. We sat down at the kitchen table and began chopping up the remaining vegetables. After a while, Elora stopped and cleared her throat.

"I heard that he might be alive," she said. "I have to do something."

"I understand but that's difficult because, technically, you're dead."

"But I'm not! I'm not dead."

"Yes, we've established that. We've also established that if you show yourself as living, you will certainly be killed, again," I said, "or whatever. Look, I'm sorry, I don't mean to be crass, I just don't know what to say."

"I can't live like this. I can't," she said.

"You can and you will. You already are," I put my hand on hers. "Listen to me. It's awful that life struck you before you had the chance to thicken, but flesh grows around the axe, Elora, until the axe becomes inseparable from the tree. This will become you. It will never leave, but you will heal around it and to heal you need to turn it into something, something you can stand to look at, whatever that might be. Jacques was right, don't you see? You need to create yourself again."

"I am creating myself again! I'm taking loads of photographs! I rarely go outside in case I'm seen, I'm stuck in here, like some crazy woman. I think I am some crazy woman," Elora said. She said it, not me, I thought.

"It's like I'm creating a gallery or something, a gallery of emotions like a reference library, with frames with staged faces, where I can see myself," she said. "I don't know what it is, but it's helping."

"That's great Elora, honestly, but I think it's time we left now."

"I'm not sure I can," Elora said.

"I know it's hard," I said. "Hard to let go. You both resembled the world in your own special way, you had that in common, saw things with an artist's eye and there is no sick like lovesick, but you are wasting yourself here, wasting away. There is no need for it. You could start again."

"There is nowhere to go."

"You are young. There is everywhere to go, but start with Chicago, I could get you a job there, nothing fancy, but it would pay the bills and get you out of the house, out of here."

"I don't even know where I'd begin."

"I'd help you. You know I would," I got up and put my arms around her. "Here is what I've learned, you see, the trick is to only love the things that love you back, that's it, that's the trick for relationships, friendships, work, hobbies, everything. Get yourself a bit stronger first, heal and consider yourself first, then, if he's out there, you'll find him. I have no doubt about that."

Elora Winter

I can still remember how the wheaten sun had pressed the afternoon into his bedroom like steam. I had come in the morning and lay on his bare chest. He slept. I listened to the culvert of his body reverberating and his breath. So much was working beyond my control. I felt waterlogged and swung my wooden legs out of the wet sheet, then rolled off the bed like a tree off a cliff, boom, I crashed and moved towards the hallway's cave, shadowed and fresh, cold hands on my shoulders, cold breath coiled around my neck like an eel of white air.

There was the sensation of sinking as I made my way to the bathroom, splashed water on my face. The hand towel smelled of damp dust, outside the air was ready to cook; through the window I could see leaves hanging from branches, grey inside the house's shadow. The sun, a giant leech, sucked the blood from everything.

I poured two glasses of water and went back to bed. He was just waking up and I handed him one and he drank.

"Thank you," he said, and plumped the pillows up behind himself.

I placed my glass on the bedside cabinet.

"I heard you were in town the other day," I said.

"I needed some things."

"You could have asked," I said.

"I didn't think I needed permission to buy toilet paper."

"CC said you were bold, that was his word, bold,"

I underlined an imaginary word in the air. "Arlo told me."

"CC was an ass."

"Bold, ass," I underlined two words.

"It's not like I lied about going," he said.

"Lying and hiding the truth are the same things, Jacques."

"I hate it when people use my name to make a point. Fine. You are right, Elora. I kept it from you. I lied. We all lie," he said. It was not how I planned it.

"How am I lying? I just want to know if you are going into town, so I can prepare myself when Arlo mentions your name."

"You're lying because you're hiding your truth: me. I'm the one that's stuck out here like some stallion lover," he said, and I laughed at his drama.

"Oh for Christ's sake. You are bold. Don't you know anything? You're out here to keep safe. You were crazy to move here in the first place and you're even crazier to stay."

"Maybe I'll just leave then."

"Okay big baby, don't let me stop you and certainly don't let me take advantage of you," I rolled my eyes.

He put his hand on my stomach and stuck his finger inside my belly button. "You can take advantage of me," he said.

"Get off."

He turned over and pulled me to him. "I don't want to argue. Something's changing."

"What do you mean?"

"I'm not sure. It's strange, but I feel like we're waiting. I keep hearing this sound, this music, when I'm working. It's synonymous with you." He kissed my hair.

"What do I sound like?"

"Let me listen," he put his ear against my forehead, adjusted my nose like a dial. "Ah there it is, seagulls."

"There are no seagulls in Callisto."

"Lost seagulls then."

"I have something for you," I said. I got up, went to my satchel hanging on the bedroom door handle, and pulled out a small cigar box. "It's not for you exactly. Inside are my most precious possessions. I would like you to keep a hold of it for me, you know, in case Arlo does find out. In case something happens."

And I handed it to him. He kissed it and put it under the bed for safekeeping.

Callisto, Illinois

Elora has pictured the evening of the fire a thousand times. It was the first real day of spring. A dry winter had waned and left the fields a brown, dehydrated flat, but the air was warm enough for birds. The whippoorwill's song had already begun.

The seagulls were circling. All night they had called her, roused her from her bed, and she watched them from the window. They dipped and skimmed the river and perched on Jacques's eaves. The spread of their wings, bright white against the off-white sky, like sheaves of paper with written messages she could not decipher.

They were from him. She dressed, stuffed her camera, Callisto, a candle, and matches into a satchel and walked out the door. Birdie kept a gallon of gasoline in the garage. Elora picked it up and entered Jacques's studio.

The piano stood in the corner like a living beast. The rustle of a hundred seagull wings and feet meant the roof felt alive. She moved the piano into the centre of the room where the lit rectangles from the windows joined. She placed Callisto on top of the piano's lid and set up the photograph. She sat on the windowsill. The shadow of her body fell across the dusty lid. In the centre of her outline stood Callisto. She sat still, photographing the light as it moved through the morning and afternoon like a sundial, circling Callisto, reshaping shapes, reshaping her.

Birdie came and stood at the door, "I'm saying goodbye," said Elora, so Birdie nodded, then walked away.

When the photo was finished, Elora went upstairs to Jacques's bedroom and retrieved her cigar box from underneath the bed. She put the box and a towel from the bathroom in her satchel, and then soaked the bed with gas. Then she poured gas all the way down the stairs, circled the piano, splattered the drapes, emptied the rest on Jacques's chair, and lit the candle. Dusk was hours away and the sun was behind the house. The living room was cold, and the candle splayed a golden circle on the piano's lid. Callisto stood behind it and she took the final photograph of the house's interior and placed Callisto inside her satchel.

She stood with the candle at the window and placed her palm on its glass, then dropped the candle in the seat of his chair and left the room. Behind her she heard the fire crack, like an old door opening, she walked down the porch steps. She needed air, distance, and scope.

Across the yard, a low beam of sun caught the tin watering can and filled her eye. She turned away, the air was cool on her cheek, and then it was gone.

The air was still, so still it polished trees, the dark shed.

Dry grass broke underfoot, crunched like a shelled bug, she walked. She could feel the hard knots of earth underneath her feet, like jutting bones poking the undersides of her boots. Her feet slid inside her sweat. Her whole body had begun to sweat. She wanted to be clean, baptized. Behind her she could hear the house burning.

She ran until she hit the road and the sharp grind of gravel, then she stopped, dust whirled around her, collected on her swelling tongue, soaked the wet from her eyes, pores. She turned off the road and entered the prairie's hiss where the grasses rubbed against one another like a crowd of hands planning something sinister. A cloud of gnats rose from its soggy bottom and with them the smell of decay, she heard small animals dart out of her way.

She moved through the prairie until she reached the creek. Roots from a few pine trees bent towards the shallow water as it twisted along its pebble and mud bank. Their shadows encased the pungency of pine and turned earth. The pines broke up an otherwise overcast blue sky, their needles spiked the blue, and she was thankful, for the sky was too big to look at, an echoing, sorrowful melancholy that fell too low and reached too far in every direction. So, she followed the creek, carefully stepping over anthills and hedge balls, sticks dipped and raced on the shallow water's spine, minnows and frantic water beetles nipped from tiny inlets where the water pooled a murky brown. She walked slowly, she cultivated solitude, and after a while the birds resumed their singing.

She followed the creek all the way to the pond and stopped on a flat dried patch of mud around which tufts of sickly grass were trying to grow. She undressed and walked towards the pond. The mud cracked all the way to the water's edge, where she stood, as if she had reached the end of a map and had to step off into murky oblivion. She entered the water up to her neck. It was as brown as dark chocolate, though not at all silky, as there was a cool fine grit to its ripples. Pebbles lodged and dislodged between her toes, then she lifted her feet and did the breaststroke. Water bugs skipped out of her way, her head was constantly parting a cloud of hoverflies, her foot scraped against something hard, possibly the shell of a snapping turtle. She turned to look back at a row of snapping turtles sunning themselves on a nearby log.

You can scare yourself silly swimming in a pond, a reed gently brushing against your leg can easily be exaggerated into a snake, a leaf clinging to your stomach becomes a leech. She had come here before, always when she was on the edge, teetering; the dark water challenged her body to reconnect with her mind. The dark water forced reason to emerge. She was not a strong swimmer, so she needed to ease into herself and relax to remain afloat and usually this trick worked. In the early days of her father's illness, miscarriage, and Arlo, she'd come here when she didn't have wounds the water could infect.

Her heart had refused to slow despite her rhythmic and steady breathing. She swam until she was too exhausted to continue, then wrapped herself in a towel and sat on the bank. She could feel a thin residue of mud drying on her skin, later it would brush from her arms like salt. She sat on the cracked ground and pulled her dress over her head, the dress clung to her damp patches of skin. She untangled her hair with her fingers, lay on her back, and fanned her hair across the ground to dry. Her hair soon felt crunched like black straw, her heart beat quickly. In her mind played a succession of small bells, she thought of nothing, yet could not sit still, so continued walking along the creek.

She saw the chimney stack first, an unsupportable presence hovering in the air. She stepped away from the creek and out into the prairie to have a better look. A large oak hid the shape of the house, but the chimney stack was unmistakable, a brick finger pointing up.

The house had silvered from the wind's touch, a smooth bone. It's back half had collapsed so that when you looked through the front door you saw the sky, splintered gray bones and rusty nails were weed-gripped and scattered across the ground. There was no sign of glass as sparrows flew in and out of windows and eaves were stuffed with nests. Weeds sprung up through cracks and holes in the porch. As she approached, she heard a steady drone and saw, in the corner, an enormous hornets' nest, like a clay tornado plastered to the wall.

She stepped back and turned towards the tree. A barely visible fence had long ago broken under the weight of brambles, red stalks and green leafy heads of rhubarb were scattered across the yard like giant spiders, and patches of green onions sprouted over mounds. She sat down facing the house. The sun was beginning to set, its golden head was framed by the door and the house beamed with a rich internal light. Everything blackened against its gleam. Shadowed birds dipped in and out of golden pools and a breeze blew shadowed grasses and shadowed branches, hornets like black dots pinged inside the gold. Even Elora became a black mound that sharpened against the gold until the gold began to burn out, handing the world's details back to her softened by twilight. With full eyes she watched the sun melt through a magenta sky, thick as a garment from which clouds, like plums, hung.

Overhead a flock of birds flew north. She knew the house had burnt to the ground.

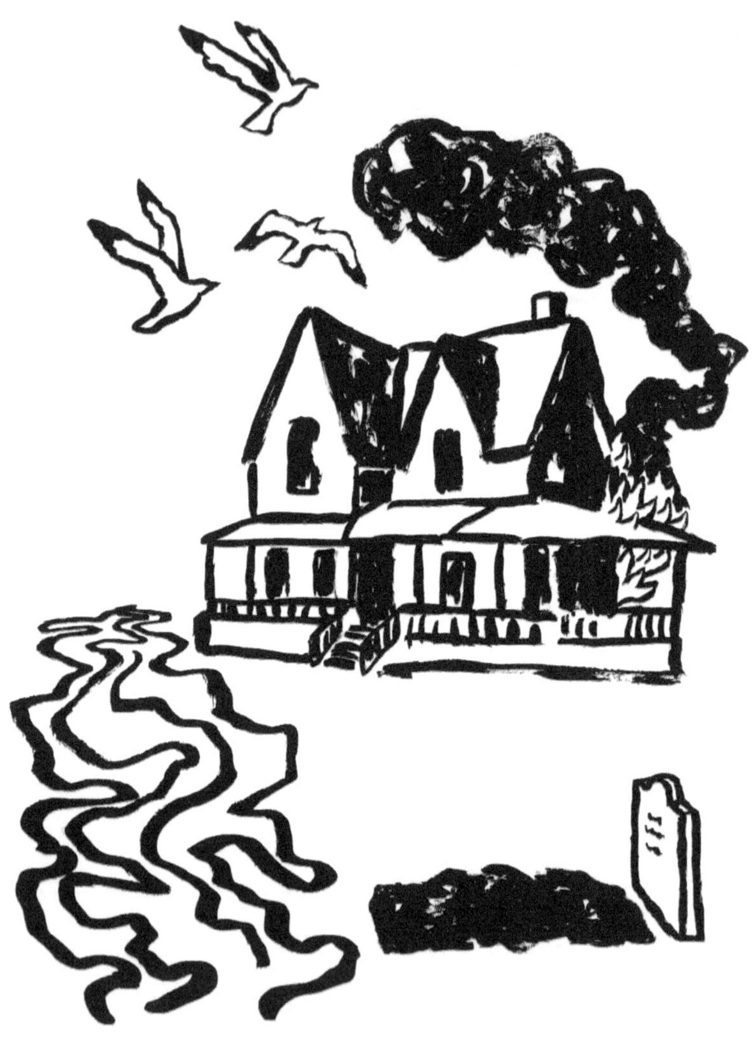

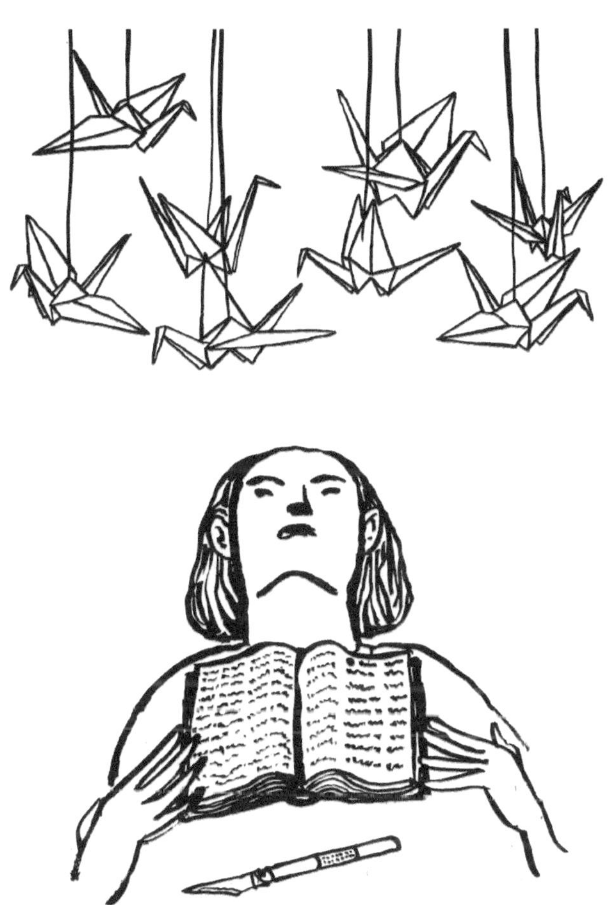

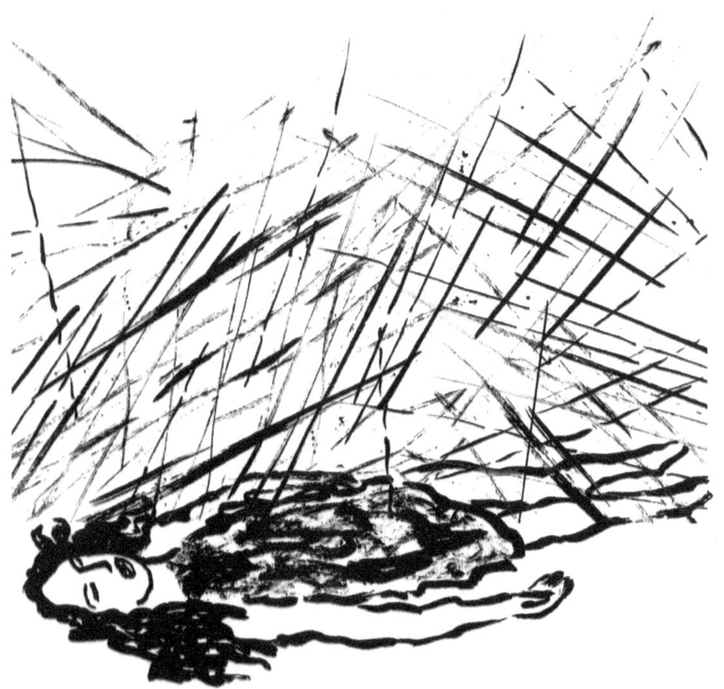

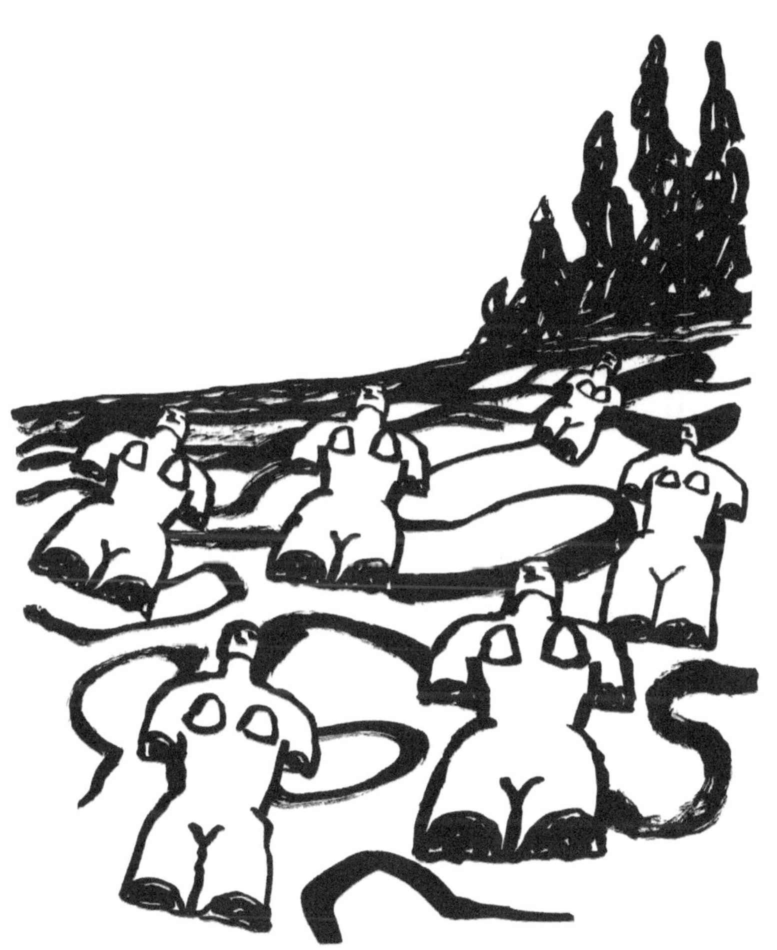

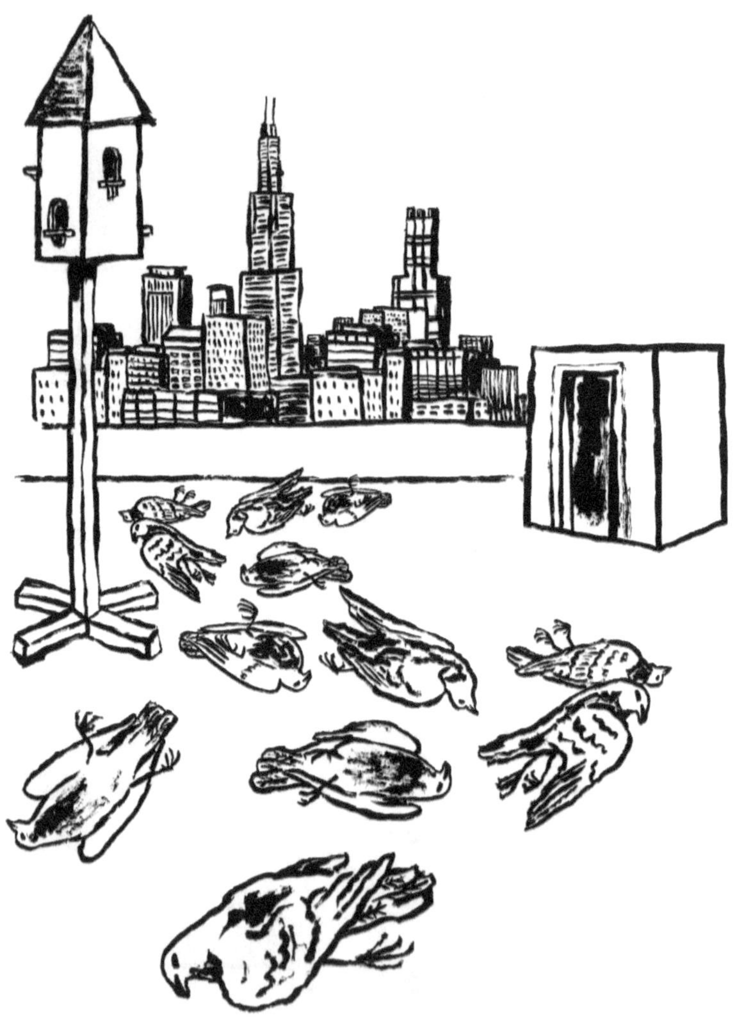

Elora Winter

Imagining myself starting the fire is now like reassembling a dream, blindness then fuzzy images, a glimpse caught in a mirror or a shop window, how you can look vaguely familiar to yourself, a nose, cheekbones, parts you recognize as your own, but then a certain slope of the neck, the way the eye is caught, something new, alien, what you do not know but adorn. His face, a reflection in the water, the form of a child, waiting. Jump, he says, jump. I remember that there was an emotion that I waded through, as if hanging from a shaft of atmosphere.

The fuming heat. The blinding sunset. A resigned evening. As if whatever change had occurred had been completely accepted by the twilight, almost casual, yes, the world seemed casual, suspiciously casual. I noticed no strain, but for a few tense stars dimly shining through the heat like small hearts trying to beat on the outside. It made them seem violent. Violent because of their delicacy. Brooches of light pinned to a pink neck strung with crimson, violent. Doves locked in a hot cave. No not that, rather the eyes of trapped doves glaring through a hot cave and out into a blackening night.

You see, even though I had yet to understand how the world hints, I remember taking notice of those stars, which is why I must recall them exactly. Even though I did not heed their warning, instead left them, barely flickering, too pale to shine and penetrate my thick chest of understanding, even so, they caught my attention. Then nothing seemed as important as a living membrane thin against the earth and open. How else? How else to receive clues? Look. The clues are everywhere.

I followed the creek back to the house, the roots were more twisted than I had remembered, so I had to plan where I placed each foot. The trees' shadows were thicker, the mud thicker, mosquitoes whizzed small jet songs past my ears, the sound of crickets turned the darkness into a single animal. I could hear the earth opening its pores to the night's cool touch, I loved the solitude, I accepted the night, welcomed the night. I ate the night. I ate and ate until I was only night covered with a transparent skin; to look inside of me one would see stars. I was nobody. I was timeless. Not even rabbits seemed shocked to see me.

I couldn't take in exactly what I'd done. Alteration is as simple as a flick. The mind allows only what it believes the body is capable of managing, it is a censor with the ability to disconnect, to foresee, predict, conclude, long before the body realizes how it has changed, why it has changed. Then it filters out our lives and gives it to us in chunks small enough to swallow.

I saw the hill glowing, then the fire whipping out and up through the studio with orange arms, red arms, and black bursts of kicking. It was kicking. It was pounding. The fire fighters were there, keeping the flames at bay, Birdie's house was intact.

Birdie came running across the field, shouting indecipherable words.

Birdie grabbed me and held me close, sobbing.

"It's over now," I told her. "It's all over."

Something had already died, and this was just the finale, the sacrificial burning of a body, hollowed and done.

A heart does not admit, cannot dismiss what is seen, could never say that stars do not exist, that what is seen is a remainder, a bright remnant of light, left, left burning a dark sky, left to prove a body of fire that once existed, that had died, too soon, perhaps, so that it decided to leave a bit of its presence behind: a flicker, a lantern, the lighted window of a distant house, as if to say, I was here, I was here. What we wish upon is only a memory, what we wish upon is gone.

Without speaking we watched. The smoke burned the back of our throats, we were too close, yet could not move. Our eyelashes, our cheeks seared, yet we did not blink, could not blink, could only stare and stare at the flames arching uniformly towards the sky. A raging tulip, beating, eating, disintegrating the house back to nothing and, slowly, slowly, it was over. Embers. "Hide," Birdie said as she walked down to the fire brigade.

They put out the fire, I watched from the grove, but I do not remember seeing any water. Only the smoke, billowing, billowing smoke, clouds of smoke, mountains. The moon was high in the sky. Seen through the smoke the moon grew small, so small it became a pupil, and the sky was an eye that glared at me.

A weak star, that's what our child was like, what I had been like, no, not stars, but constellations. Untouchable because we had been punished, burnt out.

I had found a way to own my body, celestial or not, I took up my camera and photographed the burning house. With the camera in my hands, I had found a way to feel.

Listen. I asked myself a couple of questions. What is death? The sacrifice of a body. What is life? The sacrifice of a body. And love? The sacrifice of a body. The answers are all the same. Then there was a battle. How could I fear what had always been present? Loss has been present, has constantly grown inside of me, silently as hair, as fingernails. It has grown so long that I can feel it snarl, scratch, and cut.

I can hear it. The seagulls. Were his. How do I make this skin mine?

I sound very similar to coyotes. Every evening I wait for them to come close. They scope for prey over the grave of my child. They paw, back and forth, the night. Out of the window the sun is low, and I hear them coming.

The ground beating underfoot. My heart. It is true, true – My heart has not allowed his words. His yes or no.

My heart has not allowed false words.

They took him, her, they took them away, beating underfoot, beating.

And he made me again. I drip them into my black dollop, fill it like an empty sack. They drip into my black. Pit. Fall. Hit and fall through my black, black. Where song once hid.

They took the song, all of it. Now.

This tongue is a dead snail. A locked flower. A fist that cannot open.

But it is not silent. What I mean my body infers:

Look at me, moving from ice to fire. It is the moving that matters.

The photographs like an ice covering.

Beneath my ice, a river of shiver, I shiver and bones. As if they were full of cracks. Underneath my surface I see his face. My face. Frozen. Icy eyebrows like white splinters.

Her small human shape. His mouth echoes my name. Erodes the blue flesh preserving me. Thaw, he says, thaw, she says.

And then. A flame. A way to extinguish.

The enchantment before the burn. Fire melt me.

The burning escape. To drip until I run, my wax dreams run. We run. It is what humans do. They ran after him and he keeps running. There are places where he feels alive, brings life, can bring her back and in them, in me, an army gathers drive.

I point my finger towards the disease. Prepare to attack this disease, I say.

Here. It flicks in the eye's corner.

Red. Red. Watch him go.

I run with my body as a shield. Towards victory. There are horse clouds alongside me, alongside the blue, bugs fly out of the grass like rockets and the coyote in my chest howls as though it's cheering.

Everything is red rimmed, meat around an eye and him running.

Underfoot, they beat.

Pound through the timber. Snap twigs, stamp mud. Pound through the prairie. Break stalk, bend grass. They howl. They howl like someone wanting out.

In need of a place to enter. In need of a place to exit. The answers are the same, remember?

I light a candle. I wait by the window. Come here. This way. I speak to who I am now. This is the way. In the window my golden face quivers just beneath a black pool. It does not look like me at all. But another woman, a watery glow, a light behind cloth. She reaches her hand towards mine. Our fingertips touch cool glass. Why have I not seen her before? Beautiful, muted, a bubble rises from her lips. A reflection. A photograph.

The candle on the curtains, the candles on his chair.

And the fire crawling like red spiders crawling across the wall, like blood spilling, soaking up through the curtains, like an idea – the idea that it could die, all of it, could die and live again.

I let the fire burn.

Without the fire she would have vanished. Our fingers were touching. The glass was so cool between our fingers. Together we slowly placed our palms against the window.

I set the house on fire. so that the part of me hanging, the only part of my life, of my person that the world could see, the disgusting bit that hung, limp and oily like fatty gristle from the meat of my soul, could sizzle, writhe, wilt, and die. I want to be. Again.

Quiet. Quiet. So quiet that birds land on me.

The Sculptor - Gret Heffernan

The morning sun rose as the bust of a dead fish floats to the surface of a still pond. Ash, ash, ash like silver fish scales coated everything, my face, leaves, grass, bushes, the river's edge. Ash collected in droplets of dew before running in clear lines down the shed. Pale bronze in the morning sun, it was early, the moon still bold in the sky, the clouds thin in the brown sky like white plastic bags floating beneath a watery surface. I walked to the pile of smoking wood, wind blew the ash in visible currents down the hill and above the prairie, they were being scattered, thrown, given back. Using a stick, I searched through scarce remains. Like an insect on bone, looking for things to keep, a way to digest what had happened, meat, anything, anything to sustain me.

I grabbed a garden spade and walked to the grave of our child.

I dug a small hole, placed a blue cornflower inside it and filled the rest with ash taken from where Jacques's studio once stood. Fire, they say, replenishes the earth for regrowth, yet there was nothing left, save a suffocating flower.

I have thought about this, about flowers and what they need, about sun, and about soil and rain, stems, and petals. How we exchange breath with plants and how, we, too, shrivel without sunlight, and hide in winter. How our hair can be the colour of a marigold, a hyacinth, our skin, pale to the shade of hibiscus, or dark as bark and orchids, our lips, when pressed, become the tight folds of an unopened rose.

How we can die screaming, but without a voice.

It is how they killed me. Voiceless. How they thought they'd killed him.

I have seen this, I have seen unnamed, undocumented, unborn flowers in the eyes of the silenced, their eyes and their pupils like seeds. Their fingers, roots, reaching in the dark, waiting, our child and countless quiet ones before her fertilizing the ground with their bodies, for others to plant in.

I could not sing, so I recited the final verses I'd written while I'd
carried her:

Cut Backstrand, green kelp and sand
Dune wind and sorrow fed
swim the bay without dismay
just sing to the undead.

'Tis song you need, go, God speed
I pray you dream no beast
When tide is high, scarify sky
Steer clear of Passage East.

And this came to me:

Lorelie, sweet Lorelie, daughter dearest ghost.
Lorelie, please Lorelie, rise, restore your host.

I repeated it many times, a part of me broke off and flew away, a
harpy, she repeats it still. Then, I just stood, listening, for a long time.
I listened as far as I could until I could hear the drone of silence.
Goodbye, I said to the silence, goodbye. Goodbye. And, I started
walking. Birdie was waiting in the car.

Birdie Dubois

The plan was that Elora would stay in my apartment until she felt able to find her own. I drove her there the morning after the fire and left her to her own devices, which I wasn't entirely comfortable with, but I'd given Stan full parental responsibilities and a key. I had to go back to Idlewild for a couple of weeks and pack up. In reality, I wanted her out of the house so I could clear her room and, well, energy from the place. She'd burnt my mother's studio to the ground, and I needed to process this. Also, I needed some time to myself. To think, to rage, to mourn. I was experiencing a kind of emotional inertia that takes over when you've gone into overload. In short, I needed to feel again. I think of it now and I wonder if anything would have been different had I stayed. I probably wouldn't have been able to convince her to stay and I'm not sure I'd have wanted to. The postcard from Jacques arrived at the apartment while I was at Idlewild. It was a drawing of Ursa Major. That's all. Elora left it propped up on the table as a way to say goodbye. I'd been at Idlewild for a few weeks when Stan rang me from the pay phone to tell me she'd left. The first thing I had felt was relief, which wouldn't have been the case if I'd known I'd never see her again.

Elora Winter

After the fire I took a fresh look at myself and what I saw there I kept hidden. Birdie let me stay in her apartment in Lincoln Park.

She thought I needed to be around people. In the beginning, I thought that too, so I'd stand in the centre of a busy sidewalk and let the people cut around me like a tide, people splashed against me, roared at me, and tried to pull me down. The people were angry. I put my arms out, I wanted to touch them as they passed, to contact anger, to let my own anger out; I did it to feel. The people stormed and crashed into me, they bruised me, but it was just the thing I needed, a good long scream.

Thank you, I said to the people, I hate you, I love you.

After that, I climbed to the top of the stairwell and out onto the flat black roof of the apartment building where brick chimneys stood in a thick collection of bird droppings like tall red trees with white flowers growing at their bases. The buildings reminded me of grey stalagmites; all around me drains dripped, grey water swirled into gutters, down pipes, and calcified crevices as if the city was melting. I pretended to be a bat hanging from the top of a cave looking down at the cement stalagmites.

Each morning, I returned to the roof where the clouds hung in the low, gritty heat. On the street below the pigeons cooed and picked through garbage bins with mangled, broken feet, and I'd crouch there, watching them, blowing into my coffee cup, waiting to hear the footsteps of the first morning commuter. Usually, it was the same blond woman, whose passing caused the pigeons to flare up and flap like a quite applause.

Eventually more people would trickle down the sidewalk. Two people walking side by side, two here, one there, a handful of people, multiplying until their footsteps became one giant footstep and the street was full. Pigeons dove in and out of the crowd.

The people moved like a shoal of fish and the pigeons were pushed to the side or suffered broken toes. The people were in unison but remained unattached, only the birds communicated, cried their small warning cries. After a while I felt the need to nullify and disappear inside human cohesion. So, I stopped climbing to the roof of the building and learned to walk a city street, shoulders square, quick paces, head down.

I knew nobody. Not really. Nobody knew me.

Having the loss of Jacques and our child was like having a cat in a bag at the bottom of myself. It was there kicking and gasping, yet I knew I needed to let it die, so trained my brain to shove it down and press and press it into the deep excess of my mind. But always I thought of it, carried its claws, I dreamed it awake and dreamed it asleep, as though the acid of my loss had liquefied the creature. It became the place where I'd sink into the details of despair. Him.

A whippoorwill, an eyelash seen and then blown from a fingertip, rain on tin, wood, and rivers. All these little details, glistened like sweat on skin, were the exterior did not represent the whole. The whole was something else. Something I couldn't make out, but felt huge and unimaginable, a beast, and I was simply the wind its thrashing disturbed.

The photographs helped. While taking the photographs I hovered in the balsam-like wilderness between sleep and coherence where the mind exchanges dreams for reality.

I tied my dressing gown around my waist and walked into the kitchen. Coffee. Coffee monster, black river of sanity. Last night had been difficult and long.

I looked at the empty bottle of wine and single glass posed like conscience on the countertop. I knew I'd been drinking too much lately, but it seemed the only way to deaden my dreams. I had frequent nightmares, where I felt like I was drowning in the river, where I feared Arlo was close. I dreamed of wooden women and hands around my neck.

Last night I was lucky. The thought had left as quickly as it had come, as if it were a red ribbon of ticker tape that I had to pull from my mind until it ran out and plunked my fears down like shiny pennies on the table. Where I could see what they cost me.

Last night's heat was stifling. My body had searched for coolness. I pressed my cheek against the white wall and opened the window. The smell of hot asphalt was a gel through which sounds dropped like bricks through the night's air: a motorcycle's engine, a car horn, a dog's bark. Sound was a rock in my throat.

I felt the urge to flee, so grabbed the keys, my camera, and walked into the street. There had been a short burst of rain and a moon floated inside each puddle like a white petal in a fishbowl. I took a photograph. A police car sped past; its blue siren was a frantic bird flapping against the sky, my chest. I watched a street of watery moons shake.

I walked to the river and stood expectantly at the bridge. I put both hands on its cement railing, leaned over, and breathed in the deep water. It smelled muddy and sour, even putrid, but I needed to see natural movement, I needed to see something flow its natural course. I looked up. The moon was low and hanging between two buildings like a silver portal that extended its rippled arrow, its path across the river towards me. I felt as though I could jump into the moon, become a myth, retold, reinvented, and time enhanced. I looked down at the water and saw my reflection, like a trembling black thumb that white shards of light lapped against, then closed my eyes, two moons burning through my pupils and out the back of my skull like headlights.

I clicked the shutter down and captured myself, again and again, until I made it through.

Apart from my own shadow, I resisted photographing living forms and concentrated on movement instead. The empty carriages of the L, the waves of Lake Michigan, flags, trucks.

My ongoing series titled "Hanging Smoke," where I suspended a black metal hanger with fishing line attached to a curtain pole. I dangled the hanger above the chimney stacks and waited for the smoke to curl around the shoulders of the hanger like a bolero, a dress, a scarf, a necklace. Ghosts. When I developed the photos, I could see the current of a person inside the space, arms, neck, chin, because that's what my mind expected of the view. And when that happens, when we see only what we expect, truth becomes its own deception.

All the while, something was waiting inside of me like larvae underground, every photo I took felt like the process of scratching out, where I was becoming stronger and stronger, until finally, my gift was revealed. I didn't notice my transformation at first.

One of Birdie's neighbours kept homing pigeons on the rooftop. I was eating a sandwich and waiting for the furnace to release its steam around my wire hanger, when the neighbour asked me to photograph his birds. I took a bit of bread and fed it to them as I circled the pigeon loft and photographed them preening. They had just returned from a flight and each cubbyhole was full.

"Stand next to them," I said to the neighbour, but he declined.

I took a single group shot of the birds before I heard the furnace kick on and release its steam across the shoulders of my hanger.

In the evening, as I was developing the film in the darkroom, I could hear the birds plucking seed from the rooftop. It was distracting and as I dipped the paper into the chemicals, I beckoned the birds to be quiet, then clipped their photo up to dry.

A cry reverberated from the pigeon loft, and I ran up the fire escape. The neighbour stood helpless with his head in his hands, a few birds lay lifeless at his feet. I looked inside the loft and saw the other birds dead inside their nests.

"What happened?"

"They just died," he said. "All at once. They dropped dead, as if their hearts stopped beating at exactly the same second."

I knew I had silenced them.

The following day I walked to the pet store and bought two mice in separate cages. I had three pictures left on the roll of film inside of my camera. They rattled inside their cages on the kitchen countertop. I photographed the brown mouse once and the white mouse twice.

Inside the darkroom I tried to clear my mind and think of nothing as I shook the developing tank. I sat in the dark and waited for the chemicals to activate. Show me who I am, I asked. I want to know who I have become.

When the timer rang, I opened the tank and cut the film. I submerged the photo of the brown mouse into the solution and summoned it to die. I sank one of the white mouse's photographs into the dish and bid it to live. Then I clipped the photos onto the string and studied them. There was no difference between the two. The brown mouse's photo hadn't begun to fade or change in any visible way, as I imagined it might do, yet when I left the darkroom and entered the kitchen, the brown mouse was dead in his cage. The white mouse, however, was scurrying along happily.

"I'm sorry little one," I touched the white mouse's cage. "Don't take it personally."

Back in my darkroom, I dipped the second photo of the white mouse into the developing solution and told it to die.

In the kitchen the mouse lay in a ball of white fluff, still warm, but completely dead. Awestruck, I removed the two mice from their cages and laid them out on the table. On their backs with their paws touching as though they were brothers. Their small stomachs were still soft and white. The light from the extractor fan was artificial and perfect. I reloaded my camera and took a single photo, then scooped the mice into the trashcan.

There was no remorse to feel. This was my true nature.

And the world that I had once been a victim of, now seemed as vulnerable as a small throat inside my clutch. I could make the ultimate decision. Power was the first feeling to come back to me. This must be how Jacques feels, I thought, and remembered the words he had whispered to me. Now, we can both escape.

It wasn't the existence I'd expected, but I had certainly escaped, and now that I was beginning to understand my new ability, I felt responsible for providing a particular type of justice.

I had a reason to live.

Now I know it was not a coincidence. I knew that having had Jacques inside me, having carried his child, meant that I had resurrected inside his realm. The cat in its bag kicked all the way to the surface. Kicked open my throat.

Jacques Beaumont, Pine Creek, Ontario

He has loved them all. Truly. He looks across the valley dotted with his sculptures and watches the sun lower below the mountaintop like the yellow arc of a reptilian eye closing the mountain grey. Each one of them a different character of Elora, each one, designing her memory. More than love. Love when it's explosive.

He sands her down with long raspy sighs. The wood underneath is fresh and perfect and untouched. I'll keep the first piece I chisel out of her, he thinks, curled as a child's tendril, I'll keep it close to me.

He's been saving this piece of wood for Elora for nearly a year. He's felt her waiting, tiptoeing like a cat, along the periphery of his creative view. He labels each log with a date and place of discovery and files them in his woodshed. He has it all planned. This sculpture will focus on carving her head, chest, and waist. She will have two metal posts for legs, as he perfected her legs on another sculpture months ago, and a floor-length nightdress composed of wooden medallions, each engraved with a symbol.

He'll drill a hole in the top and bottom of each medallion and fasten them together with wire, like chainmail. She'll stand in the garden with her emblem nightdress circling around her. She'll have a view of the mountains and the others to keep her company, until she completely turns.

Until she comes back to him.

Elora Winter

The postcard arrived in the morning. Conclusive evidence and an address. I traced my finger over his drawing, his handwritten address, and a part of me softened. A part that had not been accessible until then. Maybe, this, I looked at my arms, life like this could work?

I remembered how we used to play this game.

"Hold out your arm, palm up, and close your eyes," Jacques would say. Then he'd softly move his finger from my palm up to my armpit.

"Say 'now' when you think my finger has reached the inside of your elbow," he said. When I whispered "now," his finger would stop and I'd open my eyes to find it far from my inner elbow.

"Let your skin be sensitive," Jacques would say, "you need to soften." He'd shake my arm, "soften and receive things."

I stretched my arms out into the air and gently stroked them one at a time.

"Now, now," I say aloud, as I pass my inner elbow. Now, my skin was so thin that I could see two thick purple veins running from wrist to elbow. I stopped stroking, placed my right forefinger on the thickest artery and waited to feel my heartbeat.

I'm alive. You're alive, I said, I'm coming.

To leave a place is simply to turn direction, for it only feels as if we are moving forward because of our relationship with time, but often we leave to re-enter the past and attempt to correct it. The mind knows no difference; the mind is a compass needle that points in the direction of growth. To reach him I will follow the river.

I packed most of my photographs between blankets inside the trunk of the car. The rest I left for Birdie. I rented a Buick Skylark, just like Marge's. It would be less conspicuous when I drove into Callisto. All my clothes fitted into a single suitcase.

The cigar box was underneath the bed. Black and the size of a book, it wasn't heavy; I could hold it with one hand. All these years, I'd kept small pieces of myself inside it like flowers pressed in a dictionary: that delicate. Like the little abbreviated notes people make to themselves: that personal. Like the leftover shapes of a cut paper snowflake: that random. The carving of the bear was inside the box.

The first night I was alone in Birdie's apartment, I dumped the contents of the box onto the bed and ran my hands, new hands since the river, over them one by one. The objects seemed to belong to a different person. Touching them seemed to initiate a need to do something destructive and fierce. It sounds ridiculous, but I began jumping up and down on the bed as hard and as high as I could, knees to chest, then slamming my feet against the mattress. The bedsprings barked like beaten seals. The relics crashed against the sheets like wreckage inside white waves. I was a storm. I thought I would go through the floorboards and pictured my femurs splitting as I pushed like a drill through the ground. I wanted it. I wanted the pain. Pain meant life.

"Come on!" I shouted. Higher and harder I jumped, until my hands could smack against the ceiling, until my breath spiked my lungs and I had to quit to breathe. My collection had been flung and scattered across the room. Quickly I jumped down on the floor, scooped the items into the box, slammed it shut, and pushed it under the bed.

From then on, whenever the box entered my mind, I immediately shoved it out, though sometimes it wouldn't leave graciously. Sometimes it beckoned me to sit upon the bed with my knees under my chin, perched like a hawk, over my evidence. I could feel it burning under me. See? You were there. You were there, it seemed to say. There is proof that you existed in another light.

I put my hand under the bed, pulled it out, dusted it off with toilet paper, and carried it like a baby in the crook of my elbow to the door. I stopped and looked in the hallway mirror, with one hand I pinched my cheeks until they went pink and then pressed my fingertips into my eyes for a few moments. When I opened them, I saw fuzzy black spots, waited to regain a clear picture of myself, and slammed the door shut.

The café was crowded but I needed to eat breakfast. I poked a fried egg with my fork and its sun spilt a golden puddle across my white plate. The rest of the world was grey. I looked out the window at the other windows, each as greyrimmed and shadowed as tired eyes. The city pushed its steel wave against me. Waves, colours, sounds, now arrived in undertows that swept me somewhere unknown. I took it all in. A garbage truck beeped while empty bins bounced back to their places on the pavement and drivers shouted unrecognizable words. Chains scraped and clanked against the concrete. In the café, sausages and pancakes sizzled. People murmured and newspapers were opened, shaken, folded, and tucked under arms in tan overcoats. Someone coughed a phlegmy cough then lit a cigarette. The waitress rustled as she walked, her thick knees rubbed in their pantyhose. She wiped her thumb across her blue apron, the smudge like a red cloud against a dusk sky. Water hit the burner and the coffee pot popped.

I held her cup with both hands and blew. Steam entered my nose. Steam reached my empty stomach before the coffee's acidic swish. I leaned over and ate my egg. My body worked. Everything functioned. It seemed a miracle and perhaps it was. The morning's light was different, it was a bright washed yellow, and the sky had cleared. After so many days of hot suffocating rain it felt revolutionary. Perhaps it was a miracle, but how? To what purpose? I lifted my finger and ordered toast.

Outside the sun glared off the hubcaps of my car, causing my eyes to water as I fumbled for my keys. The smell of warming asphalt made me nauseous. I carried a polystyrene cup full of coffee and a map tucked under my arm, which I unfolded over the hood of the car. I took a pen and the postcard from my pocket, and traced the highway parallel to the Mississippi, stopping when I reached Pine Creek, Ontario.

Jacques Beaumont

Jacques was in his workroom when the doorbell rang. He stood up and registered the sound. A doorbell. He had forgotten he had a doorbell. He put his knife down, pulled a sheet over the figure that lay on his workbench and walked into the kitchen.

A young policeman squinted through the window. His solemn face made Jacques hesitate. He felt light-headed as if stepping off the tightrope of Before and into the free-fall of After. There was a second of mid-air before he reached the door; he held his breath and suspended.

"Hello, I'm looking for Jacques Beaumont?" He straightened his spine.

"I'm Jacques Beaumont."

The officer had heard he was a sculptor and a recluse. He looked at his hands. They were split along the creases, calloused and blunt ugly sausages. Jacques lifted one up and ruffled sawdust out of his hair.

"Can I help you?"

"Mr. Beaumont, I'm John Andersen, with the Police Department," he took a badge from his breast pocket and showed it to him. "Mr. Beaumont is there anyone at home with you?"

"No, just me."

"Do you mind if I come in?"

"After you," he made a sweeping gesture with one hand and stepped aside. "I need a cup of tea, would you like one?" Jacques asked as he placed the kettle on the stove.

The kitchen walls and cupboards were painted white. The floors and countertops were wooden. A table made from an old door and two sawhorses was pushed against a bare window. The table was covered with palm-sized wooden circles stacked in rows like collapsed dominos. A book was open to a page of writing he'd never seen before.

"No thank you. I'm fine," he said.

He found that uniform pleasantries were the worst part of job. They both watched the kettle until it whistled. Jacques wouldn't have made a cup of tea if he'd known John would decline. He could feel the officer peering over his work.

"That's Sanskrit. It's for a project I'm working on. Each word is a symbol of sorts, a meditation. I sculpt," he said, taking the spoon out of his mug and placing it in the sink.

"I know," John said, and Jacques arched his eyebrows in surprise. "I mean, I gathered as much from all the sculptures outside."

"Ah, detective work," Jacques said.

"If only all detective work were so obvious," John laughed. Jacques took the milk from the fridge and mixed into his tea.

"Let's talk in the living room. I don't want anything said in front of my medallions," he said and pointed to the wooden circles on the table. "Wood absorbs."

It took John a moment to realize that he was serious. He followed him through a hallway lined with overstuffed bookshelves. Jacques carried his steamy mug of tea like an extinguished candle and sat on the edge of a tan sofa, placing the mug on his knee. John sat across from him on a blue recliner. It was the only other piece of furniture in the room, no pictures, no television, no curtains, no nothing. Jacques knew what John was thinking.

"Renunciation," Jacques blew into his mug and took a drink. "It's for my work. The idea is that I have nothing, so I resist distractions. Now. What have you come to tell me?"

"Right. Well," John cleared his throat and took a manila envelope out of his breast pocket. "It's difficult, but I'm here to speak to you about Nora Beaumont."

He nodded slowly. "My mother." The kestrel, he thought.

"Yes," John said allowing the word space enough to sink, then removed a few sheets of paper from the envelope.

"I understand how hard this must be Mr. Beaumont, but I do need to go over a few things with you. It says here in the file that she was suffering from dementia when she disappeared?"

"That's correct."

"And you reported her missing on April 14, 1952?"

"Yes."

"And you've had no contact with her since then?"

"No, none." He could feel his mouth line with the saliva that precedes vomit.

"Well, there's really no easy way to tell you this Mr. Beaumont, but we've found her remains."

Her remains. I remain, he thought. I am all that remains of her, of a time so long ago it feels like never. He'd spent years designing an alternative story for that time and now the truth, flung out before him like a writhing being, as though she were born again.

"I'm so sorry Mr. Beaumont. Here," he handed him a tissue from his pocket.

Jacques took it. "I knew she was dead. It's been nearly two years, so of course I knew it, but all the same. You have no idea." He did not sob. He caught the tears that spilled down his cheeks with the tissue.

He had carried the guilt of his relief. He wasn't proud of it, but it was true. When she finally left he had felt relieved, as though he had been wearing the wrong skin and could take it off and set it down. He thought he could come out of himself and simply walk away, but she had felt like a small animal in his hands. He never forgot. And now his mother was telling him that it was over. That he was forgiven.

"Mr. Beaumont," John's voice was a trained softness as he handed him another tissue.

"It was a freak storm," Jacques said.

"Mr. Beaumont, it's in the file, you don't need to explain."

"No. I do. The snow was heavy and her tracks were everywhere. Like a rabbit, you know? Zigzagged like that. She was frail by then, unreachable, one day there, the next day, gone. Just like that," he snapped his fingers. "I did what I had to do."

"Of course you did Mr. Beaumont. It would have been dangerous to go after her in those conditions. You did the right thing. You reported her absence and got on with your life. And, your father, Mr. Beaumont?"

"My father is on expedition, he's a photographer. He left before my mother, and I haven't seen him since. I think she was looking for him."

"Well, sometimes people just don't want to be found," said John, he didn't feel the need to tell Jacques that his father's photographs, postmarked a few months ago, so proof that Mathis was likely alive, had been returned to the post office from authorities in Illinois. Nobody, thought John, deserves to find out their mother is dead and their father has skipped out on them in a single day.

Jacques looked at John. He knew nothing, nothing. He was a dweller of a single dimension. The type that looked at a hand and saw only a hand, not a tool that could build, that could create life, or take it away. The room changed its axis.

"Where did they find her?"

"In a ravine not far from here," John said, and scratched his knee. His sympathy was waning. He coughed and his breath smelt of sweet, digested coffee.

"Do you know who found her?"

"A group of hikers, geology students actually. Amazing what you can study these days. It's heavily wooded up there, as you know, anyway one slipped and fell down the ravine. He broke his leg and, incidentally, discovered your mother."

"That must have been a shock."

"Yes. I'm sure it was. Listen, Mr. Beaumont, there is something else. It was raining and Matt, the student, saw a cave along the bottom of the rock face. He dragged himself there to wait for the paramedics. That's where he found her."

As a child Jacques had named that ravine the Bandit Trap because it was hidden by snowdrifts in the winter and covered with vine in the summer. You had to fall into it to know it was there. He hadn't known about the cave. He looked out the window towards the forest. It pressed and threatened the house like a green and black glacier, and he felt the split of erosion, of time. Maybe she crawled, he consoled himself, but it was a lie. In his heart he knew. He knew she'd been moved.

"It appears they were brought there by an animal and, well, I need to tell you that they've been tampered with."

"Tampered with?"

"There are, ah, quite a few post-mortem claw marks, mostly on the larger bones, made by a bear or possibly a cougar, it's hard to be absolutely certain. Mr. Beaumont, I'm so sorry, I really am. It's just dreadful after all this time. But it's my job to relay the facts. Do you have any questions?"

He thought of her piled up inside the cave like a game of pick-up sticks. He remembered her falling, how her white nightdress had caught in the wind and for a moment she'd begun to rise, again glowing in the moonlight like a paper lantern. Her defiance included gravity. It made him breathless still.

"Can I have them? Her bones I mean, for a proper burial?"

"I'm sure that won't be a problem. Although it might take some time, you know, with the paperwork and all. I'll phone you in a week or so. Is there anything else I can do for you? Anyone I can call?"

"No. No, thank you," he said, and John stood to leave.

Jacques walked him to the door. A pheasant shrieked outside. The sun had dropped.

"Looks like it's going to be a nice evening," John said, instead of goodbye.

He wanted to leave him with something positive, poor man, out here all on his own. John was grateful he had his wife Martha at home. Life wasn't fair sometimes, he thought, but you can't help everyone. He opened the car door.

"She would hate to be boxed up," Jacques stepped out onto the porch and called after him.

"I beg your pardon?" John stood with the door open. The wind spun a pine-shaped air freshener from his rear-view mirror.

"She would hate to be in some laboratory somewhere, boxed up and tagged, she'd want to be here. In this soil. Under this sky," he pointed to the clouds.

"Okay Mr. Beaumont. I understand. I'll do my best to get her home as soon as possible," he stepped into the police car. He was already thinking about what Martha might be cooking up at home. Crossed his fingers for lasagne.

"Thank you," Jacques said, and raised one hand to say goodbye. John lifted a finger from his steering wheel.

Jacques watched the police car shrink until it was the size of a bug. Perception is everything, he thought, and walked back to his workroom and lifted the sheet from Elora.

It made sense that his mother would arrive first, he thought, as he laid his hand on Elora's wooden torso.

The Sculptor - Gret Heffernan

He had found this particular log for Elora the morning after a thunderstorm. It had been a night of terrific calamity, but the morning was as cool and smooth as a rock scraped clean of its moss. The morning stayed pressed against his cheeks even after he'd entered the forest. It was difficult walking, as many trees had been struck or wind torn, and their limbs lay scattered everywhere. He had adapted an old sledge attached to a chest harness to help him pull out logs. The wood for his larger sculptures often arrives this way. It's hard work that he finds incredibly satisfying. He wants to build relationships that will last with his Elora's and has moved beyond frivolous, easy commitments. He hopes he has given her a sustenance that's meaningful.

Anyone who has spent time with trees knows that each one has a different personality, so when he's searching for a piece to sculpt, he's also searching for a tree that can cope with change. Some simply can't, some roots are too deep and want to die and feed the soil to which they were born. He respects that. He leaves them for the beetles and searches for the logs that secretly wish they were birds.

She was in a clearing, lightning-struck and still smouldering on the ground like a fallen warrior. He touched her and sensed her bravery, her flight, and her bird dreams. She sighed when he sawed off her damage, she fell asleep as if to convalesce, and he saw the woman within, her face creased inside the bark like a face pressed against glass. At once, he recognized it as Elora and although he had been carving her for two years now, he had never seen the face that she'd resuscitated. It meant that she was close, and although it was what he wanted, the idea of her arrival left him unable to move, unable to speak. He just stood there and let the past land on him, all at once, a flock of birds and it was deafening.

He was a sculptor that removed. That's what he did. He cut, he shaved, and sanded away all that was unnecessary (however luscious, however fleshy) from his object until it had the required space to open. Like years that eat away at a memory, like ants that eat a fruit, entirely, until they reach the stone, the truth, the seed. Each sculpture was a seed and with this one he'll plant Elora. Again.

He gives new life to the fallen, an artistic decomposing because wood was always changing, always moving and, for years, remained alive. He liked the fact that it was only the solidity, not his marks, that could remain permanent. It filled him with a strange hope. Nobody wants the full truth, like a pause, it weighs too much.

He caught them at their heaviest. It was a service really, a bit like a chaperone or a bellhop. If you broke art, if you broke death down, it was ordinary. He painted X while eating toast. X died after making a bank deposit. The ordinary facts were the most haunting. One reason for this was because they hid the creator, the exterminator, the devil in the details. The other reason was because they brought the unimaginable close enough to recognize.

Always in the wood he recognized the tree, the thing it had been, which was already a measure of perfection that he didn't dare to compete with, like life and its perfect design, his art was the other side to the story, the other face. There is never only one. The idea of one perception is impossible, so each tree was also designed for the body that he gave it, a secret longing perhaps, an underbelly, the thought churning inside it as changing as erosion. It is a type of love in the way that it cannot be sequestered.

It belongs to him, is vital to him, and this idea pleases him as he imagines a companion might. He has many things in common with his father. The main thing being that they both shared a need to physically hold their feelings through a created object.

Jacques detached to visualize, then recreated, the parts of himself that he needed to understand. He was a tactile man. He needed to hold his emotions, cut, mould, chisel, and rearrange them so that he could control them. Sometimes he imagined that he sculpted himself out of form and into nothing, a zip of light that simply burned to black. The thought was both sustaining and horrible.

He took the postcard from the desk drawer, drew Ursa Major over it, and sent it to Birdie's address in Chicago. Elora must be ready now.

Elora Winter

I followed the Mississippi along a stretch of highway. I opened the windows and concaved my brain. My photographs, my library of emotions, hung from my mind like a row of drying hides, rawhide, I thought, as the wind slapped against them, a thumb across cards. I could be anything. Few things allow the mind to detour like driving. I like to sit in the middle of windows, like to speed to the end of the city and will the countryside to move. It makes me feel linear when I am otherwise not. Sometimes you need to move towards the bull's-eye. Arlo won't recognize me like this. He won't recognize me with influence.

The night before I left, I dreamed a highway lay across my body. It began on my forehead, spread over my nose, lips, and chin, and then ran across my chest and stomach. At my throat and pelvis, it branched into two and stretched down my arms and legs. In my dream I kept driving and driving along myself. Above me, bulbous cartoon clouds sped across a blue sky, a cartoon sun and moon exchanged in seconds, and day quickened to night and back again. Time rushed outside my window, and I was alone in my car whizzing down the empty highway with grass-bending force. A steel finger parting hair.

When I reached the turning for Callisto, I drove off the main highway and down the back roads towards the side entrance to my father's old land. I drove until I saw the iron gate at the top of a grassy hill. I parked the car alongside the road and began to climb, swatting mayflies from my face. Crossing the field and following the track would take me to the other side of the river, where there were trees, rocky outcrops, and coves full of fish. During this time of year, I would certainly find Arlo. Photographing him on the Mississippi seemed appropriate, plus he was trapped on the boat and wouldn't be able to reach or hurt me.

There was the abandoned house and the rhubarb growing wild as anything. I sat on a stagecoach stump at the top of the hill. It was another five-minute walk to the river, and I could see it snaking through the trees. It must have been a beautiful spot to settle.

Beside the house was a little cemetery surrounded by a rusted gate and a fence. Cemeteries like this could be found up and down the wagon trail. I knew to look for the tell tale iron gate poking through a grove of scrappy pines planted to keep the soil from eroding. Not many were this lucky of course, most had only wooden crosses or just stones to mark their passing. I pictured the wind whipping off the layers of soil covering their frail bones like sheets, lost in the wind they disintegrated, funnelled, and swirled like insects in a current, then vanished. Time is lost in places like this; time means nothing. This was my epitome.

I thought of my old life and myself as a child.

In my childhood bedroom there had been a single window. On stormy nights the wind softly rattled the oval mirror above the wooden dresser. Curation and collection were aspects Jacques and I had in common. Apart from my bed I had no other furniture, just a denim rag rug and a gold hook on the back of my door. Every other inch of space was covered with magpie objects, feathers, sticks, acorns, rocks, eggshells, a piece of foil I'd found on the grass like a fallen star. Objects man had named inanimate, bones. But it's not true, for if I stared hard enough, mindfully enough, the inanimate became animate. Became a song. The rock grew a face and the chipped bone, a new skin. I digested their curves and we charted one another, became maps of the same landscape, kin. In black marker I wrote my favourite words on the walls. Then I sang them alive.

Now I could do the opposite.

I remembered the day my father returned home from hospital. The doctors had told him his cancer was irreparable. The afternoon light had already begun to muddy the stark yellow of morning. I watched the air thicken, watched the shadows lengthen in silence. Silence was everywhere and it filled me. My eyes shifted through its coating like two stealth swimmers parting water, I pored over things: a white door handle, a glass vase on the dresser holding pheasant feathers, a watermark on the ceiling's right corner that looked like a starfish or a smudged handprint. Outside a gust of wind shook the dust from the leaves' thin backs. A branch scraped the window. The knowledge that life was impermanent filled my mind like lungs inhaling air. He died within a year.

In Chicago, the same feeling of impermanence arrived as I sat at the window and watched the city hit against the night like a shine across black leather. I'd stare and listen to sounds trickle through a darkness haloed by streetlights, damp headlights, and a few other yellowed windows. Pure black existed only in patches, in parks, down alleyways, and corners, black crevices where sound and light slowed and laboured as if rolling through tar, a cough, a pair of lit eyes, cold cardboard. Elsewhere light burned through black, fusing and reinventing black as watered-down amethyst, dark gold, and army-green bruises. Sometimes I'd light a candle just to see my shadow pulse. To remind me of my power. Sometimes the wind blew this shadow, banging like a dark hand against the wall, and I'd stare at things until I no longer reacted to them. All night stripping objects of their names.

In the city I spent those few summer afternoons in the park under a particular tree; I'd sit watching its pale-green leaves oxidize to grey. I left at dusk, so never saw the leaves turn black with night, but pictured them often just before sleep, saw their yellow light draining to uncover an opaque figure, like a sunlit puddle evaporating to divulge its solid mud bottom. The person I had become. The earth of things for which there are no words.

It was time to say goodbye to my old self now.

I followed the track to the trees, sat on the riverbank, and waited for Arlo's boat to appear. The reeds harped inside the mud and swallows dipped and caught early-evening bugs. Across the water, the skeletal remains of Jacques's burnt-out studio settled into the landscape like a rotting corpse. In the distance, Birdie's house, and the grave of Lorelei. I took a photo of the grave. A remote shot was best, and then I closed my eyes and quietly revelled in the synchronization of knowing that I was putting events to rest.

Before long, Arlo's boat retched through the air. Geese flapped up in warning and I stood to face him. The engine oil was pungent as he motored into view. Look at me, I beckoned him, and he did. When he saw me standing there, like a ghost, he cut the engine and lunged forward, but the boat nearly capsized and forced him to steady himself. I smiled, waved, and brought the camera up to my eye.

I took photo after photo, capturing him inside the negative. He shook his head to remove my image. There was nothing he could do to hurt me now. He looked as silly as a toad. It was stupid how simple it was. Stupid. To make it ceremonious would add a gravitas he didn't deserve. Within minutes, the current floated him downstream and out of view. I put the camera down and walked back to the car. The sunset now was thick and red as flayed muscles through the trunks of trees. Death is the first life I have truly owned.

I sat in the car without turning it on. Across the road was a fenced field like any other. Cattle stared at me and slowly chewed, their jaws constantly grinding, turning. I had missed the infinite expanses of land and sky. The unevenness of the pulled-apart clouds as if the sky were linen too long in the sun and bleached along its creases.

The sky in Chicago was spiked with metal's posture, building, bridge, crane, all screaming a separation from the natural world. Lake Michigan had offered an indifferent respite, but it was tidal and crashed, whereas the Mississippi rolled. I was, and still am, a sky and river person.

I had died alongside the Mississippi. Seeing Arlo, the thought of him and who I'd been no longer asphyxiated me. The woman who had sung beside the river and even the thought of Jacques, had begun to recede into the obscure briars of my memory. I let them go because I had also been reborn alongside the Mississippi. For better or for worse, Jacques had wanted me to live, so here I was, inside this strange, hollowed body for which I documented emotion. Here I was with my ability to take life, but also, to chronicle it, to bring justice. Yet, would I? Would I develop the photos of Arlo? He had seemed so inane now, meaningless, and perhaps knowing that was enough. There was time to think, that was the main thing, there was time, endless time.

I stopped the car in Lake Itasca, sixty miles outside of Pine Creek. The road is empty all the way to the mountains. Lake Itasca is the headwater of the Mississippi. I leave the car and walk to the edge of the glacial lake where the river begins. Thick pines along the sides and boulders rolling all the way to the shoreline. I climb up a large rock and dangle my feet inside the cold water. The clouds are mirrored across the water's surface. I hold the cigar box in my lap, remove a silver locket from its contents, and fasten it around my neck. It had belonged to my mother.

For many years, forever, I'd wished for a child to inherit it. I also removed the carving of Callisto. I was its custodian, not its owner. I would return it to Jacques to mark our full circle.

Everything else inside the box belonged to another woman. I folded the road map of Illinois to fit, placed it inside with a few heavy rocks and shut the lid. To keep yourself open is on some level to submerge to a close, like coral can close when it's distressed, and is most beautiful when left undisturbed. Life, love are disturbing, inspirational, yes, but disturbing all the same. To see myself as closed is to admit there must be a time of opening. Maybe he had never loved me enough to be interrupted. Or maybe he had only wanted to interrupt. Well, whatever the case, I am the result of an interruption. The moon was a small C in the sky. The air off the water smelt like cool wet leaves. The mountains perched in the far-off distance like hawks. I am an interruption.

I removed a piece of rope from my pocket and tied it tightly around the box so that it looked like a present. A present for the river. Then, I pitched the box into the air as hard as I could, it flew for a second before cutting straight through the water, and it barely made a ripple. In my mind I watched it sink quickly to the bottom, scare a few fish, and lodge in the brown mud, looking as if it has always been there.

That is what my body would have done before the gas of decay rose me to the surface. That woman needs to stay here now, I tell myself, and here below the mouth of the river is where she belongs. Above her the river moved on and on and I sat there for a long time breaking back to nothing. Just breaking.

Back to that night. I would have died alongside the river. I did die alongside the river, but then I rose from it again. The first step, he had orchestrated, but every other step had been of my making. My thoughts scattered like gulls. My seagulls, the birds he had heard. I let them. I let them go and watched as they disappeared. I could feel, inside of myself, a silence pulling down like a root, a quiet knowing. Sometimes a need will go on so long that it becomes a grind that must turn itself out of you like a screw, like this, twisting through tailbone and out the balls of your feet. The resulting pattern is a coiled cavern where a new trust, like a cool stream begins to lick the splintered edges smooth. I let myself feel it and closed my eyes and breathed into the hollow.

It was nearly dawn, but still dark when I left. The river was hazy, the sky was cold. I noticed a round rock similar in shape and size to a geode and when I looked closer, I saw that there were many, clustered like black mushrooms, wet and musty. They seemed real. I watched them as they slowly begin to pinken into a patch of bald heads under the light of the sun's golden jet stream as it opened the distance with its red lashes.

I chose the rock closest and carried it back to the car and placed it on the passenger seat. I had the strange sense that it was living. I had felt this way about eggs before, as if they were asking to hatch. I knew a person that could help me crack it. When this was over, I will contact Birdie and thank her.

I started the car and drove away. It was the only car on the road. The lights on the speedometer faded as the sun came up. We are the chances we take, I said to nobody, and it felt like a mantra. The window down; the hair on my arms standing up. I could feel my chest leap; I leapt. I felt. Did you read that? I said I felt, and I hope that when you read this you will feel too.

I drove slowly down Jacques's drive so as not to wake him. Parked, picked up the wooden sculpture of Callisto, closed the car door very carefully, and walked towards the porch. I didn't rush, instead concentrated on placing each heel precisely in front of the opposite toe, linking my footprints to trail a chain behind me. The house was quiet, and I knew when I reached it everything would change, for this is what happens when pieces slide into place; they plough and unearth a rough terrain.

The garden was full of sculptures, I entered the fold, walked in and out and around their bodies. Their bodies were mine. I recognized myself as magnificent. Each of them had a feature that moved in the wind, arms that swung, or rope hair, their eyes were painted stones. They were without grime and spotless. It was like walking through my montage. I was wanted. They did not push me away.

I stood in the middle of my women, my selves, and watched the sun come up from behind the house to warm the sky, watched clouds roll behind the trees, break into kaleidoscopes, and emerge whole again. The leaves had begun to turn colours, like orange ink spilling across the green, like leaky red veins seen through the pine's thick bodies. I would have liked to watch the colour spread, I wanted nothing more than to see a cycle complete itself.

It's amazing how one circumstance, one hour, can reconstruct a lifetime, and while the moment is performing, we sit on the cusp of our own definition, isolated by magnitude and inert in time. I waited like this, watching, until he saw me.

Jacques Beaumont

He walked down the steps with soapy water and linseed oil. One of his statues caught his eye and started walking slowly towards him. Elora. He stepped down from the porch. He was wearing an oilcloth apron and had long yellow gloves on. He dropped the bucket, and the water ran down the steps. He didn't care or notice. He whispered her name.

She walked closer to him. Her flowered dress in the breeze, her laced up boots on the grass, she coughed, she was real, his head began to spin, he leaned against the banister, and she reached out her hand, as though to catch him. He dropped to the ground. She knelt beside him.

There seemed nothing and everything to say, as if one word, one single word, would act like a crack in the levee and they would drown. The soapy water soaked into the soil. He began popping the bubbles, he touched her forehead with a wet finger to make sure she didn't disappear. Didn't pop.

"You're alive," he said. "I can't believe it."

"I am," she said, and stood. "And you, too, are alive. I've brought you something," she handed him the carving of Callisto. He took it and stared at her.

He brought it to his nose and smelled it.

"Callisto?" His face was shocked. "Where did you get this?" "On the kitchen table, where you left it," she said.

"Where I left it?"

"Yes. It was there the morning after you died, or left, or whatever you did. After you changed me."

"I didn't die. And I didn't change you, I resurrected you, I saved you," he said.

"I see that," she interrupted.

"And I didn't leave this," he said, searching the grain of the bear.

He began to pry off the head.

"Stop it! You'll break it," she said as the bear head popped off in his hand. Inside its torso was a small pale shell. A white mushroom inside the knot of a tree. A white moth under a log.

"It's my father's," he said, removing the shell and rubbing it. "It has to be, he left it for me," he sat down on the steps, shaken. "Tell me what happened after I left," he said.

The stories they exchanged were not so different from the ones they'd made up inside themselves. Their child, his father, victims of place and time. When people share a death, they often share a rebirth. He took her to the sculpture of his mother.

"I knew she was returning, and she did, just like you," he waved a hand towards his garden of goddesses. "Will you be able to bring your father back?"

"He won't want to be human," he looked at the carving of Callisto, "I know exactly how he'll return."

"Shame, your father and I have things in common now. I, too, create things. Photographs," she said.

"Photographs? You're a photographer?" He looked at her and back at the sculpture of Callisto.

"Yes."

"Of course," he smiled. "Of course. Show me."

He helped her bring them in from the car and hung them on the walls of his living room. He took some other photographs from the closet, pictures of bears, himself as a child, the mountains, and his mother. He hung them beside hers. He circled around her photos, asking what each symbol meant. She found herself describing a person she admired, however despicable, and this surprised her.

"They are stunning," he said.

"They're just emotions," she said.

"No. Not just. More than that. They hide the truth by revealing half of it. It's what I do. It's what my father did," he stood in silence for a while. "I can't believe he actually came for me. All this time I thought his body was on the mountain. I've even thought that I've felt him as I harvest the wood. I assumed he had finally met his bear, and so, I didn't try to resurrect him," his eyes brimmed with tears.

"There is no way you could have known. His spirit was free because you didn't resurrect him. And you probably have felt him in the woods because his spirit went where it wanted to be," she put her hand on his shoulder.

"And you," he took her hand. "Are you free and where you want to be?"

"When I was alive, I wanted to sing and be near you, so in that way, yes, I suppose, but I don't know now. I'm not the same person. It's hard to pinpoint what you want when you have to learn how to feel. I'm still adjusting."

"I wish I could say I was sorry, but I'm not. You are standing here in front of me, without fear or secrecy, you can become whomever you want, and Arlo will never hurt you again," he went to hug her, but she pulled away.

"Do you really think it was your father that Arlo murdered?" She avoided his touch.

"It has to be. Somehow Arlo killed my father instead of me and I wasn't there," he looked out the window towards his father's work shed.

He would carve his father as a bear. Rage and its slow eternal burn, charred his inside, he would finish his father's sculpture and bring it to life.

"If you would have been there, then we both would be dead, and anyway, you can't be sure that Arlo killed him."

"I can and I am. He carved animals for me when he went away on expedition. I left him the encyclopaedia as a clue and he left me Callisto. The bear's name is Callisto. That's why I moved there in the first place. He figured it out and he came for me. You saw the photos of my father, we looked very similar."

"What will you do?"

"I'll let fate decide."

"What does that mean?"

"It means that I know where there are some eyes in the forest that can help us."

"What are you talking about?"

"Actaea pachypoda. A plant. Also known as 'Doll's Eye,'" he said, rose from the chair and pulled the encyclopaedia off the shelf, opened it to the correct page, and handed her the book.

"I've never seen anything like this before," she said.

"I can take you to them," he said.

"They would look amazing photographed, with the right light, I could make it look like an eyeball stuck on a red needle. I know that sounds a bit macabre, but in the right context, it would look astonishing," she said.

"In the right context, I can see it."

"I could do a collage or something. You know, many eyes exposed to different lights, then reattached to the same stalk. Maybe I could even paint a few," she said.

"I would even make you a wooden one. You could place it alongside a real eye. Arlo's," he said.

"What?"

"I mean the eye could be Arlo's," he looked straight at her. Outside fireflies dipped in and out of his sculptures. Elora went silent.

"It could be the one that holds the mystery," he said.

"The mystery?"

"Every work of art holds the mystery of its creation close to the surface but remains untraceable. That's the trick."

"What are you suggesting?"

"Five little eyes in a bitter wine will stop a heart that deserves stopping," he said, and took a drink. "Think of the image Elora. Think of giving birth to that. You're an artist now. We both are and this man deserves to die for what he's taken from us."

She understood exactly what he meant. Understood it completely.

They stared at one other and inside the slant of windowed sun between them, grew the image of a body, as if their veins were crocheting together and creating an entirely new person.

She felt something drop inside her, cold as a seed and black as a note of music.

"There is no need for that," she said, and took her camera from her bag. "I have a photo of Arlo in here. I can end him. That's what you gave me. That was my rebirthing. You resurrect. I take away. All I need is a darkroom."

When she spoke, the pieces of their future slotted into place like loose blocks of ice will freeze into a single sheet of glacier. The familiar feeling of frost behind his eyes began again, only this time it was shared warmth. She could understand him now. They could unite. He put his hand over hers. As true partners.

"You have no idea what this means," he said, and stopped.

How could he finish this sentence? It would take years, but that's what they had.

"I'm still learning to feel," she said. When she imagined her own eyes, they were barren like soil where life had been uprooted. Holes. Again, holes.

"Let me help you. Trust me, this is how we were meant to be," he said. "I love you. I want to learn how to love you more."

She thought about his love and its potential hope inside her own disturbed earth. Maybe. Maybe he could fill her. But it was a risk.

"We'll see," she removed her lens cap. "Stay like that. Don't move," she said, as she placed her camera against her eye and shot his photograph. Just in case.

Callisto, Illinois

Arlo sat bolt upright in bed, gasping for breath and panting in the pre-bird morning with a feeling of panic he could not explain. I'm going to die, he thought, end. There had been no nightmare, no pain, just the sense of his world being gathered up and yanked away from him as though his surroundings had been painted on cloth. For a moment he felt the fragile ripping of premonition and stared past the window frame at a windbreak of leafless trees, black branches stitched across the dawn. He thought of her eyebrows against her bloated forehead and shuddered.

He swore he'd seen her the other day. Like a damn ghost, he saw her near his fishing cove, but when he turned the boat around, she had gone. Vanished. He should cut back on his drinking.

Arlo was not a good man, not even a decent one, and had learned to shake off any earthly forewarnings that might force him to consider his own karmic comeuppance. There were things he was willing to contemplate and things he wasn't willing to contemplate. It was as simple as that. The past was in the past and when it showed signs of rearing its ugly head, he focused his mind on the thing he loved best, fishing.

It was early autumn, and the fish would still be biting.

Arlo's heart slowed as he imagined catfish waiting on the river's bottom like quiet whiskered stones. Stones that were muddied straight through to the point of putrefaction and if he had a soul, then surely, it resembled this.

There she was again.

Her white arm reaching up for him and the river, full of hooks and snags, tumbling around it like a mysterious dream. Her fingers unkempt with seaweed, her mouth opened and out floated two huge water lilies, as pink as lungs, bobbing up and down the current. Elora. He hadn't thought about her for months, and now, all the sudden, she was everywhere.

At first, he couldn't even look at the river without imagining some part of her body resurfacing and he felt the panic, then the anger. Why was she back now? He punched down his thoughts with action, pulled on yesterday's clothes, had a piss, and went into the kitchen to pour himself a scotch. These things take more time than we realize, he thought, filled his flask, and grabbed his fishing rod.

His boots broke across shards of frosty grass and his breath clouded the air. It seemed as though he were the only thing awake until his boat motor started like some faithful animal. He moved quickly across ripples.

The river's wind was a good smack across the face and cleared his mind. He took a deep breath and welcomed the return of his old self just before he was pushed into the water.

It was shocking and cold. The boat was empty and sped off without him.

He tried to swim, but his body was completely frozen and inert. He could only move his eyelids and his mouth.

He shouted for help and floated on his back. The current was as tangled as Elora's hair, and it carried him like a log downstream. Stars raced above him, fading ornaments against the pewter sky and an arrow of geese. Lines of trees shadowed the bank like a watching crowd.

He felt himself pulled under and when he screamed the water swelled into him like the sucking in of bellows. It felt purposeful as though the water were enjoying it, as though it were alive.

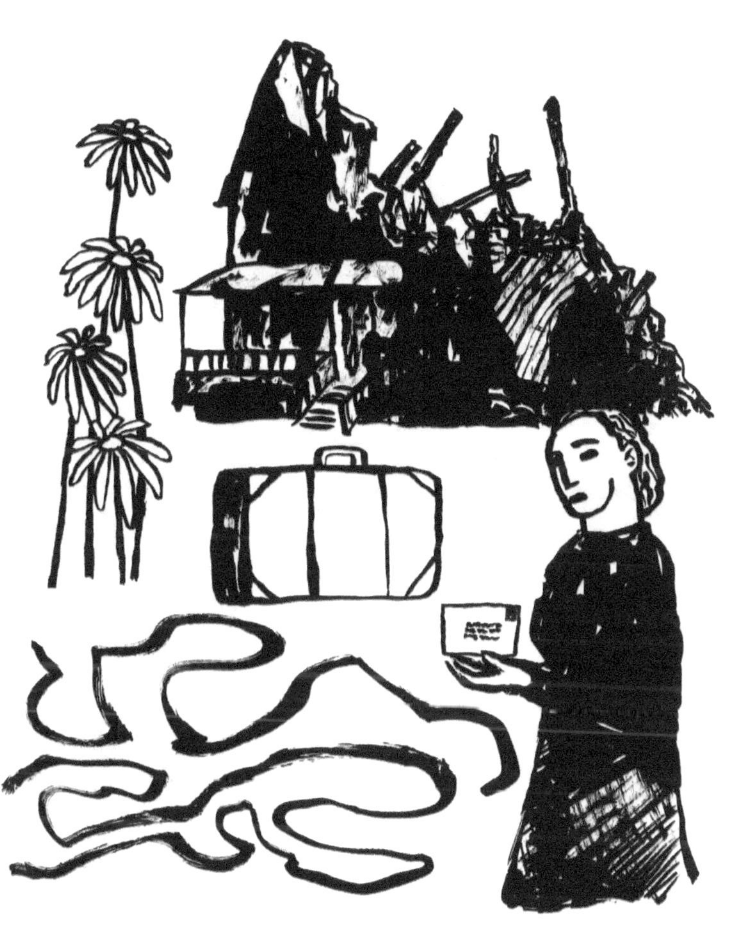

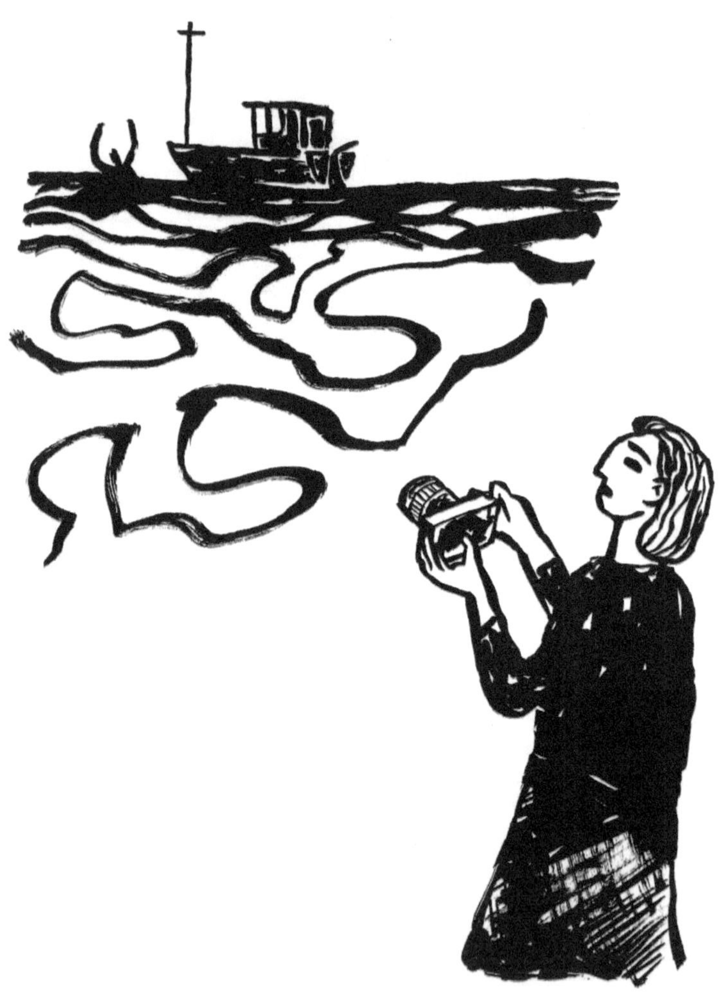

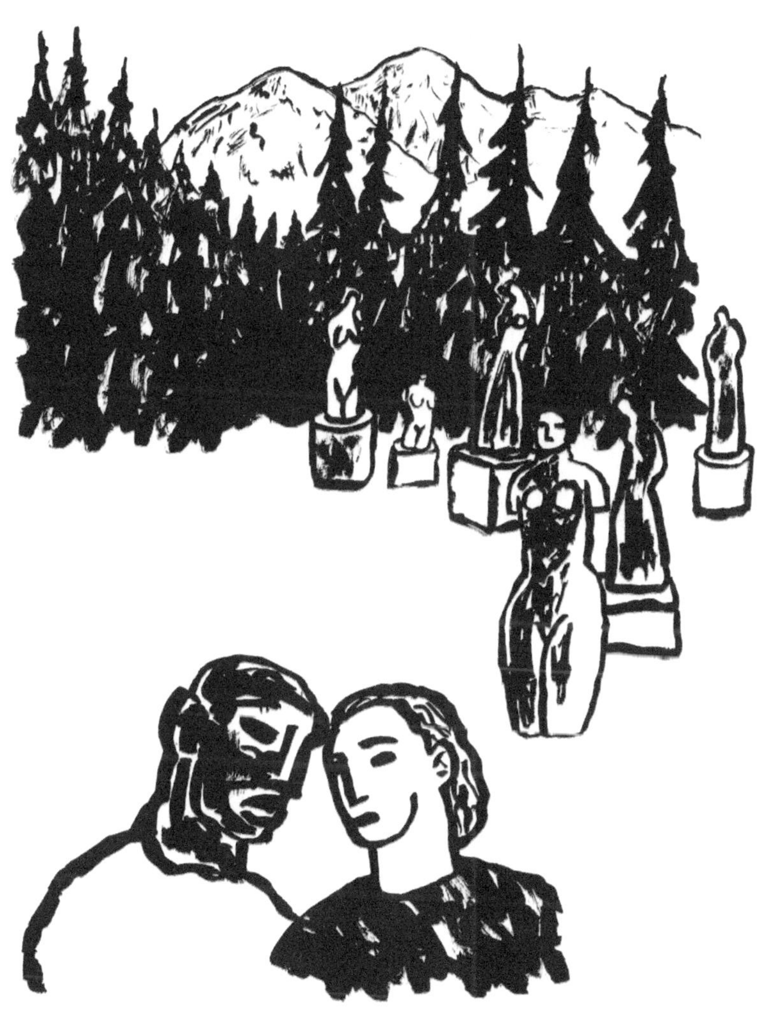

Birdie Dubois

I sat on a deck chair in my garden with two suitcases beside my feet. In the house, the possessions I've loved have been packed into boxes and labeled. The Vertical Gallery had agreed to take the majority of my mother's paintings, along with my new photo boxes. After three decades of living, sometimes actually, other times, metaphorically, inside these walls, I've kept only six medium-sized boxes of things, which feels like a meaningful metaphor for something I can't quite articulate but understand as a type of waste. How I kept waste present in my life because I feared emptiness.

It was Elora who taught me how to embrace emptiness and make the hollow sing. And now, through Elora's release, Stan is arriving in a hired removal van to move me back to Chicago. He's left Melissa and we are beginning again.

I've decided not to live with Stan straight away, if ever, and will stay in my apartment, but already the idea of him and the city has begun to seal a leak I'd purposely kept cracked. Already, I feel as though I've stopped draining. The change happened just after Arlo's funeral, when I found a package on my front porch.

It was wrapped in brown paper, tied with string, and placed next to a seed tray of tomatoes. Inside were two letters, one address to me and the other address to Lorelei. I recognized Elora's handwriting straight away. There was also an enlarged and framed photograph of Stan and I drinking coffee at the small kitchen table in Stan's apartment above the diner. That was the day I'd taken Elora to Chicago before I'd driven back to Idlewild. Two empty plates were piled beside the sink on the countertop. Behind me, a sash window was lit by the OPEN sign on the diner below and gave my hair a strange orange glow. We were caught inside a pause of a conversation, both looking up and thinking, before continuing the discussion. I remembered that talk, the peach cobbler that had been eaten off the plates, and the sound of the city street below. We had been speaking about the logistics of Elora staying in Chicago.

The brief presence of Jacques and Elora emphasized to me just how lonely I'd been. That, despite my protesting otherwise, I actually desired human companionship and, in my mind, there was no greater human than Stan. No greater place than the city, I loved to look out at all the neighbouring apartment windows, evening lit with moving shadows, and listen to pans scraping, curtains snapping, televisions, shouting and laughing, it made me feel a greater part of humanity and secure. I looked out at the place where the studio had stood. After Elora's disappearance, I had sown white oxeye daisies inside the recovering soil. They will spread prolifically and in another couple of years will take over the entire field.

I'm not selling the house. In the future, perhaps I will visit with Stan at the weekends or maybe our friends will come and stay, either way, anyone standing here, staring at a field of swaying daises, would believe that this was a peaceful place. The land is a marker of where we've trespassed and I have done my best to restore serenity. What else can we ask of ourselves? Now it is time to move on. I take Elora's letter from my pocket and read it once more.

Dear Birdie,

Many months have passed and I feel that my contacting you will no longer put you in any danger. Often, I have wanted to visit or call. You have probably felt me pining after your advice, staring out at the mountains or up at the clouds, speaking to you, asking, explaining. In many ways, you have been here with me, as though your presence were a residual force. Because I cannot think of myself as human, yet exist inside the human world, I sometimes think of myself as a rock, composed of many minerals, flung far from its point of origin. You are the quartz inside of me.

I know that you will destroy this letter once you've read it and this knowing allows an honesty to arise in me that might not exist otherwise.

First of all, thank you. Thank you for all that you have done for Jacques and me. We could not have lived without your help and will always be grateful for your kindness and love.

To think of myself then, when you knew me, is like thinking of a character in a fable, an archetype of sorts, well known and relatable, though existing inside the circumstances of another world. For a long time, I was blurry, as though seen through water, that water being, of course, the Mississippi. The river is still inside me, as the place of my rebirth, we tumble in one another's embrace, and I imagine I will carry its current eternally. It is not a sad thought.

Jacques is obsessed with making me fully human and has carved my figure inside of every emotional experience he can possibly conjure. So, in this way, I have been filled with emotion and can present, feel even, emotional responses like an actual human might. Though, they are still reactions, for in my core I am hollow, to be inside of my mind is to place your ear against the inside of a shell.

There is a whistling about me that people don't realize they notice. I think it is because I do not possess unconsciousness. When I sleep, I do not dream. I know the reason behind all my decisions. There is no sense of mystery to my existence.

Humans live in a shroud of mystery that they call presence. I do not have presence. But how to show an individual unconsciousness? It is impossible because the individualism of presence is unique, though the mystery of unconsciousness is universal. Jacques is insistent on trying to develop an unconsciousness for me through his sculpture, which has only resulted in him uncovering his own, though I suppose that is the purpose of art and I don't think he will suffer for it. But it won't work for me, plus, I don't want it. Who can live with their unconsciousness forever? It would be a cruelty.

Despite all this, we have found a way to live in peace without complete isolation. We have a garden. We visit Montreal once a week for supplies and a few galleries have begun to stock Jacques's carvings of unconsciousness. Many of them are in the form of Callisto, who you will remember is the bear his father tracked seasonally. Tourists like the carvings and some people travel to Montreal specifically for his sculptures. It seems that the story of his mother's death, in particular her clawed bones, has circulated and developed into a lure of ghostly intrigue. Nora, Jacques's mother, is said to haunt the mountain beyond the Bandit Trap, where her bones were found, and a travel agency in Pine Creek recently asked us if they could run a hiking tour during the high season. We objected at first, but it brings in revenue, plus, I think Jacques is lonely for his own kind.

This is not to say that I don't respond to his love for me or return it in my own way, of course I do, but the truth is that it took a while for us to get to know one another, being that we were reunited as entirely different people.

It is relieving when you consciously choose to remake your life and we have been living in what feels like a huge exhale, just examining moments as they come. I suppose I've always had that choice, but didn't know how to actively pursue it, perhaps I was too overcome with immediate concerns, fear, guilt, obsession.

Now, my days are mostly slow and languid. I often walk the mountains photographing trees. I am especially intrigued by decay, by how a living beast breaks back into the elements of itself, of every self, as a form of return. I guess it is my way of accepting that I will never experience this particular rot. A woman such as I has her own form of decay, but it is not physical.

Which brings me to Lorelei, our daughter. Jacques resurrected me by carving a child in my arms. I know that his gift did not reach Lorelei in time, that she had died inside of me pre-birth, and so, I suppose in this terrible way, I do know a type of physical decay. However, Jacques has told me that Nora returned as a kestrel. We can only guess that this is because her body was not suitable upon her renewal. I am hopeful that this is the case for Lorelei and like to think of her as an otter twirling around my mind. Keep an eye out for her, will you? She will be magnificent. In many ways, she was the lucky one. Jacques and I are stuck in our forms. And, please, place Lorelei's letter into the Mississippi where, I believe, it will have the best chance at reaching her.

As for me, my life could go in one of two ways. Either I'll develop the ability to drown my own photograph and, hopefully, die that way, or I'll go on living. Someday, when Jacques is old and in pain, I will develop his photograph peacefully and move to a city.

Recently, I photographed a small beech tree, a single leaf really, spawned beside its fallen giant ancestor, which gave me the idea for a generational study. I would like to photograph a family throughout generations, centuries, and by keeping this archive, creating for myself a type of soul. I think about this family often and although I don't know them, I believe that we will find one another.

For now, it is enough that they exist in the same way that I exist, inside a tunnel, half in the world and half beyond it, at the end of which waits the tragic ecstasy of eternity. I feel we are forever walking, walking towards one another. And I imagine that when we meet, we will fold into ourselves and disappear like a collapse of time. Perhaps, I do dream after all. Perhaps, my dreams are the desires I have while awake. In any case, there is but a whisper between dreaming and desiring and I hope you often hear it. Be well and know that I have willed you a long life my dearest friend.

Love, E

I placed both letters in the river. I stood and watched as the ink and paper dissolved into indivisible filaments of meaning, of history, breaking apart and mutating into an abiding current of time. What we know of life is that it changes form. Change is all that is certain. Behind me, Stan pulled into the drive with a swirl of dust. I heard his tires against the gravel, picked up my suitcases, and turned away from the water, that exposed and unstoppable artery.

www.ingramcontent.com/pod-product-compliance
Lightning Source LLC
Chambersburg PA
CBHW021240060726
47590CB00005B/1831